SHARING THE PRIZE

SHARING THE PRIZE

THE ECONOMICS OF THE
CIVIL RIGHTS REVOLUTION
IN THE AMERICAN SOUTH

Gavin Wright

The **BELKNAP PRESS** *of* **HARVARD UNIVERSITY PRESS**
Cambridge, Massachusetts & London, England
2013

#809789684

Library of Congress Cataloging-in-Publication Data

Wright, Gavin.
Sharing the prize : the economics of the civil rights revolution in the American South
/ Gavin Wright.
    p.   cm.
Includes bibliographical references and index.
ISBN 978-0-674-04933-8 (alk. paper)
    1. Civil rights movements—Economic aspects—Southern States.   2. Civil rights
movements—Southern States—History—20th century.   3. African Americans—
Southern States—Economic conditions—20th century.   4. Segregation—Economic
aspects—Southern States.   5. Southern States—Economic conditions—20th
century.   I. Title.
E185.615.W69 2013
323.1196'073075—dc23   2012033549

For Daisy and Agnita

CONTENTS

PREFACE

It is customary to open with a remark about how long this study has taken, but the present work may approach an all-time record. My interest in the American South, and in the connection between the race issue and economics, goes back to the summer of 1963, when I traveled to Warren County, North Carolina—a black-majority, tobacco belt county in the northeastern part of the state—to join a voter registration project sponsored by the American Friends Service Committee. Our interracial group of college students was warmly welcomed by the local black community, and by the end of the summer we felt we had made some progress in laying a foundation for more ambitious registration drives in the future. But we had no sense that revolutionary change was imminent in the South. As wholesome as our efforts were, the deeper problems seemed to be economic in nature, specifically the decline in farming and an absence of opportunities for young people, who were then leaving the region in large numbers. My realization that I had little understanding of the underlying issues was an important factor in my decision to pursue graduate study in economics.

Mainstream economics did not have persuasive or satisfying answers to my questions, however, and so I became an economic historian. My research on the antebellum slave economy and on southern regional development might be seen as an effort to probe the deep background reasons for the problems I observed in the 1960s. But in truth the connection was remote. Writing in the 1980s, I concluded (as did many others at that time) that the historical underpinnings for the South's distinctiveness had disappeared, so that the region as a political-economic entity had ceased to exist. This diagnosis now seems to have been premature.

What brought me back to Civil Rights history was learning in 1992 that Eva Clayton, who as a young mother in Warrenton had been the local sponsor of our 1963 project, was running for Congress in the First Congressional District of North Carolina. In November of that year she was elected, as one of the first two African Americans to represent the state in the twentieth century (the other being Mel Watt) and only the second African American woman in history to be elected to Congress from the South (after Barbara Jordan). The idea that something I was connected with so long ago, however briefly, was linked to such an outcome decades later was deeply moving to me. And so I returned to the subject in my 1998 presidential address to the Economic History Association in Durham (published in the *Journal of Economic History,* June 1999); since then I have pursued my renewed interest, though somewhat sporadically, whenever time allowed. Thus although I try in this book to present the economic history of the Civil Rights revolution as objectively as possible, I cannot claim to be unbiased.

The more I considered the evidence, the more impressed I was with the economic and political gains that resulted directly—though often not quickly—from the Civil Rights breakthroughs of the 1960s. What also came through strongly is that these accomplishments could be seen clearly only by taking a regional approach. Contrary to my earlier view that the South was disappearing, many regional dimensions of change became stronger rather than weaker over time. Once you begin to notice them, regional features of the story become more and more obvious, yet they are often missed by observers based in northern or western cities who typically work with national data. The most compelling of these is the post–Civil Rights black migration into the South, roughly two million people since 1970, reversing the direction of more than half a century, and convincing me that this was not merely a figment of my own wishful thinking. Retelling this neglected southern story became my main objective in writing this book.

I also found that by and large these gains did not come at the expense of white southerners. Instead this was a revolution in which almost all parties gained. Thus we have a case in which interest groups, including profit-seeking businesses, pursued political goals that did not advance their own economic interests, not because they favored racial supremacy over economic gains but because they did not understand the situation fully and could not picture an acceptable new way of conducting business and politics in the South on an integrated basis.

I am certainly not the first to argue that desegregation served the economic interests of white southerners, especially business interests. Many view the idea with some bitterness, either because it is evidence of hypocrisy or because it confirms that black well-being can be advanced only when it serves the interests of influential whites to do so. But I prefer to view the record more positively because the Civil Rights Movement deserves much of the credit for realigning interests and perspectives to make this mutually beneficial exchange possible. Opening the eyes of white southerners to the possibility of a prosperous, racially integrated South is one of the signal achievements of the Civil Rights revolution.

As the last chapter is at pains to emphasize, this analysis is not to be understood as a triumphalist celebration, a tale of heroic struggles that vanquished the segregationist foe for the rest of time. The book is a work of economic history, set in a particular historical context that could not be re-created even if we wanted to do so. Some of the achievements of the Civil Rights Movement have endured, while others are now receding or in jeopardy. As interpreted here, the Civil Rights revolution does not provide a well-defined set of policy lessons to be applied to our current economic and political problems. But even one historical example of realigning perspectives and interests to build larger coalitions and advance the common good should be a source of encouragement. As much as things have changed, this broad principle can be put to use again and offers us hope for the future.

SHARING THE PRIZE

CHAPTER 1

CIVIL RIGHTS,
ECONOMICS, AND
THE AMERICAN SOUTH

The Civil Rights revolution of the 1960s is firmly embedded in American civic culture, an inspiring example of virtue and courage rewarded and age-old injustices finally set right. Accounts and pictures of the Montgomery bus boycott, the Greensboro sit-ins, the Freedom Riders, and Martin Luther King's soaring speech at the Lincoln Memorial feature in textbooks and classrooms throughout the nation, including those in the southern states, where most of these famous events occurred. Civil Rights heritage sites in Atlanta, Birmingham, Memphis, and other cities attract more than a million tourists each year, who come to see and hear tales of the epic struggle and to absorb lessons in what one historian calls the "new regional civic ideology" of tolerance.[1]

Those who lived through the era know that these popular histories are highly condensed and simplified, conveying little sense of the raging controversies of the time or the perspective of the white southerners who resisted the revolution so strenuously. But one can hardly object to the veneration of Civil Rights heritage on these grounds. Textbook histories are always simplified, and to some degree one can measure a country's character by the quality of its mythic narratives. American Civil Rights stories are fundamentally true and powerful, and their propagation has served laudatory purposes ever since. Domestically the revolution for African American rights offered a model and an inspiration for the campaigns for women's rights, gay rights, and the rights of the disabled. Around the world, the Civil Rights revolution has been invoked and emulated by liberation movements in such disparate lands as Northern Ireland, South Africa, eastern Europe, China, and, most recently, the Middle East.[2]

The question remains, however, whether the substantive accomplishments of the Civil Rights Movement measure up to its iconic status. Specifically, was it an *economic* as well as a moral and legal revolution? Did it bring significant advances in the material well-being of ordinary people? Did it open new opportunities in education, employment, and occupational status for African Americans? Perhaps most challenging, did the revolution live up to the oft-repeated claims that the movement was "good for the white South," that by accepting black rights white southerners would "lift a burden from [their] own shoulders, too."[3] These are the questions explored in this book. And if all three can be answered in the affirmative—as will be argued here—then an economist is obliged to address a further question: Why did white southerners defend so passionately and for so long an inefficient system that evidently failed to serve their own best economic interests?

One of the obstacles to understanding this history is that acquiescence in the Civil Rights revolution has been so complete, at least in public discourse, that it is difficult to find white southerners willing to acknowledge, much less explain and defend, their earlier choices. One black southerner who remembered the Jim Crow era all too well complained, "when [segregation] ended you can't find a single white person who remembers it."[4] Historian Jason Sokol writes, "Many years after the Civil Rights movement, white southerners made a concerted effort to forget the very past that continued to define them."[5] Some political figures whose segregationist past could not be denied offered abject apologies. A dramatic example was Mayor Joe Smitherman of Selma, Alabama, of whom it was said, "He can do the reformed redneck segregationist almost better than anybody." Smitherman once confessed to a local congregation, "My hands are as dirty as the others. I ordered the arrest of Dr. King. We were wrong. I did it. I'm sorry."[6] Similarly the *Jackson Clarion-Ledger,* Mississippi's most influential newspaper and an outspoken supporter of "massive resistance" to desegregation in the 1960s, declared two decades later, "We were wrong, wrong, wrong."[7] How many revolutions win such uncoerced testimonials from spokesmen for the ancien régime?

Because the economic and political motivations for these statements are often transparent, they invite the suspicion that the so-called revolution may have been merely superficial, a change in tone but not substance. Many observers are inclined to support this skepticism, suggesting that little of economic consequence actually occurred. The distinguished historian Leon Litwack writes, "Even as the Civil Rights Movement struck down legal barriers, it failed to strike down economic barriers. Even as it ended the violence of segregation, it failed to diminish the violence of poverty."[8] After a lengthy stint in the South, *New York Times* correspondent Peter Applebome concluded that although the Civil Rights revolution was "the best thing that ever happened to the white South," it was "a mixed blessing for Southern blacks," for whom pining for the old segregation era is "a common theme across the South."[9] Of race and schooling, historian Raymond Wolters states flatly, "Integration has been a failure."[10] The catalogue of similar sentiments could be extended almost indefinitely.

Because this book reaches very different conclusions, it makes sense to begin by identifying and elaborating the core propositions underlying the analysis. The most important are these: (1) the Civil Rights revolution was in essence a southern regional phenomenon, calling for a consistent regional focus in assessing its impact; (2) from the beginning the Civil Rights Movement had economic motivations and goals, which were primarily realized in the South; (3) it was a true revolution, that is, a fundamental break with past trends and behavior that cannot be explained away as the inevitable consequence of market forces or modernization; (4) the landmark federal legislation of 1964 and 1965 was essential for the success of the revolution, but although some effects were almost instantaneous, the longer-term consequences required ongoing political and legal mobilization and played out only across many decades.

WHY THE SOUTH?

At one level, a focus on the South hardly requires extended explanation: this was the region with a legacy of slavery, segregation, disfranchisement, and violent racial suppression. Southern denial of basic constitutional rights to African Americans is where the Civil Rights Movement got its name. Into the 1960s, national political campaigns for racial justice overwhelmingly targeted the South.

It was of course well-known that African Americans also experienced prejudice, discrimination, and various forms of exclusion in northern and western states, phenomena dating from before the Civil War. Not only did economic and political inequities in these areas persist through the Reconstruction and Progressive eras, but in many respects, race relations and practices worsened with the onset of massive black inflows from the South during and after World War I. The reality of northern discrimination is undeniable, but regional differences in racial structures and in the rigidity of these structures were also fundamental. Outside of the South, blacks were not denied the vote, so they could organize politically and in time exert significant pressure on city, state, and national policies. One result was that many northern cities and states passed (or revived) laws against discrimination in public accommodations such as restaurants, hotels, and theaters. Such segregation practices had been common, though never as pervasive as in the South. The mobilization of legal infrastructure and moral pressure supported significant progress on this front during the 1940s and 1950s.[11]

In labor markets, racial discrimination prevailed in all parts of the country, but its forms differed by region. Job categories in the South were explicitly racial (though rarely codified legally) and by the 1920s were marked by a visible "racial wage differential." In contrast, employers outside the South rarely differentiated wages by race explicitly, but blacks were commonly excluded outright from a wide range of occupations and firms. In Philadelphia, for example, most manufacturing companies did not hire a single black worker until the late 1930s. In some ways, the southern structure might have been preferable, and indeed, even before the Great Depression, unemployment rates in northern cities were 50 to 100 percent higher for blacks than for whites. In the South the rule may have been "Know your place," but in the North it was not clear that the economy really had a place for black workers.[12]

But the northern structure was more susceptible to change in response to economic, political, and moral pressure. Economic historian Warren Whatley shows that for Cincinnati firms that first hired African Americans during World War I, the learning experience had a lasting effect on employment policy. The Ford Motor Company broke the color line in the auto industry in the 1920s and profited in so doing. Political mobilization led to greater black representation in municipal jobs in such cities as Chicago, Pittsburgh, and Detroit. According to William Collins's detailed econometric study, the Fair Employment Practices Committee established in 1941 had substantial positive effects on black employment in defense-related industries, but only outside the South. Subsequently most northern states with large black populations adopted fair employment laws with at least modest impact on employment opportunities for black men and women. The cumulative result of these forces was that black occupational

attainment as of 1950 in northern states—limited as it was—
markedly exceeded that of black southerners.[13]

In contrast to this path of steady though slow racial progress,
the white South dug in its heels in defense of its racial order. Writing in 1942, the Swedish economist Gunnar Myrdal observed "an
increased determination on the part of white Southerners to defend unchanged the patterns of segregation and discrimination."[14] Taking a long view, one may cite various positive trends
even in the South, such as improved health, higher relative school
spending, and the decline of lynchings. But blacks were severely
underrepresented in the growth of southern nonfarm employment between 1900 and 1950, a gap that cannot be explained by
differences in education.[15] On matters of policy, there was little
sign or promise of change. Myrdal quoted a letter from a white
liberal southerner who had previously been hopeful: "The South
is becoming almost unanimous in a pattern of unity that refers to
white unity. The thousands of incidents and accidents in the South
are being integrated into the old pattern of Southern determination against an outside aggression."[16] The growing regional isolation noted by Myrdal is what made the southern Civil Rights
revolution both necessary and possible.[17]

The preceding paragraphs may not be particularly surprising
or contentious. It is well-known that the pre–Civil Rights South
was more overt in its racism, and it is perhaps not unexpected as
a corollary that its racial economic constraints were also more
severe. An issue arises in the late 1960s, however, when historical coverage tends to follow the attention of the media in shifting
from political confrontations in the South to the violent upheav-
als in northern cities. With the "discovery" that the race issue was
not confined to one region, subsequent analysis typically draws
upon national data, conveying the impression that the landmark
legislation of 1964 and 1965 was ineffective and unappreciated.
The "civil disorders" in Watts, Newark, Detroit, and many other
cities were certainly major events in American racial history, but

they were far more frequent and severe outside of the South.[18] Civil rights legislation had little immediate impact in these areas, and this neglect may be justly criticized. The question raised here is this: Where is the follow-up on the economic and political effects *within* the South, which was the primary target of the new laws? Subsequent chapters will show that the historical substance of the Civil Rights revolution looks very different, and on the whole more encouraging, when viewed from a southern regional perspective.

As incorrigible as the white South seemed during the 1960s, an oft-heard comment within the movement was that the South had a better chance to "make it" in race relations than the rest of the nation. Benjamin Muse, tireless organizer for the Southern Regional Council, wrote in 1968, "Over the South as a whole a gentler wind was blowing. There were indications, in fact, that this region might yet arrive at a Negro-white relationship of equality and friendship sooner than any other."[19] The precise basis for such hopeful observations was often unclear. White southerners, presumably hoping to encourage racial goodwill, often suggested that after centuries of coexistence, black and white southerners "know and understand each other more fully."[20] This analysis may contain some truth, but because dubious claims to "know the Negro" were themselves a long-standing southern tradition, they cannot be taken at face value.

A more plausible basis for regional differentiation lies in the quality of southern black political leadership and organization, traceable to the experience of the movement itself. Leslie Dunbar, executive director of the Southern Regional Council from 1961 to 1965, wrote, "If we try to make clear what we mean by the 'Civil Rights Movement,' I think we must say that it was defined by Southern problems and given character by the qualities of Negro Southerners. The movement did, of course, spread beyond the South, but always the cohesion was the South."[21] Distinguished interpreters such as Clayborne Carson, Aldon Morris, and Charles Payne have argued that the southern movement drew upon indigenous black organizing traditions that reached back for decades, if not longer.[22]

One of the hallmarks of the southern movement between 1954 and 1965 was the commitment to nonviolence, an approach that did not transfer smoothly into northern settings. To be sure, historians have refuted the idealized conception that the southern movement was entirely nonviolent, pointing to the militant Deacons for Defense and noting that most activists accepted nonviolence as a tactic more than a philosophy.[23] This corrective is appropriate, but it does not gainsay the regional contrast. In the South, self-defense groups supported and complemented nonviolent protest and voter registration, in contrast to the revolutionary and defiant Black Panther Party, most active in northern cities. As Peniel Joseph points out, Civil Rights–era organizing in the South was not abandoned after 1965 but "updated with a new face and political edge."[24]

Indeed the active black presence in the South is one important basis for the persistence of regional distinctiveness into the twenty-first century. Yet somehow "region" has ceased to be an acceptable category among American social scientists. From the 1970s onward, observers have periodically announced the impending demise or disappearance of the South.[25] Some historians proclaim it emphatically: "The era of southern exceptionalism is over."[26] This perspective is understandable, since regional patriotism no longer serves as the ideological basis for southern politics—by 2001 the percentage of blacks in the South who identified as southerners was actually higher than that for whites—and the region is no longer isolated from inflows of population, capital, and information. Adherents correctly point out that merely declaring a phenomenon to be "southern" hardly constitutes an adequate explanation for it. Nevertheless the desire for greater explanatory depth does not justify glossing over pronounced and persistent regional patterns that fairly leap from the data as soon as one begins to notice them. It is not unusual for analysts using state data to find that "percentage black" is a powerful variable accounting for political and economic outcomes, without considering how strongly this index is correlated with location in southeastern states. In 2010 the ten states with the highest African American population shares were all located within the census South region.[27]

Region is not merely a proxy for race. Investigators continue to find, often to their surprise, distinct southern configurations in voting, health, tax, and environmental policies, incarceration, and school desegregation, among many others. The degree of regionalism varies among these indicators, and the forces at work are not always obvious. But regionalism is evident in one major development that is closely related to the subject matter of this book: the migration of African Americans into the South from all other regions of the country, reversing more than fifty years of sustained outflow. In some areas, the reversal began directly after passage of the Civil Rights Act; since 1970 net black migration has been persistently southward, increasingly so over time. The causes and consequences of this shift are discussed in greater detail in later chapters, where it will be argued that the phenomenon is a direct consequence of the Civil Rights revolution, understood as an essentially regional phenomenon.

In a study drawing upon sources both multiple and diverse, it is not always possible to maintain a consistent definition of the South as a geographic entity. Because it is often necessary to work with state data, and the main focus of this book is on states that practiced Jim Crow segregation through the 1950s, a useful working definition is the eleven states of the former Confederacy. For practical purposes, it is sometimes necessary to use data for the South as defined by the U.S. Census (which includes the border states of Delaware, Maryland, Kentucky, West Virginia, and Oklahoma, plus the District of Columbia). The Bureau of Economic Analysis has its own grouping, called the Southeast, which adds Kentucky and West Virginia to the Confederate list but assigns Texas to the Southwest (see Map 1.1). Fortunately,

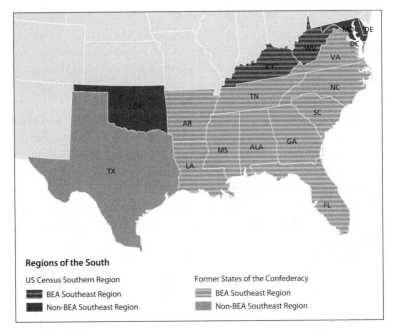

Regions of the South

US Census Southern Region

███ BEA Southeast Region

███ Non-BEA Southeast Region

Former States of the Confederacy

▓▓▓ BEA Southeast Region

▒▒▒ Non-BEA Southeast Region

Map 1.1 Regions of the South.

none of the major theses of this book rise or fall on the precision of regional boundaries. The analysis applies most directly and fully to the former Confederate core; no attempt is made to cover the unique experiences of the border areas, though this neglect is not meant to imply that racial issues in these places were minor or economically insignificant.

DID THE CIVIL RIGHTS MOVEMENT HAVE ECONOMIC GOALS?

A common perception is that the movement of the 1950s and early 1960s focused primarily on *rights*, turning only belatedly to matters of economic justice. The implication is that the major issues were legalistic and essentially symbolic, driven more by middle-class concerns over status than by the material struggles of ordinary people. James MacGregor and Stewart Burns write that the black freedom movement "did not make economic needs and aspirations a high priority. At first glance the abundance of movement rhetoric about black poverty and joblessness and the obligatory demands for economic betterment seem to belie this. But if one looks at deeds not words, and to the deployment of movement resources, it is clear that economic rights were slighted—until it was probably too late to make a real difference."[28]

This really is a misperception. The *Brown* decision of 1954 did not represent a desire for "social equality" or "race-mixing" but grew out of the decades-long struggle for racial equality in education, fundamentally an economic goal because of its importance for life chances. The National Association for the Advancement of Colored People (NAACP) argued, and the U.S. Supreme Court agreed, that segregation on the basis of race deprived black children of equal educational opportunity. One may question the integrationist strategy, as skeptics have done from the beginning, but not the economic character of the objectives.

Similarly, from the bus boycotts of the 1950s to the sit-ins of the early 1960s, demands for equal access to services were almost always coupled with demands for jobs providing those services. In December 1955 the Montgomery Improvement Association called for "employment of Negro bus operators in predominantly Negro residential sections," a demand that was actually quite radical for the time because of the quasi-legal powers bus drivers held. Flyers like the one from Warrenton, North Carolina, were circulated during public accommodations disputes throughout the region (Figure 1.1). The appeal for "equal opportunity for employment" and the complaint that stores "do not hire any Negroes in responsible jobs" are, if anything, more prominent than the demand for fountain service. In Birmingham, pickets wore sandwich boards reading "Don't buy where you cannot be a salesman" and continued their pressure until each downtown department store hired at least one black clerk. Every school child knows that

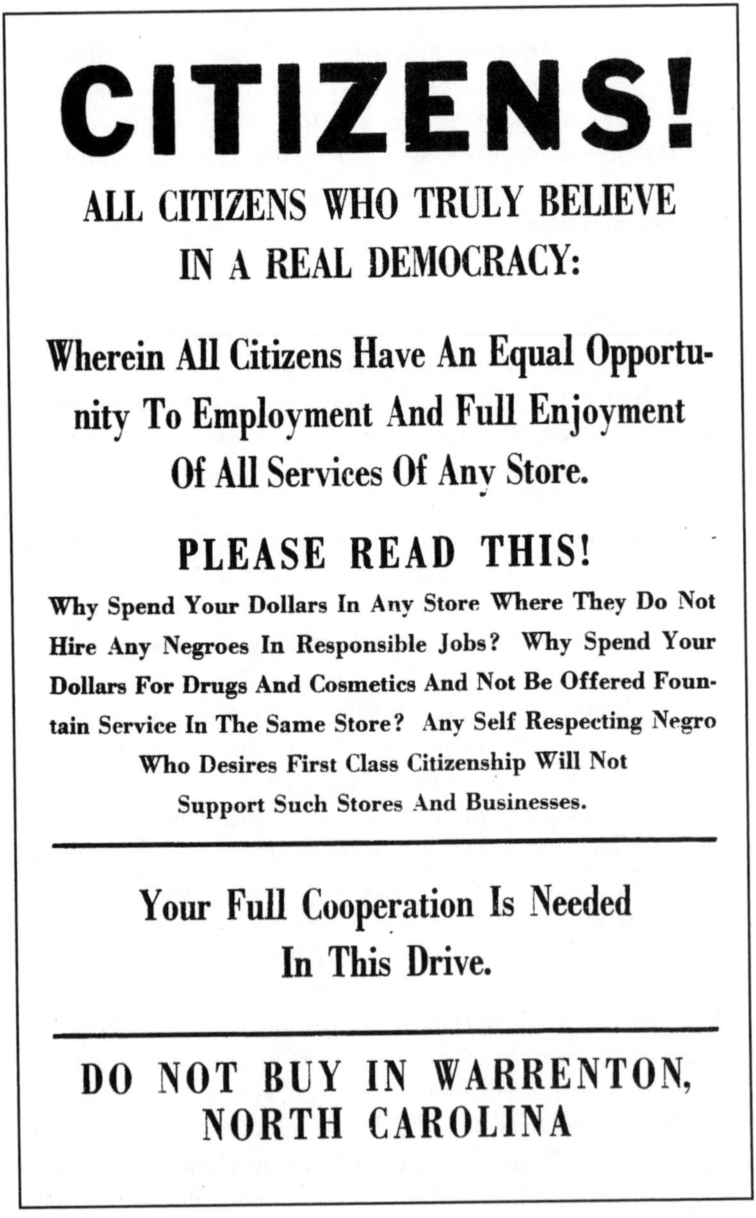

CITIZENS!

ALL CITIZENS WHO TRULY BELIEVE IN A REAL DEMOCRACY:

Wherein All Citizens Have An Equal Opportunity To Employment And Full Enjoyment Of All Services Of Any Store.

PLEASE READ THIS!

Why Spend Your Dollars In Any Store Where They Do Not Hire Any Negroes In Responsible Jobs? Why Spend Your Dollars For Drugs And Cosmetics And Not Be Offered Fountain Service In The Same Store? Any Self Respecting Negro Who Desires First Class Citizenship Will Not Support Such Stores And Businesses.

Your Full Cooperation Is Needed In This Drive.

DO NOT BUY IN WARRENTON, NORTH CAROLINA

Figure 1.1 Boycott flyer from Warrenton, North Carolina, Summer 1963.

Martin Luther King's "I Have a Dream" speech was delivered at the Lincoln Memorial on August 28, 1963, but it is often forgotten that the event itself was billed as a March for *Jobs* and Freedom (emphasis added).[29]

The public accommodations issue itself certainly had economic content, reflected in the hardships experienced by black travelers who could not count on finding a place to eat or stay overnight. It was not uncommon for families to pack meals, blankets, and even containers of gasoline in their cars for long trips. Playwright Alexander Ramsey recalled, "We didn't want to stop anywhere and get into a situation where we didn't know how it was going to turn out."[30] It is true that media attention tended to focus on human-interest aspects of racial issues, and movement leaders often catered to this tendency. In Nashville, some activists argued strongly for an emphasis on economic issues, but as Reverend Kelly Miller Smith, chaplain of the local chapter of the Southern Christian Leadership Conference (SCLC), recalled:

> We did not disagree with the fact that [the economic issue] was most important, but our view was that sit-ins would lend themselves to a kind of public presentation of the issue. Kind of a dramatizing of the issue that would be better than any procedures of which we were aware when dealing with economics.[31]

However valuable as theater, participants clearly understood that sit-ins represented "something bigger than a hamburger," as Ella Baker put it, launching an attack on racial discrimination "not only at lunch counters but in every aspect of life."[32]

The claim that the movement neglected economics only persists because most standard narratives omit the black labor struggle entirely. Black workers in southern industries fought against discrimination even in the 1930s and 1940s, an effort labor historians have called "Civil Rights unionism."[33] The fact that white fellow workers (as well as employers) were often adversaries does not deny the goal of economic advancement. Although these efforts were often thwarted, labor activists frequently supplied foot soldiers for the Civil Rights Movement, attending meetings, writing letters, serving as guards at mass meetings and demonstrations, in one case even directing the choir of the Alabama Christian Movement for Human Rights! A press release issued by the ACMHR at the height of the Birmingham conflict specified, "Chief among the Negro requests are the immediate desegregation of lunch counter facilities and the establishment of fair hiring practice and job upgrading on a non-discriminatory basis."[34]

The grain of truth in the "rights to economics" scenario is that activists changed their line of attack from enactment to enforcement after passage of the Civil Rights Act. But there was no discontinuity in the underlying goals, since Civil Rights pressure was directly responsible for the strength of the antidiscrimination sections of the Act. Because of the Kennedy administration's deference to southern power in Congress, early drafts contained no fair employment provisions, but this omission was reversed in response to vigorous lobbying by groups allied in the Civil Rights Coalition.[35] The postenactment effectiveness of Title VII required grassroots mobilization and extensive follow-up litigation, which were genuine though often overlooked parts of the Civil Rights revolution. Willie Boyd, the Duke Power janitor who initiated the landmark *Griggs* case, was a veteran of NAACP youth work and sit-ins. Boyd and his fellow plaintiffs closely followed the course of the Civil Rights Act through Congress. Although the decision was announced in 1971, the job transfer application that launched the case was submitted on March 1, 1966, directly invoking the new legislation.[36]

Allegations that the movement neglected economics often boil down to a complaint that federal legislation mainly targeted the South, when the "big problems," as Whitney Young said to President Kennedy, were northern. Southern economic problems were as big or bigger, but it is true that the Civil Rights Act avoided distinctively northern forms of discrimination, such as de facto school segregation and union seniority systems. Young's warnings of a "tinder-box of racial unrest in northern cities" proved prophetic, but that is not the same as saying that the southern movement favored rights over economics. Economic goals were fundamental, and the Civil Rights Act was a true watershed in pursuing them.[37]

EXPLAINING AWAY THE REVOLUTION

Despite, or perhaps because of, the momentous impact of the Civil Rights revolution, observers from various perspectives have been attracted to the possibility of attributing these changes to something other than the passage of powerful federal legislation in 1964 and 1965 and the robust enforcement of these acts in subsequent decades. One common tactic is to identify the movement as a straightforward campaign to eliminate state-sanctioned or legal segregation. For example, Stephan and Abigail Thernstrom write, "The racial segregation that was the organizing principle of southern society had largely been created by law—by Jim Crow codes."[38] It is understandable that many economists are also drawn to this formulation, because it underscores the strong belief that in the absence of legal sanctions, market forces would undermine unjustified discrimination even in the presence of race prejudice.[39]

But to view the Civil Rights revolution as primarily a dismantling of legal barriers is deeply misleading. It is true that the legal codification of segregation between 1890 and 1910 was something of a watershed in consolidating the Jim Crow regime, though in most cases the statutes merely ratified practices already in place. As the decade of inaction following the *Brown* decision showed, however, mere federal invalidation of segregation laws had little effect on behavior. State and municipal segregation statutes were occasionally invoked in response to the Freedom Rides and sit-ins of the early 1960s, but these laws had little if any bearing on the struggle for equal access to public accommodations. Most laws *requiring* segregation had been repealed by that time, precisely to avoid *Brown*'s proscription of state-sponsored segregation.[40] Southern workplaces were even less subject to legal regulation. A 1940 legal survey concluded that "the problem of industrial segregation in the South is usually left in the hands of private business" and noted only three exceptions.[41] The point is not that segregation laws were unimportant. The essence of the problem, however, in both consumer and labor markets, was persuading or compelling profit-seeking businessmen who believed that desegregation was economically threatening.

More challenging is the argument that the Civil Rights revolution was largely a byproduct of economic change, reflecting deep incompatibility between the emerging urban-industrial society of the South and the traditional racial caste system. Derrick Bell writes, "Finally, some whites realized that the South could make the transition from a rural, plantation society to the sunbelt with all its potential and profit only when it ended its struggle to remain divided by state-sponsored segregation. Thus, segregation was viewed as a barrier to further industrialization."[42] Sociologist Jack Bloom puts it this way: "When the agrarian elite was finally faced with the political and social ramifications of the trend towards industrialism in the region, it dug in its collective heels to fight, and it was defeated" by a new coalition of southern business and middle classes, aided by the federal government.[43] Labor historian Paul Moreno suggests that "a new generation of southern business leaders put economic rationality ahead of racial order."[44]

This style of analysis poses a problem familiar to economic historians: it posits an association that seems forcefully compelling in retrospect, but despite the apparent logic, it does not describe the historical record accurately. The demand for spatial separation known as segregation originated not in rural but in urban settings, in an attempt by leaders who considered themselves progressive to adapt the racial order to the modern world. Segregation was stricter in newer cities like Atlanta and Nashville than in older centers like Charleston. Atlanta's civic leaders were among the first to join the new southern bandwagon court-ing conventions, tourism, and industry, yet in its racial order the city remained thoroughly southern. Hotels and convention cen-ters were rigidly segregated. Even in the 1950s, many Atlanta jobs, such as firefighting, truck driving, clerking, and auto repair, were closed to blacks in both public and private sectors. Despite its progressive, cosmopolitan image as the "city too busy to hate," the response of Atlanta's business community to desegregation demands in the 1960s was openly hostile and resistant, until (and in some cases after) passage of the Civil Rights Act in 1964.[45]

In labor markets, job segregation lines proved remarkably per-sistent through the 1940s, 1950s, and into the 1960s in southern industries both new and old, even including plants managed by outside firms. As economist Donald Dewey found in the mid-1950s, in most plants "the racial division of labor . . . has re-mained fixed as far back as anyone can remember."[46] If employ-ers were inconvenienced or distressed by this system, with rare exceptions they kept their opposition secret. They certainly did not testify in favor of federal equal employment initiatives, but instead typically responded at most with tokenism and foot-dragging. Although fear of adverse reaction by incumbent white workers undoubtedly explains some of this employer behavior, the deeper explanation is that the assignment of workers to jobs roughly matched what employers took to be the inherent capaci-ties and potential of the races.

One might suppose that racial differences in expected job per-formance would be subject to change through education, train-ing, and work experience, but as products of their time and place, southern employers thought such investments in black workers were pointless. Thus the hard-won improvements in black schools and gains in educational attainment had little ef-fect on job opportunities because the prevailing white vision of the emerging modern southern economy had very little room for educated blacks. In retrospect, the massive out-migration of southern blacks between 1940 and 1970 (disproportionately those with schooling) was wasteful. In practice, this outflow may have provided the safety valve that kept the southern system running smoothly.

The Civil Rights revolution could hardly have been an inevitable byproduct of economic change, because if the white South had been left to its own devices, the revolution would not have happened. As David Chappell points out, in every major Deep South election in which segregation was an issue between *Brown* and the Voting Rights Act, the segregationist candidate won.[47] Jason Sokol, who emphasizes the diversity of southern white responses, nonetheless writes, "All but the most liberal of southern whites opposed school integration."[48] With rare exceptions, southern business leaders held very similar views, acting first to delay and then to minimize racial change. Only the prospect or experience of economic losses—from boycotts, from the effects of turbulence and school closures on the climate for investment, and from the threat of withdrawal of federal contracts and funding—induced some business groups to support moderate accommodation to the cumulating pressures.[49]

To be clear, the foregoing summary is not meant to downplay the significance of the belated conversion of southern business to desegregation, nor even to belittle the ex post facto efforts to rewrite history and celebrate the Civil Rights revolution as a proud chapter in regional history. The point is simply to reject claims that the transition was merely an epiphenomenon driven by deeper economic and demographic forces. The clearest indicator of a true revolution is when prevailing norms of behavior and rhetoric change and participants "imply that they had known for an age what they had discovered only yesterday."[50] In the end, there is a core of truth in the assertion that southern business chose "economic rationality over racial order," and for some readers, the timing and order of events may seem of secondary importance, compared to understanding that the system moved from one political-economic equilibrium to another.

But the historical details are important to economic historians. We normally analyze political processes in terms of interest groups vying for economic advantage, yet here we have a case in which groups fought tooth and nail against changes that turned out to be good business moves. A closely related lesson is for economists, who tend to assume that business firms know best how to maximize their own profits. Contrary to the economic tradition descended from Gary Becker, which treats racial discrimination as a noneconomic preference, most southern firms and most white southerners believed that desegregation was economically threatening. The Civil Rights revolution shows the possibility of collective learning in a positive direction, even where profit-seeking entities are at the center of the action.

THE CIVIL RIGHTS AND VOTING RIGHTS ACTS AS WATERSHEDS

This book treats the Civil Rights Act of 1964 and the Voting Rights Act of 1965 as watershed moments that reshaped all subsequent events in southern history. After a seminar I gave a few years ago, a friendly critic remarked, "Your methodology seems to be to attribute everything that happened in the South after 1964 to the Civil Rights Act." In a sense this shorthand summary is not far off. Obviously the South was also affected by all manner of economic and political developments that were not caused by Civil Rights laws and that for the most part could not have been anticipated at the time of enactment. But southern responses all looked different after the revolution.

It is true that pressure for federal action on Civil Rights was building over time, so that one might reasonably argue that if Congress had, for one reason or another, not passed that particular bill in that very year, something like it would surely have happened sooner or later. Perhaps so. On some economic indicators, one can detect the beginnings of change prior to the Act itself, developments described in Chapters 3, 4, and 6. A more econometrically oriented study might attempt to identify the effects of the legislation more precisely and to distinguish them from trends that were already under way. My belief is, however, that such an approach would not do justice to the status of these two pieces of legislation as historic, game-changing breakthroughs.

In making this case, one can begin by noting just how unanticipated the Act and its consequences were to both advocates and opponents of change until shortly before its passage. The Montgomery bus boycott of 1955 was a remarkable victory, though it required a federal court decision for a successful conclusion. But this outcome was followed by a wave of bombings, for which the perpetrators were quickly acquitted. Lawsuits to desegregate the city's parks got nowhere, and Montgomery saw no further progress on integration for the next five years. Historian J. Mills Thornton writes, "The white supremacist who surveyed the situation in Montgomery at the beginning of 1960 could do so with considerable satisfaction. . . . The prospects for the ultimate victory of Jim Crow looked bright indeed." This status quo prompted the Citizens' Councils to declare that history would describe Montgomery as the place where "integration efforts were stopped cold."[51]

Nor, as of the early 1960s, did the prospects for effective federal legislation look any better from outside the South. President Kennedy was known to have strong political ties to southern Democrats, confirmed by his appointment of five segregationist judges. (His five black judicial appointments were in other parts of the country.) Kennedy did announce plans to introduce a Civil Rights bill, but with polls showing that a majority of Americans believed the nation was "moving too fast" on racial issues, it was widely believed that it would have no chance of passage until after the election of 1964. It was also anticipated that the Act would be watered down by Congress, as had happened in 1957 and 1960. The 1963 explosion in Birmingham dramatically changed the political atmosphere, but at least some of the events that brought about "a tougher bill than anyone had imagined the previous year"—the Kennedy assassination and the unique leadership exerted by Lyndon Johnson—were surely historical accidents. The overall legislative record supports the conclusion of political scientist Mark Stern; after years devoted to analyzing the black vote and Congress, he wrote, "When I examined the quantitative studies, what struck me was that they did not predict or explain the Civil Rights revolution of the 1960s, nor the sea change in black voter enrollment that followed the Voting Rights Act of 1965."[52]

The Voting Rights Act was even more contingent than the Civil Rights Act. The Johnson landslide of 1964 can be read as a triumphant national ratification of the Act, but the magnitude of the victory reflected numerous unrelated factors, particularly the perception that Barry Goldwater was a dangerous extremist. Once returned to office, Johnson had many other legislative priorities. The violence at Selma gave him the occasion to push voting rights forward, but Johnson and his advisors were keenly aware that the window of opportunity for successful action was brief. With race riots in the cities and the rise of militant groups like the Black Panthers, they knew that a backlash in northern public opinion was inevitable. With a different leader and smaller Democratic majorities, it is easy to picture an alternative history in which the window had closed without major legislation. Political scientist Richard Valelly writes, "In retrospect, of course, there is an air of inevitability about the Voting Rights Act. It is hard to imagine that something so important to American national life could not have happened in the end. Quite possibly, though, the compelling nonviolent protest in Selma that did so much to empower Johnson to procure the act came at the last possible moment."[53]

Important as it was, passing the legislation was only the first step in a new phase for the movement. Having seen a decade of court rulings and Civil Rights laws resulting in little real change, both activists and resisters had reason to doubt that this time would be different. Even where there was substantial voluntary compliance, as in public accommodations, extending desegregation into smaller towns and rural areas required testing, filing complaints, and a serious commitment on the part of the Department of Justice. In employment, some textile firms responded quite quickly to the new law, but in most industries, significant progress came only in response to grassroots activism and litigation, extending into the 1970s and beyond.[54]

On voting rights, the jump in black registration was rapid and dramatic, but realizing genuine returns from the political process was a protracted struggle across subsequent decades. Thus to identify these acts as watersheds is by no means to say that they constituted one-time, self-contained historical phenomena. Their meaning and long-run impact depended crucially on political and organizational follow-through, for the most part visible only with a consistent regional approach. As Thornton observes:

> An examination of the southern communities that generated the direct-action campaigns reveals that the presumed decline of the civil rights movement is far more an artifact of the recounting of history from a national perspective than it is an accurate portrayal of the experience of southerners during the twentieth century's final three decades. At the level of southern municipalities, the struggle for civil rights continued to play out in numerous electoral contests for town councils, county commissions, and state legislative office and in the debates over measures in those and comparable bodies. In that sense, the death of the civil rights movement has been greatly exaggerated.[55]

But community and state forces within the South could not have accomplished much without outside help. The Civil Rights and Voting Rights Acts provided the statutory foundation, but more often than not, genuine progress in employment, school desegregation, and voting was achieved only through strong rulings by federal courts and strong actions by administrative agencies charged with defining and enforcing rules of compliance. Impatient with years of foot-dragging and evasion and empowered by the new legislation, federal courts during the late 1960s and 1970s demanded concrete, verifiable steps from southern employers and school districts. In the process, compliance rules often went well beyond the assurances of restraint made by supporters at the time of enactment. The Voting Rights Act was a particularly aggressive incursion by the federal government into areas long reserved to the states. But the expectations of change developed sufficient momentum that enforcement efforts were largely continued by the federal bureaucracy, even while President Nixon was carrying out a "southern strategy" in political rhetoric.[56] The tide of judicial assertiveness had begun to turn even before the end of the 1970s, and the national political climate turned decisively with the election of Ronald Reagan in 1980. But as will be shown, by then most black economic progress within the South had become established and difficult to reverse.

Thus it would not be quite right to view the two major acts as pure historical accidents, made possible only by a unique and fleeting conjunction of circumstances. The determination of courts and federal agencies reflected a deeper resolve to carry out the reconstruction project then under way. Congress too confirmed and extended their actions, by strengthening the enforcement powers of the Equal Employment Opportunity Commission (EEOC) in 1972 and by renewing and strengthening the Voting Rights Act in 1970, 1975, and 1982. Nonetheless the window of intensive federal enforcement was not open long, perhaps fifteen years, and most of this energy derived from the legislation of 1964 and 1965, which could easily have been derailed, delayed, or watered down. This perspective justifies an approach that regards the acts as historical turning points and the revolution as what was done in their wake.

A BRIEF SYNOPSIS

As a work of economic history, the analysis begins in Chapter 2 with an interpretation of the political-economic origins of the

Jim Crow South, during the era when the region was dominated by plantation agriculture. A crucial feature of this period of Civil Rights insurgency was that the South was then a rapidly developing economic region, whose growth prospects were particularly strong as it escaped decades of backwardness and isolation. Figure 1.2 shows that, as measured by per capita income, the most dramatic break from the past in all three census subregions occurred during World War II, though key structural changes began earlier. Between the 1930s and the 1950s, many of the foundations of the old regime were undermined by mechanization, migration, urbanization, war, and other federal policies. But the figure also suggests that the wartime growth spurt had slowed by the mid-1950s, especially in the South Atlantic and West South Central subregions. Economic analysts of the time portrayed the South as a region struggling to overcome outdated thinking, rigid

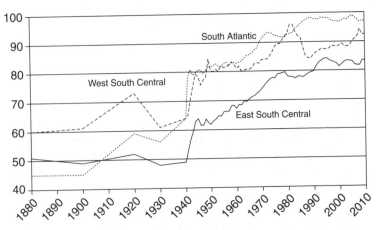

Figure 1.2 Income per capita as percentage of U.S., 1880–2010.
   Sources: 1880–1940: U.S. Bureau of the Census. *Historical Statistics of the United States: Colonial Times to 1970*, Series F287, F292, F293, F294; 1941–2010: U.S. Bureau of Commerce, Bureau of Economic Analysis. *Annual State Personal Income and Employment*, Interactive tables website, accessed April 4, 2012, SA1-3 Personal Income Summary.

social structures, and substandard school systems in the interests of economic progress.[57]

One should not leap to the conclusion that an intensified drive for economic growth fostered moderation in racial attitudes or policies. Although the economic base was changing, the superstructure of segregation by then had a life of its own, embedded in norms, perceptions, interests, and institutions of remarkable persistence and resiliency. Analyses of growth strategies within the region rarely considered the role of African Americans in the emerging economy. The *Southern Economic Journal,* though preoccupied with regional issues, never published an article on race. Most white southerners saw no integral place for blacks in the new urban-industrial economy, and this implicit exclusion was evidently ratified by the departure of four million black southerners from the region, even while educated white professionals and retirees began to move southward into fast-growing cities and Sun Belt areas. Mechanization certainly did not convert wealthy planters into racial progressives. The southern political and economic leadership largely changed its tune from "Negroes are necessary for the South" to what Civil Rights leader Aaron Henry summarized this way: "They wished we'd go back to Africa, but Chicago was close enough."[58]

Nevertheless black southerners mobilized politically and economically to break down racial exclusions and improve access to economic opportunities. The region's new hunger for economic growth provided great leverage for the Civil Rights Movement in these efforts. Only after experiencing economic pressures over months and years through sit-ins and boycotts did southern business groups acquiesce in desegregating lunch counters, restaurants, theaters, and hotels. Racial progress in employment and schools required more than local economic pressures, coming only in response to new federal legislation, and even then requiring years of litigation and the threat of severe financial consequences for continued defiance. Even after legal issues related to public accommodations, employment, and schools had largely been settled, black voting rights generated new rounds of opposition and vote dilution, so that southern black political representation advanced only across three decades or more. The political narrative of how the country arrived at the culminating legislation of 1964 and 1965, and then enforced these laws in a purposeful way through several administrations, has been recounted many times by able journalists and historians. The economic consequences in the South have been neglected by comparison.[59]

Chapters 3 through 6 present an economic interpretation of four major areas of conflict that were central to the Civil Rights revolution: public accommodations, labor markets, school desegregation, and voting rights. The focus on economic aspects of these issues certainly does not imply a belief that all actions by the major players were driven by a narrow calculus of pecuniary benefits and costs. Such a claim would be absurd in realms of behavior soaked with emotion, fears, and concerns over status and respect. Yet an emphasis on economics may still be justified, on the grounds that, as will be argued, most southern whites did not see themselves as sacrificing material gains for the sake of racial status. Instead they saw Civil Rights demands as economically threatening, and their ultimate acquiescence required seeing the economic world in a new way. Despite appearances, this book is more about white southerners than blacks.

Although the timing and mechanisms varied widely, the record shows strong gains on each one of these fronts for African Americans in the South—relative to earlier levels, relative to southern whites, and relative to national standards. Advances in incomes, educational attainment, occupational status, political representation, and black-owned businesses have been strong enough to be sustained, even in the face of marked changes in the political and economic climate.

The chapters go on to ask whether these gains were won at the expense of white southerners. In each case, the finding is that, contrary to prior fears, the Civil Rights revolution was economically beneficial for whites as well as blacks and for the regional economy more generally. Such a claim must be advanced and understood in moderation. Hypothetical alternative scenarios are necessarily imprecise, and one can always point to exceptions in particular times and places. But aggregate indicators point clearly to a post–Civil Rights growth acceleration. One index that captures the region's goal of attracting capital and high-income migrants is total personal income, expressed as a share of the U.S. total in Figures 1.3, 1.4, and 1.5.[60] Rather than steady progress, all three graphs suggest that the period between 1950 and the mid-1960s was a time of relative stagnation. In the East and West South Central regions, acceleration occurred only after the political breakthroughs of 1964 and 1965. In the South Atlantic the break may have happened slightly earlier, but in each case the major relative gains largely postdated the Civil Rights revolution.

Why and how did Civil Rights foster regional economic progress? It would be a mistake to claim that changes in the racial

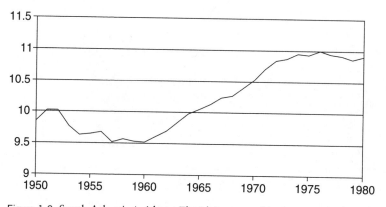

Figure 1.3 South Atlantic (without Florida) personal income as percentage of U.S. personal income, 1950–1980.
Source: U.S. Bureau of Commerce, Bureau of Economic Analysis. *Annual State Personal Income and Employment.* Interactive tables website, accessed April 4, 2012, SA1-3 Personal Income Summary.

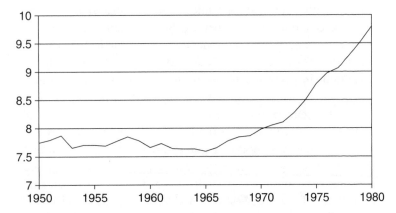

Figure 1.4 West South Central personal income as percentage of U.S. personal income, 1950–1980.
Source: U.S. Bureau of Commerce, Bureau of Economic Analysis. *Annual State Personal Income and Employment.* Interactive tables website, accessed April 4, 2012, SA1-3 Personal Income Summary.

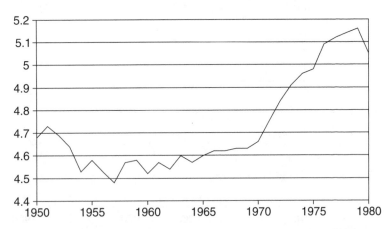

Figure 1.5 East South Central personal income as a percentage of U.S. personal income, 1950–1980.
Source: U.S. Bureau of Commerce, Bureau of Economic Analysis. *Annual State Personal Income and Employment.* Interactive tables website, accessed April 4, 2012, SA1-3 Personal Income Summary.

order *caused* accelerated growth directly. There were many sources of southern growth potential in the 1960s; low-wage manufacturing was one, but the list also includes natural resources, real estate, retirement and vacation communities, and the prospect of new business and technological clusters in metropolitan areas. As much as we might like to believe that the inefficiencies and barbarities of the Jim Crow era were incompatible with modern economic life, the more immediate stimulus was that settling the most contentious racial issues allowed political and business leaders to resume their pro-growth agenda. As Chapter 3 shows, cities that acquiesced in desegregating public accommodations enjoyed growth spurts in sales, as black customers returned with little apparent discouragement to white patronage.

Desegregation also opened clogged channels for outside investment into the region. In some instances the payoff was almost immediate. In 1965 the Milwaukee Braves announced plans to move to Atlanta, giving the South its first major league sports franchise. Star player Henry Aaron, who grew up in segregated Mobile, Alabama, at first expressed displeasure at returning to the South. But after local businessmen took him around town several times, Aaron said he wouldn't mind playing in Atlanta. Within five years major league teams were playing in New Orleans and Dallas, moves that would have been unthinkable under segregation. Another liberating moment was the first performance of *Porgy and Bess* in Charleston, South Carolina, before an enthusiastic integrated audience on June 26, 1970. A 1974 *New York Times* article reported that "the arts have become the hottest growth stock in Dixie," featuring Birmingham's newly dedicated concert and theater hall. The story noted that public theater in Birmingham had been desegregated since the mid-1960s, when arts patron Mrs. Cecil Roberts walked down the aisle of an auditorium on the arm of Dr. John Nixon, local president of the NAACP.[61]

Subsequent chapters discuss longer-term linkages between the Civil Rights revolution and regional progress. By broadening political representation and thereby assuring that blacks would share in new jobs and business opportunities, cities like Atlanta, Charlotte, and Birmingham were able to unite in support of growth-oriented projects such as airports, roads, health facilities, and municipal buildings. Acceptance of desegregation lessened local opposition to the pursuit of federal funds, a major source of infrastructure support in that era. Federal agencies insisted on nondiscrimination as a condition for funding, reinforcing local power-sharing even though enforcement was not always strict. The advent of black political power in cities was often viewed with deep suspicion by white business leaders. In time, however, the two sides found that mutually advantageous cooperation was better than protracted conflict or abandonment. The result was resumption of growth on a more racially inclusive basis. Ultimately Civil Rights tourism itself became an important component of the biracial agenda, reshaping the region's civic self-image even as it augmented revenues.

To be sure, the case for mutually beneficial progress is clearer for business and professional classes than for working-class white southerners. But as will be shown, regional growth generated gains for all major segments of the population. One never observes white wages falling while black wages rise, nor black employment growing at the expense of white jobs. Despite the contentious debates over race and schools, southern white test scores continued their progress toward the national average throughout the period of desegregation. The course of progress since the 1960s has certainly not been smooth, but the fluctuations for both races have largely reflected higher-level forces affecting regional and national economies. In other words, the Civil Rights revolution was not a program of redistribution but an integration of blacks into the mainstream of a regional economy from which they had long been excluded.

Chapter 7 considers three common criticisms of the Civil Rights Movement: that desegregation wiped out black-owned businesses and the communities around them; that the economic gains from the revolution served only the middle class; and that the universalist ideology of the movement was betrayed or abused, so that it came to stand in the way of further progress. On each count, my conclusion is that the criticisms do not have much force when assessed in historical context. But the discussion brings out an aspect of the Civil Rights revolution that is often not acknowledged: that the movement's successes did not come through diffusion and adoption of the principle of color blindness in political and economic life. Racial tensions have receded and tolerance has greatly improved—truly historic achievements. But race remains highly salient in political and economic life, in the South as in the rest of the nation. The region's remarkable record of achievement is closely associated with the presence of strong middle-class black communities, and the vitality of these communities has attracted African Americans into the South from all other regions of the country.

Chapter 8 reflects on the viability of this form of progress in the changing economic and demographic context of the twenty-first century. The deepest cultural and ideological legacies of the Civil Rights revolution have endured. But the success of race-based reforms in sharing economic gains among broad segments of the population reflected features of the Civil Rights era that have now passed into history. Most if not all of these conditions cannot be re-created. But in searching for ways to adapt the policy agenda to the challenges of harsh new times, such efforts will need to draw more than ever on the highest ideals of the Civil Rights Movement.

CHAPTER 2

THE POLITICAL ECONOMY

OF THE JIM CROW SOUTH

Abolition of slavery in the United States was swift and thorough, in contrast to other emancipations cushioned by gradualist timetables, compensation, or periods of apprenticeships. Slaves in the rebellious states were legally freed by the Emancipation Proclamation on New Year's Day 1863, and this radical step was reaffirmed by the Thirteenth Amendment to the U.S. Constitution in 1865 and by the first state postwar constitutions under Presidential Reconstruction. The Fourteenth Amendment, granting citizenship and equal protection of the laws to freedmen, was ratified in 1868; the Fifteenth Amendment, prohibiting denial of the vote on the basis of "race, color or previous condition of servitude," passed in 1870. Although these measures seemed definitive and were intended to be so at the time, the political and economic character of the postemancipation South was hotly contested for a full generation thereafter.

It would not be accurate to say that the region settled into a new form of slavery. Labor mobility was high in the postbellum era, and the new systems of sharecropping and tenancy emerged as a kind of market-generated compromise between the freedmen's goal of independence and the planters' quest for cash crops.

But the abandonment of plans to distribute land to the former slaves meant that blacks entered such contracts from a position of weakness. At the same time, high postwar cotton prices encouraged many smaller white farmers to take up cash-crop production. Subsequent stagnation in world cotton demand combined with high rates of population growth to bring blacks and many whites to a regional economic standard that was low relative to national norms.

Active African American participation in politics during the 1870s and 1880s could not change these deep background conditions, though a more equitable distribution of farmland might have altered the racial and class basis for southern politics over the longer haul. As events unfolded, when it gradually became clear that neither the federal government nor the U.S. Supreme Court would intervene, southern states were emboldened to disfranchise black voters, beginning with Mississippi's constitution of 1890. By 1910 the exclusion of blacks from southern politics was nearly complete, and the devices adopted effectively disfranchised large numbers of poor whites at the same time. The result in virtually every southern state was an undemocratic political structure dominated by large landowners with an interest in maintaining the isolation of their tenants and laborers.

These patterns can be understood as a kind of political-economic equilibrium. Elite planters dominated state and local politics. The farm labor force was by no means exclusively black, but disfranchisement aggravated the racial divide. Spending on black schools fell to a bare minimum, especially in black-majority plantation counties. New urban and industrial jobs were claimed overwhelmingly by whites, whose living conditions gradually improved, thus ratifying and seeming to justify the divergence in schooling. Racial separation was the rule in most spheres of life throughout the Reconstruction period, but its formal codification came relatively late in the process. Legally mandated segregation ultimately extended not only to schools, churches, and eating and drinking establishments but also to public transportation, hospitals, prisons, cemeteries, and recreational areas. Although their promoters saw these as modern, progressive measures in the interests of better race relations, the effect was to reinforce the economic confinement of most blacks to the countryside.

Notions of societal equilibrium always do some violence to history, and it would be wrong to think that the Jim Crow South ever settled into a condition of rigid stasis, impervious to larger economic and technological changes. World War I marked a turning point of sorts, because it triggered the first great outmigration from the region. Diffusion of the automobile in the 1920s increased individual mobility and sparked new rounds of road building by the states. The pace of change accelerated in the 1930s, when federal farm policies induced a drastic restructuring of plantation labor systems, and federally funded infrastructure investments modernized southern cities. These developments set the stage for even more massive out-migration during and after World War II.

As dramatic as these developments were, the important lesson for Civil Rights history is that by and large they did not disrupt the racial order put in place at the turn of the twentieth century. Economists with the aid of hindsight may see the system as costly and inefficient, but as an empirical matter, southern economic development did not undermine racial segregation, and few southern whites saw any incompatibility between the two. Statements of faith in such an effect were most commonly voiced as rationalizations for leaving the system undisturbed in the here and now. In this setting, racially selective out-migration was seen not as a cost to the region but as a mechanism that maintained the viability of the Jim Crow political-economic regime.

TENANCY, SHARECROPPING, AND LABOR MARKETS IN THE POSTBELLUM SOUTH

The belief that the federal government would distribute "forty acres and a mule" to give former slaves a new start in life was no mere wishful figment of newly liberated imaginations. General

William T. Sherman's field orders of January 15, 1865, distributed confiscated lands in coastal Georgia and South Carolina (and some army mules) in this way, and similar plans were widely discussed in Washington as the war drew to a close. But President Andrew Johnson revoked Sherman's orders, and in the end most confiscated lands were returned to the former owners. As an alternative vehicle, congressional Republicans approved the Southern Homestead Act of 1866, opening more than forty-five million acres to settlers in five states (Alabama, Arkansas, Florida, Louisiana, and Mississippi), with preference to loyal whites and blacks until 1867. The intentions were no doubt sincere, but the Act was a dismal failure. By the end of 1869, only four thousand freedmen had filed entries. Accounts of the time suggest some of the reasons: only one land office per state was opened; the land itself was remote from the plantation belt and of poor quality; no means of finance was available for seed, implements, work stock, and subsistence rations prior to the first crop; and there were few opportunities to combine wage-earning employment with part-time homesteading.[1]

Land ownership was thus a distant dream for most freedmen, who had to come to terms with the need to find employment on someone else's land. A number of scholars have traced the path of employment relations over the formative period from 1865 to 1880. According to economist Gerald Jaynes, plantations were initially reorganized on the same centrally managed basis as under slavery, using labor contracts supervised by the Freedmen's Bureau. These were not, however, cash-wage but share-wage contracts or, less frequently, the "standing wage." In the first, the entire labor force contracted for a share of the crop; in the second, a significant portion of the wage was withheld until after the harvest. Both systems were mainly postharvest payments, reflecting the landowner's effort to secure continuity of labor while reducing credit requirements. Both systems broke down over time. The centralized system using share payments suffered from poor work incentives and gave way to an intermediate "squad system," with foremen subcontracted to act as a buffer between employer and worker. Decentralization continued through the 1870s, culminating in family-based sharecropping. The standing wage system might have been a feasible alternative, but crop failures and falling prices during 1865–1867 caused widespread planter default on wage payments. In this setting, the popularity of shares to freedmen is largely explained by the legal status of the shareholder's lien on such contracts, which gave the worker property rights in his share of the crop. These rights, in turn, allowed workers to borrow from third parties using the crop lien as collateral.[2]

The postwar setting of crop failures, falling prices, disrupted credit, and mutual suspicion help to explain the shift to payment on shares. But freedmen continued to enter such contracts long after credit conditions had stabilized and property rights in the crop had been firmly assigned to landlords by "redeemed" white legislatures.[3] Its persistence may be explained by comparison to other contract forms with which it coexisted in most parts of the South. Agricultural wage labor was an option chosen by large numbers of young black males. But wage labor was not attractive to married men with families, because it offered neither security nor work autonomy. True tenancy, on the other hand, with tenure secured by contract, legal title to the crop, and managerial autonomy on the farm, was the preferred option for anyone with the assets or creditworthiness to obtain it. Sharecropping was in the middle—a contract form adapted for married men with families but possessing no property. Legislatures and courts might have endowed sharecroppers with more extensive rights, but that possibility would have made the transaction highly unattractive to lenders. Sharecropping, as it came to be defined in the South, was essentially a logical corollary to the status of *propertylessness* in the mainstream of Anglo-American legal history. This is what southern writer R. P. Brooks meant when he asserted that "the law only crystallizes the actual economic facts as they have worked out."[4]

But sharecropping was not slavery. State-to-state migration rates were high throughout the period, for blacks as well as whites; prior to World War I, the great majority of these moves were from the low-wage Southeast to the higher-wage South-west.[5] Moves within local areas were also frequent, in what one analyst called the "great annual reshuffling of black families."[6] Both contemporary and historical observers often depicted this intrasector labor mobility as economically pointless, perhaps re-flecting an irrational restlessness because the benefits seemed so limited. Economists, on the other hand, presume that people move when they expect to gain by doing so. And indeed many black farmers did succeed in working their way up the agricul-tural ladder over time, to tenancies and even to ownership, albeit on what usually were small and low-quality pieces of land. At least the agricultural sector offered some possibilities for ad-vancement to some black farm families.[7]

Thus the deeper barriers to black advancement during this era were denial of access to education and restricted job opportuni-ties outside of the agricultural sector. Elements of monopsony power in local labor markets were undoubtedly present, but the larger regional class interest of planters was in maintaining these sectoral restrictions. This interest was exercised directly by con-trol over local schools, but it was complemented by racial segre-gation in workplace settings and in the cities.

Segregation and Labor Markets in the Jim Crow South

Extensive as the scope of legal segregation became, its limits were equally notable. Racial aspects of employment and work relations were virtually unregulated. The only industrial segrega-tion laws of any importance—a North Carolina statute requiring separate toilets and a South Carolina law requiring segregation in cotton textiles—were adopted only in 1913 and 1915, respec-tively, long after prevailing racial patterns were established. Yet despite the absence of legal enforcement, segregation was the norm in southern industries. In his study of Virginia firms in 1900 and 1909, Robert Higgs found that "occupational workforce segregation was overwhelmingly the rule."[8] Even more dramatic illustrations may be found at the state level: in Florida, Georgia, Louisiana, Mississippi, North Carolina, Tennessee, and Virginia, the U.S. Census of 1930 recorded over four thousand male telegraph operators, not one of them black; the southern states reported nearly fifteen thousand locomotive engineers, but less than fifty were black (0.3 percent); only four of the 5,600 loom fixers were black. These extreme cases may involve access to special skills, but the evidence is nearly as strong in unskilled and semiskilled categories: more than 90 percent of the operatives were white in such industries as furniture, textiles (including cotton, silk, knitting, and rayon), shoes, printing, and car and railroad shops. At the same time, more than 75 percent of the laborers were black in tobacco manufacture, iron and steel, fertilizers, and turpentine.[9] These patterns of segregation, which persisted for decades, cannot readily be attributed to legal barriers, unions, or an absence of labor markets.

Interestingly, racial separation was more prevalent and more clearly delineated by industry than by location. White cotton mills and black tobacco factories coexisted in places like Durham, North Carolina, and Danville, Virginia; in Birmingham, Alabama, where two-thirds of iron and steel workers were black, the Avondale cotton mill was 98.1 percent white.[10] The persistence of these configurations indicates that labor market segregation was a regional phenomenon, not just a response to varying local conditions.

Explaining segregation in labor markets does not pose a serious challenge for economic theory. Discrimination models by Becker and Arrow, among others, show that if whites demand a premium for working in close association with blacks, segregation dominates mixed alternatives.[11] The issue that economists have wrestled with is not segregation per se but wage discrimination: Did segregation serve to support an "unjustified" wage differential, or was it merely the market's way of avoiding the costs of mixing the races? The perhaps surprising finding of numerous studies is that, despite the prevalence of racism in the South before World War I, racial differentials in the open (unskilled) labor market were small or nonexistent.

In agriculture, wage labor coexisted with sharecropping and other forms of tenancy. Although whites had a large overall advantage in farm property and incomes, with rare exceptions black and white farm laborers were paid the same wage. For example, in 1887 the North Carolina Bureau of Labor Statistics posed the question of racial wage differences to landlords as well as to tenants and laborers. In ninety-four of the ninety-five counties, the landlords reported "no difference" between the races, and in seventy-seven of the counties the tenants and laborers gave the same response.[12] Agricultural department wage surveys for 1899 and 1902 show racial wage differentials averaging less than 10 percent by state, and even these were probably attributable to geographic variations within states. As Georgia planter R. J. Redding explained:

> We have white men working on the farms. We frequently have applications every day. But when the white men come and are willing to work we have to say: We cannot afford to pay you any more because I can get a negro for 60 cents a day; if you are willing to work at that price the first vacancy we have you can get it. We occasionally put a white man on that way.[13]

The great majority of farm laborers were black, but even in the plantation states as many as one-fourth were white in 1890.

Perhaps even more surprising, evidence from Virginia shortly after the turn of the century suggests that wages were equilibrated for unskilled black and white workers, even across highly segregated industries such as cotton and tobacco manufacturing. The frequency distribution of white wages was bimodal, with one peak at about seven dollars per week (the unskilled market) and another at two to three times this level (representing the skilled and often unionized market in the iron industry and construction). The black distribution was unimodal, but its peak was virtually identical to that of the white unskilled workers, at just over one dollar per day (Figure 2.1). If we eliminate the iron industry and the building trades, the black and white peaks were remarkably close (Figure 2.2). The large intermediating agriculture sector may have been important in maintaining this equilibration for men, because the same data suggest a 25 percent wage gap in favor of white over black women, who did not have access to farm labor jobs.[14]

As noteworthy as the finding of no wage discrimination, however, is the virtual exclusion of blacks from higher-paying skilled jobs. In the Virginia sample, skilled jobs were primarily in iron and construction, which had highly structured job hierarchies controlled by craft unions. In these respects they resembled the job structures of the railroads. William Sundstrom finds a high degree of discrimination in railroad work, generated by an extreme racial exclusiveness in promotion to the top jobs, as well as by unequal pay within job categories. Whites often argued that blacks were not qualified for these jobs, but Sundstrom points out (and cites evidence to this effect) that poor black work performance may have been attributable to the absence of a promotion incentive.[15]

If one could trace the evolution of such a structure, one might find an increasingly close match between the racial distributions of skills and of wages. But it is evident that the skill distribution was endogenous to the structure of segregation. Elsewhere blacks were held back even in the absence of unions and even where skills were largely acquired on the job. Thus despite the efficacy of labor markets in equilibrating unskilled wages, access to skilled positions was distinctly unequal between the races.

DISFRANCHISEMENT AND SCHOOLING

White control over industrial skills occurred in a larger political context of ascendant white supremacy. This movement took many forms, but the capstone was the effective disfranchisement of black voters. Between 1890 and 1903 every southern state

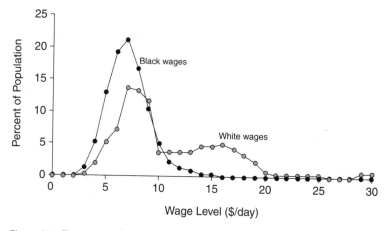

Figure 2.1 Frequency distribution for black and white wages, Virginia, 1908.

Source: Compiled from the Annual Report of the Commissioner of Labor for the State of Virginia, 1909.

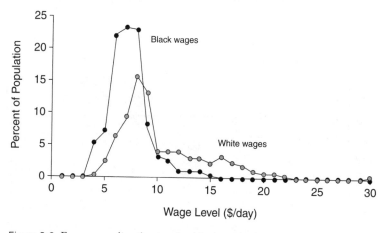

Figure 2.2 Frequency distribution for black and white wages, Virginia manufacturing, 1908.

Source: Compiled from the Annual Report of the Commissioner of Labor for the State of Virginia, 1909.

adopted legislation (and in many cases new constitutions) limiting the vote. In ironic deference to the Fifteenth Amendment, the laws were ostensibly race-neutral, but black voters were the clear and openly acknowledged targets. In the process, many poor whites were also disfranchised. It is sometimes held that de jure disfranchisement was a mere formality ratifying a de facto exclusion that had occurred much earlier. But blacks participated vigorously in many localities despite discouragements, and in many states the disfranchisement impetus emerged in the wake of biracial agrarian insurgencies during the 1890s. Figure 2.3 displays estimates of adult male turnout in presidential elections for the South and non-South, showing a decisive break after 1896.[16] Table 2.1 shows the impact on school spending by race in six states.

For decades historians have debated the motivations and class origins of the disfranchisement movement. Classic treatments by C. Vann Woodward and V. O. Key emphasized the leading role of planters from black-majority counties, who were most threat-

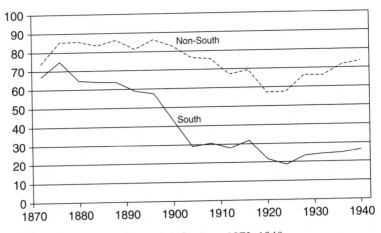

Figure 2.3 Turnout in presidential elections, 1872–1940.
Source: Carter et al. *Historical Statistics of the United States, Millennial Edition.* Vol. 5, Series Eb115 and Eb116.

Table 2.1   Per Pupil Expenditures by Race, 1890 and 1910

	White Expenditures	Black Expenditures	Ratio
Alabama			
1890	3.14	3.10	1.01
1910	10.07	2.69	3.74
Florida			
1890	9.42	4.63	2.03
1910	11.58	3.11	3.72
Louisiana			
1890	5.85	2.92	2.00
1910	11.54	2.07	5.57
Mississippi			
1890	18.62	9.27	2.01
1910	27.88	7.67	3.63
North Carolina			
1890	2.71	2.74	0.99
1910	5.20	2.52	2.06
Virginia			
1890	7.08	4.93	1.44
1910	11.59	4.10	2.83

Source: Margo, *Disfranchisement, School Finance, and the Economics of Segregated Schools,* Table I-1.

ened by the prospect of democracy.[17] These interpretations were largely confirmed by Kousser's 1974 landmark study in quantitative history, which stressed that planters and their elite allies actively intended to disfranchise "not only the ignorant and vicious blacks but the ignorant and vicious whites as well."[18] More recently, Glenn Feldman argues that these historians have "failed to see the forest for the trees," giving class considerations exaggerated attention while glossing over powerful evidence that black disfranchisement had broad support "among all classes of whites" in the turn-of-the-century South. In Feldman's reading, white Populists were never committed to biracial politics. They fiercely opposed the 1890 Lodge "force bill" (which would have sent federal registrars into offending districts) and quickly learned the riskiness and futility of even tentative appeals to black voters. The typical white voter responded to emotional, hot-button issues rather than appeals based on interracial economic interests.[19]

This is where the concept of societal equilibrium is useful. The detailed political dynamics of disfranchisement differed widely from state to state. In Alabama it is clear (as Feldman acknowledges) that black-belt planters and their industrial allies (known as the Big Mules) were the movers and shapers of disfranchisement. In North Carolina, where the planter class was small, fusionist insurgents actually took control of the state legislature and governorship between 1894 and 1898, raising taxes on railroads and business to support public schools. In Georgia the issue was debated as late as the 1908 gubernatorial campaign, when Joseph Brown defeated incumbent Hoke Smith, architect of the state's disfranchisement constitution. With all of these variations, however, the ultimate outcome was essentially similar in every southern state: black voting virtually eliminated; poor white voting drastically reduced; political power firmly lodged in the hands of wealthy planters and their business allies. Questions of timing and poor-white psychology seem distinctly secondary in the face of a powerful class onslaught.[20]

The economic motives of the planters could hardly have been clearer. They wanted to solidify control over tenants and laborers, avoid having to deal with contrary public officials, and keep taxes low. Not only did they prefer to keep as much of their income as possible for themselves, but landlords actually had a positive interest against the most likely object of state and local spending: public schools. As a South Carolina planter put it in 1900, "My experience is that if you educate the negro he is of no account."[21] These sentiments were not confined to the largest landowners. The North Carolina state labor commissioner reported in 1905 that nine of ten farmers opposed compulsory

Table 2.2 Per Capita Expenditures for White and Black Schools

County Groups	Per Capita White	Per Capita Black
Counties under 10% black	$7.96	$7.23
Counties 10% to 25% black	9.55	5.55
Counties 25% to 50% black	11.11	3.19
Counties 50% to 75% black	12.53	1.77
Counties 75% black and over	22.22	1.78

Source: Jones, *Negro Education,* 1:28. The figures are for 1,055 counties where per capita expenditures were available in 1911–12 and 1912–13.

education for blacks because "educated Negroes, in nearly all cases, become valueless as farm laborers." A Virginia landowner queried, "If we educate the Negro out of being a laborer, who is going to take his place?"[22]

Table 2.2 illustrates a crucial aspect of discrimination in schooling, first clearly described by Thomas Jesse Jones in 1917: the spending gap between white and black schools was far higher in black-majority plantation counties than in small-farm areas. As overall regional school spending began to rise after 1900, differentials between rich and poor whites were often as large as those between whites and blacks.[23] Jones wrote:

> In practically all the Southern States the State funds are assigned to the counties on the basis of total population without regard to race. In this way a large Negro population is as much of an asset to a county school system as the white population. These funds are then divided between the races by the county board of education and supplemented by such local taxes as the county may decide to vote. The appropriations for Negro schools are therefore almost entirely dependent upon the local sentiment of the white school board.[24]

Statistical studies show a strong three-way association among disfranchisement, plantation tenancy, and educational inequality for both blacks and whites.[25] The dual-inequality pattern extended even to North Carolina, exemplifying what Kousser calls "progressivism for middle-class whites only."[26]

Should we understand this outcome as confirmation that lower-class southern whites cared more about racial status than economics, that they sacrificed their own economic self-interest on the altar of white supremacy? The power of emotional appeals to disrupt political cooperation can hardly be denied. Only as of the late 1890s, when the last interracial alliances had collapsed, did lynching become clearly identifiable as an expression of southern white supremacy.[27] But before attributing white responses exclusively to psychology, we should recall that no policy reforms within a realistic horizon would have altered the fundamentals of the world cotton market or the hierarchical structure of the southern agrarian economy. To believe otherwise would have been to envision an ambitious long-term political agenda that southern whites had very little reason to buy into. Furthermore many southern whites of middling status had good reason to feel that they themselves occupied relatively privileged positions in the emerging Jim Crow economy. That list would include both small landowners and skilled industrial workers. As the southern development process unfolded, the racial divide became more economically salient rather than less, as large categories of the white working class, such as cotton mill workers, pulled away from blacks in their living standards and economic aspirations. In this setting, divergence in schooling paralleled and reinforced divergence in the labor market.

Race, Schooling, and the Labor Market

Economists often identify poor schooling as the primary reason for low black incomes throughout the Jim Crow era.[28] This interpretation meshes comfortably with a perspective emphasizing that barriers to black progress operated through political channels rather than discrimination in markets. It also offers a simple explanation for the qualitative change in the southern industrial

THE POLITICAL ECONOMY OF THE JIM CROW SOUTH

labor market as of the 1920s. Figure 2.4 displays black and white wage distributions for 1926 for the same set of Virginia industries covered in Figure 2.2. Although there was still considerable overlap between the two, it is evident that a "racial wage gap" had come to prevail, in contrast to the "skill gap" of the prewar era. This new formation was of fundamental importance, less for its direct income effects than because it represented the crystallization of a racial stereotype that made the low-wage status of black workers self-justifying.

In trying to identify the reasons for the new racial wage divergence, many proximate factors can be listed: the stagnant world market for cotton had a disproportionate effect on blacks, as did depressed conditions in lumber and saw milling; real wages in cotton textiles, on the other hand, rose to a relatively high plateau during the wartime boom and proved resistant to downward

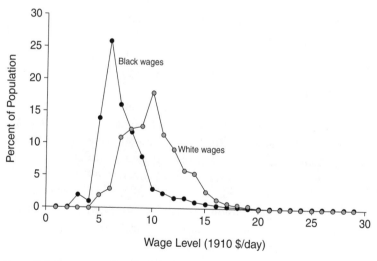

Figure 2.4 Frequency distribution for black and white wages, Virginia manufacturing, 1926.
Source: Compiled from the Annual Report of the Bureau of Labor and Industrial Statistics for the State of Virginia, 1927.

adjustment for reasons both internal and external to the industry.[29] Invoking these immediate circumstances, however, begs the question of why segregation could support a racial wage differential in the 1920s, when it had not done so earlier. Among many possible answers, the one most congenial to economists is education, specifically the wide racial gap in years and quality of schooling for the cohorts entering the labor force after World War I.[30]

The key role of public schooling was to alter the "ability" level that firms could expect from a randomly selected new employee with no previous work experience. The basic issue is not whether education was "required" for work in (say) the textiles industry; job specifications can be adjusted to accommodate the background of the average worker in the relevant labor pool. But if employers could safely assume that the ability of the average white was higher than that of the average black, they could set wages so as to equate the price of an efficiency unit of effective labor for each group. In such a setting, segregation could actually be productive, by reducing heterogeneity within workforce units, as well as conducive to good relations with white workers.[31]

Educational discrimination was a crucial link in the system, but it should not be understood as an exogenous force driving all subsequent outcomes. Rather education policies were largely endogenous to the previously established racial division of labor by industry and occupation. The self-interested opposition of planters and farmers to black schooling is clear. But when northern reformers began to pour money into southern schools, they too regarded the policy implications of the labor market as self-evident. Philanthropist William H. Baldwin, for example, advised recipients to "avoid social questions; leave politics alone . . . know that it is a crime for any teacher, white or black, *to educate the negro for positions which are not open to him.*"[32] When the Rosenwald Fund sought to support black high schools during the 1920s and 1930s, it sponsored a series of surveys of "negro jobs" in various cities so that curricula could be adapted to jobs actually available. In place after place the response indicated that there were no black jobs for which a high school education would be useful.[33]

Perhaps the clearest illustrations of endogenous schooling, exceptions that prove the rule, are cases where black workers did maintain a niche in industrial employment. Cities with a substantial black industrial labor force, like Durham, became centers of black education as well. In Birmingham, Alabama, schools for both blacks and whites were better funded than in rural areas. The largest employer, Tennessee Coal and Iron (part of U.S. Steel as of 1907), played an active role in promoting, funding, and administering black schools, primarily to stabilize its labor force. Although school quality was by no means equalized between the races, "the superiority of the TCI schools was undeniable," according to Bond, a claim supported by test scores relative to those of black children in other county and city schools and in the South at large.[34]

Another example is provided by economist Price Fishback's study of educational discrimination in West Virginia. That state's economy was dominated by coal mining, in which the majority of the workers were laborers, including many blacks recruited from plantation areas. Fishback finds little evidence of wage discrimination against blacks. Schools were segregated, but West Virginia schools came closer to parity with white schools than in any other southern state. Indeed the quality of black schools was used in recruiting efforts by the mining companies.[35]

Over most of the South, however, the emerging logic of racial dualism was the more powerful tendency. Table 2.3 displays average wage rates for entry-level workers in twenty industries as of July 1937, from a rare Bureau of Labor survey that requested race-specific information. Nearly 60 percent of southern firms reported hiring only whites or only blacks; those hiring only

Table 2.3 Average Hourly Wage Rates for Entry-Level Workers
Twenty Industries, July 1937

	White ¢	Black ¢	% difference
United States	53.4	42.0	27.1
North	55.2	56.6	–2.5
South	43.4	34.5	25.8
Virginia	37.6	34.6	8.7
North Carolina	33.1	25.8	28.3
South Carolina	29.8	22.8	30.7
Georgia	30.5	26.0	17.3
Alabama	41.5	38.9	6.7
Mississippi	36.5	30.2	20.9
Louisiana	36.9	30.5	21.0
Texas	48.2	39.0	23.6
Southern Firms Hiring:			
Whites only	44.4	—	
Blacks only	—	29.6	
Blacks and Whites	42.8	35.8	

Source: Perlman and Frazier, "Entrance Rates of Common Laborers in 20 Industries."

blacks paid starting wages fully one-third lower than those hiring only whites. Of the firms hiring both blacks and whites, nearly 30 percent paid blacks a lower starting wage, a figure that must be regarded as a lower-bound estimate. Equally striking in the table is the absence of an explicit racial wage gap in the northern states, despite black educational levels far below national standards at that time. Looking only at this table, one might attribute the regional contrast to "southern racism." But there was no comparable wage gap thirty years before, when "southern racism" was surely at its historic peak. The "separate wage rates for Negroes" that observers took to be "a fixed tradition" had in reality developed and become institutionalized in the twentieth century.[36] Thus divergent relative wages should not be understood as a direct expression of southern racial hostility but as a sustainable market outcome that crystallized what had come to be prevailing expectations about the quality of black workers and the types of jobs to which they would be assigned.

LEGAL SEGREGATION AND SOCIAL DISTANCE

Roughly coincident with disfranchisement, southern states and municipalities enacted legislation codifying racial segregation in wide swaths of social and economic life, such as public conveyances, schools, hotels, restaurants, parks, and cemeteries. Here too historians have debated the timing, intent, and effects of these laws. In *The Strange Career of Jim Crow,* published in 1955, C. Vann Woodward suggested that the period between the end of Reconstruction and disfranchisement was marked by "experiment, testing and uncertainty" in race relations, "quite different from the time of repression and rigid uniformity that was to come towards the end of the century."[37] Coming just after the *Brown* decision, the impact of this thesis was powerful: segregation had not always prevailed in the South, as its defenders claimed; racial patterns had changed radically in the past, and therefore the region could adjust to equally radical changes in the future.

A generation of critics successfully demonstrated, however, that there never had been a hopeful interlude of "human contact and association" when racial integration was genuinely open as an option. Historian Howard Rabinowitz argued that although the term *segregation* did not appear until later, in most facets of southern life racial separation was the de facto rule from earliest postbellum times—most emphatically in schooling, which was the immediate object of attention in 1955. Indeed according to Rabinowitz, the most common practice prior to codified segregation was *exclusion* of blacks from both public- and private-sector services, so that requiring "separate but equal" services for both races was often an improvement on the status quo, despite the glaring gaps between ideal and practice.[38] This thesis was elaborated in a comparative analysis by

John W. Cell, who argued that, as in South Africa, codified segregation was not the most extreme expression of racism but was instead an effort by moderate elites to reduce racial conflict and adapt white supremacy to the conditions of a modernizing urban society.[39]

There is no doubt that patterns of racial separation, both informal and codified, reflected deep-seated attitudes and emotions on the part of white southerners. For our purposes, the important point is not to determine the immediate psychological and political motivations behind segregation but to ask how the emergent structures were related to economic incentives and behavior, and how they affected and were affected by the process of economic development. This issue arose with the first state segregation laws, which pertained to the railroad, the very symbol of economic development in the nineteenth-century South. Every one of the southern states ultimately passed laws requiring separate coaches for black and white passengers. According to historian Michael Perman, passage of a law requiring separate coaches was closely linked to disfranchisement in Arkansas, North Carolina, Virginia, Maryland, and South Carolina, often with strong reinforcing expressions of white-supremacist rhetoric. In Tennessee, Mississippi, Louisiana, Alabama, Georgia, and Florida, on the other hand, such laws were passed very early and with a minimum of dissent.[40]

Notably, in nearly every case, the railroad companies opposed these laws. As historian Edward Ayers puts it, "The railroad companies did not want to be bothered with policing Southern race relations and considered the division of coaches into black and white compartments an irksome and unnecessary expense."[41] The companies feared that they would have to add first-class and Pullman facilities of equal quality. Yet despite this powerful political opposition, the laws were passed, seen as part of the progressive drive to regulate big private businesses. One could easily take this as an indication that legally mandated segregation was a matter of race-baiting politics, inefficient, costly, and detrimental to economic progress. A closer look, however, reveals that the railroad companies did not oppose the laws because they favored racially mixed travel. Agents often refused to sell first-class tickets to black travelers, restricting them to second-class and smoking cars carrying baggage. Rabinowitz writes that "the association between blacks and smoking [on trains] was pronounced." White travelers who wanted to smoke could enter these areas, but blacks had no choice in the matter. Although railroads opposed regulation, they did not object to the more systematic and unequal segregation that ultimately emerged, ending the "dangerous and uncertain situation" that arose when a black traveler tried to purchase a first-class ticket.[42]

Concern for morale of white customers as a business matter was critical to working out the legal issues involved in interstate travel. In *Hall v. DeCuir,* decided in 1878, the U.S. Supreme Court invalidated a Louisiana public accommodations law prohibiting racial discrimination by common carriers as an unconstitutional interference with interstate commerce. The case arose in 1872, when Josephine DeCuir, a wealthy black plantation owner, was denied entrance to a steamboat cabin "specially set aside for white persons." The company's defense was that nearly all Mississippi steamboats segregated passengers at the behest of white customers who "would not like to be put into the cabin with colored passengers." The ship captain testified that the purpose of the segregation policy was "to protect a man in his business." He said, "I don't think there are many white people who would travel on a boat . . . that allowed negroes to occupy rooms in the main cabin and stay in the main cabin." Because some of these passengers were interstate (even though DeCuir herself was not), the Court agreed that the law placed an unreasonable and therefore unconstitutional burden on interstate commerce.[43]

The separate-coach laws were constitutionally vulnerable on the same grounds if they impinged on interstate travel. According to legal historian Joseph R. Palmore, Jim Crow segregation became legally entrenched in interstate travel only when the railroads themselves adopted internal rules requiring segregation. A 1909 book of company rules for the Louisville and Nashville Railroad, for example, required conductors to learn and comply with the segregation laws of the southern states. Palmore writes, "When the cost-benefit analysis reversed after intrastate segregation laws withstood legal challenges, the companies became willing and energetic segregators." The Greyhound Company adopted similar policies after losing the *Morgan* case in 1946. Like the railroads, Greyhound clearly believed that segregation in the South was good for business.[44]

The streetcar segregation laws adopted in most southern cities after 1900 were somewhat different, but the outcome was essentially similar. In an influential article, economist Jennifer Roback shows that the ordinances requiring partition of cars into front and back sections were never initiated by and were often strongly opposed by streetcar companies. Their opposition intensified in the face of vigorous black boycotts, which lasted anywhere from a few weeks to three years. Because black riders constituted a far larger share of patronage on streetcars than on railroads, the companies sometimes suffered heavy financial losses. Despite a few temporary reversals, however, all of the boycotts ultimately petered out, and streetcar companies ceased active resistance to enforcing segregation. The system became sufficiently entrenched over the next half-century that the Montgomery Improvement Association, after Rosa Parks's arrest on December 1, 1955, initially asked not for desegregation but only for a fixed dividing line on city buses so that seated black passengers would not be required to yield their seats to white newcomers.[45]

Progressive Segregation

For consumer services suggesting social relationships, such as restaurants, hotels, and theaters, the evidence is clear that segregation was the rule long before it became law throughout the

South. These practices were hardly affected by the 1875 federal Civil Rights Act, nor by the Act's reversal by the Supreme Court in 1883. Because the exclusion of blacks was entirely consistent with the profit-seeking goals of business establishments in these areas, state and municipal legislation did little more than to codify and perhaps coordinate existing and widespread conduct. But southern urban boosters could portray such laws as progressive measures, prescribing what was considered socially respectable behavior, while minimizing the occasions for dispute by making it all perfectly clear.[46]

It is true, as some writers have emphasized, that individual shop owners sometimes faced tension between maintaining the racial order and a profit-driven desire to attract black customers. But this consideration only underscores the *class* interest of urban boosters and developers in maintaining segregation. As recounted by urban historian Alison Isenberg, from the early twentieth century onward, the business strategy pursued by downtown merchant groups was to make their retail districts attractive to middle-class shoppers, especially women (whose spending decisions accounted for the bulk of household discretionary income). From this perspective, fear that a downtown area could become known as a "Negro shopping district" was a mortal threat, not just to an individual establishment but to the merchant community as a group. According to Isenberg, "Before the 1960s, only the rare white investor or consultant challenged the prevailing dogma that the presence of African Americans or race mixing on Main Street brought property values down."[47] Although the fear of blight prevailed nationwide, southern cities settled on a system that could tolerate a black presence by keeping it at an acceptable social distance. Thus lines of physical separation were stricter in New South cities like Atlanta and Nashville than in more traditional Charleston. Where tourism and conventions were core parts of city's business plan, as in Atlanta, projecting an image of orderly, segregated race relations was essential.[48]

It is a serious error to interpret segregation in public accommodations as either imposed by law on a reluctant business community or as a manifestation of "traditional" attitudes that would recede with economic development over time. Segregation was modern and progressive, an integral part of the New South creed. The progressive southerner Woodrow Wilson certainly thought so. With Presidential approval, his cabinet members introduced segregated toilets, cafeterias, and work areas into federal government departments. Wilson's response to black criticism was this: "The policy of segregation had been enforced for the comfort and best interests of both races in order to overcome friction. . . . Segregation is not a humiliation but a benefit and ought to be so regarded by you gentlemen."[49] As Glenda Gilmore writes about the 1920s, "White supremacy was not a vestigial, dying system; instead it was a vigorous, growing one."[50] In effect the Progressive era institutionalized southern segregation, and despite massive economic changes it weakened very little in the decades to follow.

THE NEW DEAL AND THE MODERNIZATION OF THE SOUTHERN ECONOMY

On the eve of the Great Depression, the South appeared to have settled into a lasting political-economic equilibrium, dominated by an elite planter class with a powerful stake in white supremacy and regional isolation.[51] Historian James Oakes argues that this group wielded greater political and economic power than their slave-owning forerunners had in 1860.[52] In the classic formulation of V. O. Key's *Southern Politics in State and Nation*, planter hegemony was maintained by the centrality of the race issue, which in turn supported undemocratic political structures in the states. In the aggregate, the economic effect of this regime was to perpetuate regional backwardness, compared to historically feasible alternatives, through underinvestment in human capital and the choice of a development path outside the mainstream of national technological development. But the majority of politically active white southerners viewed themselves as occupying relatively privileged positions, so that the system as a whole seemed stable.

Persistent regional backwardness does not mean that the South experienced no economic progress at all. Between 1869 and 1929 real value-added in manufacturing grew faster in the states of the former Confederacy than in the nation as a whole. Even though most of this growth was in labor-intensive, low-wage industries, the expansion still generated real progress in living standards compared to the impoverished farms from which most workers had come. The region also experienced gains in public health and mortality during the same historical span. A study by economist Hoyt Bleakley shows the dramatic impact of the campaign sponsored by the Rockefeller Sanitation Commission to eradicate hookworm, a parasitic disease that struck as many as 40 percent of school-age children in the South. The five-year investment beginning in 1910 had major results within a decade, and Bleakley traces subsequent county-level effects on school enrollment, attendance, and literacy. Economic historian Werner Troesken shows that at roughly the same historical juncture, public investments in water filtration systems and sewage systems reduced the incidence of typhoid and diarrhea in such southern cities as Memphis, Savannah, and Jacksonville. Troesken finds that these gains were shared by the urban black population, despite their lack of effective political representation. The main reason for this apparent anomaly was that urban whites had a strong self-interest in black health conditions, especially in cities where residential segregation was relatively low.[53]

Relative to the rest of the country, however, the South as a whole made few lasting gains. Per capita income grew faster than the national average between 1900 and 1920, boosted by strong cotton markets and the wartime boom. But these relative gains were largely reversed when cotton markets stagnated during the 1920s, confirming that the regional economy remained heavily dependent on an undiversified farming sector. Southern farm wages remained about half of those in northern states, essentially where they had been fifty years before. In terms of retail sales per capita, an indicator that reflects market development as well as income, the southern states formed a contiguous cluster in 1930, averaging about one-third of the national average.

The advent of Franklin Roosevelt's New Deal in 1933 marked a turning point in regional development, a watershed if not an instantaneous revolution. Like the rest of the nation, the South was hit hard by the Great Depression, and southerners continued to suffer throughout the 1930s. But federal government initiatives during that decade generated major changes in southern economic infrastructure, the environment, and public health and disease conditions, far beyond what the region could have or would have supported on its own. In many ways these long-term developments set the stage for the more dramatic and visible effects of World War II, launching the modernization of the southern economy in the postwar era.

In his account of the New Deal in South Carolina, historian Jack Irby Hayes Jr. writes that the Public Works Administration (PWA), created under the National Industrial Recovery Act during the first wave of New Deal legislation, "literally changed the face of the Palmetto State. Its visible legacy a half-century later included hundreds of low-cost housing units to replace urban slums, miles of modern highways, a host of schools, courthouses, hospitals, post offices, and administrative buildings, a thriving shipyard, a number of new sewage and water systems, and two huge hydroelectric projects."[54] The Works Progress Administration (WPA), launched in 1935 as the leading federal work-relief agency, had even more dramatic effects. Southern highway construction was under way in the 1920s, but the pace slackened with the Depression and then accelerated in 1933. Total southern highway mileage more than doubled during a depressed decade. An English visitor to Alabama and the Carolinas in 1938 noted that one could hardly round a curve in the highway without encountering a sign, "WPA-Men at Work." The South had been far behind the rest of the nation in roads, cars, and related institutions, but by 1939 every southern state had established a state police system or highway patrol, and motor vehicle registrations grew by 50 percent between 1934 and 1941.[55]

Highway building expanded marketing areas, prompting the appearance of chain grocery stores in many parts of the South, marking the first step toward "living out of bags" as contrasted with "living at home" or "out of the smokehouse and hen house." Sears, Roebuck also began building stores in the South in the late 1930s, generating opportunities not just for consumers but for suppliers. For example, Armstrong Rubber built a tire plant in Natchez, Mississippi, on the basis of a commitment from Sears to purchase the plant's entire capacity on a cost-plus basis for ten years.[56]

Equally important for regional development was the electrification of farms, homes, and industries. The most visible and controversial New Deal program was the Tennessee Valley Authority (TVA), which revolutionized access to electric power in a subregion featuring the highest poverty and relief rates in the country. Rapid diffusion of electric service was encouraged not just by lower rates but also by subsidized loans for rural service, initially from the TVA but after 1935 through the Rural Electrification Administration (REA), primarily to cooperatives. Electrification would have come to the South eventually, even without the New Deal, but the pace would have been nowhere near as fast nor the diffusion as extensive. By 1945, 75 percent of households in the Tennessee Valley were electrified, compared to just 2 percent in 1933.[57]

The social implications of electrification for rural households can scarcely be overstated. Nationwide the highest priorities were lights, ironing, and a radio, but southerners acquired refrigerators at a higher rate than elsewhere. The U.S. Public Health Service reported that incandescent illumination protected eyesight, promoted cleanliness, and prevented accidents. Refrigeration reduced the rate of food spoilage, making it economical (for those with funds to spend) to rely on purchased groceries for the first time. Affordable radios were perhaps equally important in reducing rural isolation. Radio provided direct access to the outside world, most notably to the voice of the president himself, thus playing a major role in the countryside's intense loyalty to FDR.[58]

The Environment and Public Health

A common feature of economic backwardness is the destruction of natural resources. Time horizons are foreshortened by the pressure of poverty, the weakness of state regulation, and underdevelopment of financial systems. This description fits the pre–New Deal South all too well. The cut-over forest area in the thirteen southern states was estimated at more than 156 million acres by 1920. One government forester described the situation as "probably the most rapid and reckless destruction of forests known to history." The picture for southern soils was just as bleak. The first comprehensive inventory of national resources, compiled in 1933 by the National Resources Board, estimated that nearly one-third of the land area in the southern states could be classified as "severely impoverished," "soil washed off," or "devastated." Altogether the South accounted for 61.1 percent of the nation's impoverished or devastated soil.[59]

The southern environment began its historic reversal in the 1930s, and the primary vehicle was the Civilian Conservation Corps (CCC), a public work-relief program that put unemployed young men to work on natural resource conservation projects throughout the nation. "CCC boys" worked for the Departments of Agriculture and the Interior, for the TVA and other agencies, on roads, check dams, terraces, pest control, and wildlife, but the highest priority was reforestation. By the time of its demise in 1942, the CCC had planted more than one million acres of timberland in the South (Figure 2.5). CCC labor was also deployed for cultural operations to improve the composition and growth of young second-stand trees, an operation known as "timber stand improvement." The remarkable success of these efforts served as a model for private forest owners, such as those associated with the pulp and paper industry. Also essential to promoting private investment in southern forests was reduction of the risk of forest fires. An educational campaign by the American Forestry Association began in the late 1920s, but it was the CCC that provided "a virtual army of fire fighters," bringing an "unprecedented sense of moral urgency" to the drive. By 1942 the southern area under fire protection had increased to almost 90 million acres.[60]

New Deal programs also reversed more than a century of southern practices pertaining to the soil. The Soil Erosion Service was created in 1933 in the Department of the Interior and was transferred to Agriculture as the Soil Conservation Service (SCS) in 1935. Using labor from the CCC and other agencies, the SCS instructed farmers on the advantages of tractor terracing, strip cropping, cover cropping, and reforestation. By October

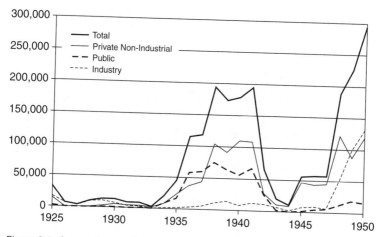

Figure 2.5 Acres of annual tree planting in the South, 1925–1950.
Source: Hamlin L. Williston. "A Statistical History of Tree Planting in the South, 1925–1979." Miscellaneous Report SA-MR 8, United States Department of Agriculture Forest Service (Atlanta), September 1980.

1936 the SCS had educated more than 90 percent of farmers within a twenty-five-mile radius of their demonstration projects, and at least one of them admitted, "Those book farmers have certainly taught me a lot more than I ever learned through experience." The shift from cotton into soil-holding feed crops such as soybeans was well under way in the 1930s.[61]

In public health, a positive trend was already under way in the South, but the New Deal accomplished the remarkable feat of maintaining and extending this progress during a decade of economic hardship. Figure 2.6 displays infant mortality rates by race for Virginia, Mississippi, and South Carolina across the interwar period. Virginia and South Carolina experienced major gains during and shortly after World War I, but almost no further progress through the 1920s. After the setback of 1933–1934, mortality rates fell throughout the South for the rest of the 1930s. A study by economists Price V. Fishback, Michael

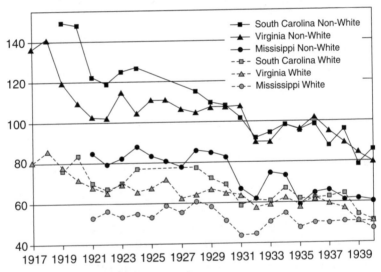

Figure 2.6 Infant mortality, 1917–1940.
Source: F. E. Linder and R. E. Grove. *Vital Statistics Rates, 1900–1940.* United States Public Health Service, 1947, Table 26.

R. Haines, and Shawn Kantor finds strong county-level association between declines in infant mortality and expenditures by New Deal agencies, particularly the Federal Emergency Relief Administration (FERA) for the earlier period 1933–1935, and the PWA for 1936–1939. The authors attribute the FERA effect largely to augmentation of household income, whereas the PWA contributed to longer-term health improvement investments in water and sewage systems and disease eradication. The gains were experienced by both blacks and whites, and in many states the reduction for blacks was the larger of the two.[62]

In South Carolina, mosquito-eradication efforts as part of the Santee-Cooper project reduced deaths from malaria by 66 percent. The TVA area recorded no malaria cases after 1949. The Memphis malaria-control project employed 25 percent of all relief workers in Shelby County in 1936, and "all but eliminated the traditional scourge of the city." Similar successes against hookworm (which continued to infest school children in rural areas), dysentery, enteritis, and pellagra were recorded, thanks to electrification, dietary improvements, and new sanitation facilities in rural areas.[63]

In many southern cities, sanitation and health facilities were completely transformed by federal funding. In Birmingham the sixteen-story Jefferson Hospital opened in 1940, constructed through PWA grants and Reconstruction Finance Corporation loans, the city's first new hospital in forty years. Health workers also conducted special testing in Birmingham schools, offering free hearing and vision tests in 1938 to twenty thousand children. In 1941 the modern Slossfield Health Center opened as one of five health centers in the Birmingham corporate limits, with clinics for maternity care, pediatrics, child health, dentistry, venereal disease, tuberculosis, and general diagnosis.[64]

Perhaps the most dramatic example of urban upgrading occurred in Atlanta. The city's top priority was a new sewer system. The old system was disgraceful, polluting streams with human and industrial waste, generating a number-one ranking for the city in diphtheria deaths and a typhoid rate twice the average for other large urbanized areas. Atlanta applied for $8 million in funding from the PWA in July 1933, but the application foundered for lack of a sufficient local contribution. Work began only when the project was shifted to the Civil Works Administration, which required no local funds. The real turning point came in 1936, with approval of a joint PWA-WPA plan, limiting the city's contribution to just $1.5 million. The Atlanta sewer system was the largest WPA project in the South, and by 1940, according to historian Douglas Fleming, "Atlanta had the best infrastructure of any southern city." Direct federal funding was particularly important for Atlanta because the state of Georgia under Governor Eugene Talmadge had no interest in such projects. As Fleming argues, the New Deal laid the basis for Atlanta's postwar growth in industrial plants, transportation, and new construction.[65]

In 1932 33 percent of the nation's urban population drank untreated water; by 1940 the rate was less than 0.2 percent. Southern cities were disproportionate beneficiaries of this remarkable upgrade. But prior to the New Deal, many of these cities lacked the fiscal capacity or political will to improve basic services. Altogether the New Deal spent more than $2 billion in the South, much of which supported "the types of services that southern cities would not have provided even in good times." Historian David Goldfield writes, "The almost-free modernization received by southern cities [in the 1930s] would prove to be an important economic advantage in subsequent decades."[66]

THE NEW DEAL, MODERNIZATION, AND RACE

If the New Deal kick-started the modern southern economy, why do so many historians maintain that the New Deal's impact on the South was peripheral if not actually retrograde, "essentially a holding action," in Anthony Badger's words?[67] The reason for this apparent contradiction is not hard to identify: historians are looking for evidence of social and political change, for progress in the status of labor and women, and especially for any weakening in the Jim Crow regime of racial segregation and subordination. On these counts, the South saw few signs of fundamental change before World War II. The elites who dominated southern political and economic life were just as dominant at the end of the decade as at the beginning, having beaten back most hopeful early signs of change. The question then becomes: Why was it that such dramatic economic change had so little effect on political and social relationships?

One group of historians does locate the origins of the modern Civil Rights movement in the New Deal era. They argue that access to federal funds through work-relief jobs and soil conservation checks was a major breakthrough for many black southerners, raising incomes and giving them their first taste of economic independence. Acknowledging the acquiescence of New Deal programs in racial segregation, these historians maintain that awareness of a potential political ally in Washington enhanced black political mobilization in the South, a formula whose ultimate impact was immense. The case for this long-run realization is persuasively articulated by such distinguished authorities as Harvard Sitkoff, Patricia Sullivan, and Glenda Gilmore.[68]

This analysis is compelling, but it would be mistaken to believe that the New Deal began a process by which the Jim Crow regime was gradually undermined by the force of modernization. Indeed the correlation often seemed to be the opposite. The vast majority of white southerners had a vision of economic progress in which blacks had no more than a subordinate role, if any. This conceptual bifurcation predated the 1930s and survived the Great Depression, in many ways actually confirmed and strengthened by the very success of the New Deal in its regional modernization objectives.

Early federal relief funding was threatening to employers in the South, particularly to landlords with black tenants, sharecroppers, and laborers. But as many historians have recounted, this challenge was largely beaten back by 1935. Southern planters were well represented in Congress, ensuring that both farm and domestic laborers were excluded from coverage under the Social Security Act, and later from the wage standards of the Fair Labor Standards Act. Within the South, local elites fought for and gained control over administration of farm and work-relief programs. One upshot of local control was that workers were dropped from federally funded jobs if farm employment was available, such as during the harvest season. In Louisiana, for example, the state WPA director advised his staff in 1936 not to wait for complaints from employers but to release workers from projects whenever necessary. The use of the WPA as a labor reserve for cotton planters facilitated mechanization of preharvest operations and the shift from tenants to wage labor, even during a depressed decade.[69]

Central to the New Deal's diagnosis of southern backwardness was the proposition that low wages perpetuated poverty, undermining living standards and health and discouraging development. The imposition of high wages on the South, however, first through the National Recovery Act and subsequently the minimum-wage provisions of the Fair Labor Standards Act, facilitated the replacement of black workers by whites as part of the upgrading process. One might consider this an example of unintended consequences from outside intervention. But the phenomenon of whites taking over formerly "Negro" jobs predated the New Deal. William Jones writes that in the lumber industry (as in others), a new pattern of vertical segregation and racial wage differentials appeared after World War I, replacing the earlier, more horizontal regime.[70]

In *The Report on Economic Conditions of the South,* issued in 1938 by the National Emergency Council with strong Presidential encouragement, the low-wage doctrine was emphatically endorsed, and the only mention of the race issue was in this observation: "Increasing competition for jobs has upset the balance of employment between white and Negro." Among the strenuous objections to the report, one of the more common was the complaint that the *regional* interpretation was unfair to south-ern *whites,* because regional differentials were largely attribut-able to low black living standards. Thus the displacement of black workers by whites in higher-wage jobs is best understood as an aspect of economic modernization that southern whites simply took for granted.[71]

There is no need to carry this argument to extremes. African Americans in the South shared in many of the benefits of the New Deal and economic modernization, such as roads, electricity, and public health. And despite segregation and local administration, blacks were included in federally funded relief programs. Evi-dence collected by Michael Brown indicates that in southern cities, the black share of the relief and work-relief programs ex-ceeded the black share of the population in 1933, 1935, and 1940. (The reverse was true, however, in rural areas.)[72] As WPA wages rose toward national standards by the end of the 1930s, the economic significance of these jobs for black southerners was immense, helping to account for Roosevelt's popularity with this group.

But blacks' overrepresentation in work-relief was largely the mirror image of their underrepresentation in private-sector em-ployment. As early as January 1931 black unemployment rates in southern cities were double those of white males, and the gap was even greater for black females. Occupational segregation was rarely challenged by New Deal agencies. Even the National Youth Administration, a WPA program offering work-training employment for young men and women, adopted a regional policy that blacks would not be recommended for positions if whites needed work. In practice, job training for blacks was of-ten limited to domestic work.[73]

The proposition that economic modernization was inversely related to racial equity may be illustrated by two showcase New Deal programs: the TVA and the GI Bill. Like the CCC and the WPA, the TVA was officially committed to nondiscrimination from the beginning. But all three agencies acquiesced in racial segregation in the South, and, in the words of Raymond Wolters, the TVA went "beyond segregation to exclusion." The history of TVA race policy was summarized by Nancy Grant as follows: "In an effort to avoid controversy and opposition from local white politicians and community leaders, TVA carefully adhered to the valley practices of racial segregation in schools and communities, and restricted economic opportunities for blacks." "Grassroots democracy" referred only to white groups. Research support and consulting relationships applied only to white universities, excluding black agricultural colleges entirely. White recreational facilities were planned and constructed as a matter of course, while their "separate but equal" black counterparts were often long-delayed or never completed. Blacks were excluded from living in the "model town" of Norris in eastern Tennessee and effectively from employment there as well. Although official TVA policy was to employ blacks in roughly their percentage of the local population, in practice this quota was achieved by hiring blacks only for unskilled and temporary positions. The discriminatory employment pattern was essentially the same in 1945 as in 1933, and indeed continued into the 1950s. According to Grant, the most harmful effects of TVA-inspired discrimination were mitigated only by abandonment in the late 1930s of the Authority's ambitious program of rehabilitation and social planning.[74]

TVA's sorry record on race might be attributable to the project's remote historical roots and its location in a southern region with a relatively small black population. The GI Bill, in contrast, was a quintessential New Deal program that looked forward to the bold new post–World War II era, an extension of benefits and access to middle-class status to a major segment of the American population. Retrospective assessments tout the GI Bill as "the law that worked," a "true social revolution," in the words of Bill Clinton. Historical research suggests, however, that although the bill contained no racial language, blacks were largely excluded from its benefits, especially in the South.

As in the 1930s, the fatal flaw at the federal level was administrative decentralization. For the GI Bill, this feature was enacted into the language of the legislation, at the behest of Congressman John Rankin of Mississippi. The key passage read, "No Department or Agency, or Offices of the United States in carrying out the provisions of this part, shall exercise any supervision or control whatsoever over any state educational agency." As a consequence, black veterans in the South were routinely discouraged from applying for loans, training programs, and employment assistance. In addition to overt discrimination by program administrators, segregation in the South meant that blacks had very limited options for utilizing the higher education benefits of the bill. Historically black colleges were small and underfunded, unable to accept even half the qualified black veterans who applied for admission. In a comprehensive econometric analysis, Sarah Turner and John Bound find that although the GI Bill had substantial positive benefits for black and white veterans outside the South, "those from the South made no significant gains in education attainment." For these reasons, an act that fostered a "true social revolution" within the white population served as perhaps the greatest instrument for "widening an already huge racial gap within postwar America."[75]

THE POSTWAR JIM CROW SOUTH

From the 1930s through the 1950s, the South was hit by a series of shocks that rocked the foundations of the regional economy. In the midst of the Great Depression, New Deal farm programs undermined the economic bases for plantation tenancy, obliterating any residue of social glue that held young southerners in farming. Then came World War II, which brought a vast expansion of federal spending on military bases, industrial plants, and infrastructure, as the Roosevelt administration consciously "used the war emergency to develop the South."[76] The wartime boom triggered mass out-migration from the region, two-thirds of it black. The resulting shortage of harvest labor induced

International Harvester to throw the full weight of its resources behind the effort to develop a commercially viable mechanical cotton picker. That research project achieved success only at the end of the 1940s, but from that point forward, mechanization diffused rapidly across the region. Figure 2.7 shows that the process was two-thirds to three-fourths complete by 1964.[77] Rewarded by generous federal subsidies, the planter class was not hurting economically, but it no longer required the services of poor uneducated workers. If one were looking for a way to explain away the Civil Rights revolution as a consequence of deep changes in technology and economic structures, this would be the place to focus: the disappearance of a major class interest in racial subordination. As Jack Temple Kirby, eminent historian of the rural South, wrote, "Change merely seemed sudden in the 1950s and 1960s, when foundations, long before undermined, collapsed."[78]

But although the historical economic base for Jim Crow had departed, it left an imposing superstructure of norms, percep-

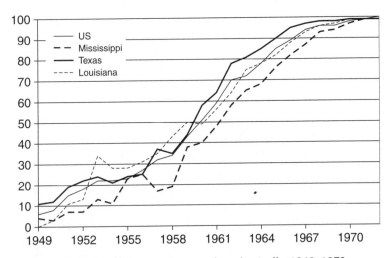

Figure 2.7 Percentage of cotton harvested mechanically, 1949–1972.
    Source: U.S. Department of Agriculture, Economic Research Service. *Statistics on Cotton and Related Data*, p. 218.

tions, interests, and institutions in its wake. The demise of plantation labor may have been a necessary condition for the success of the Civil Rights revolution, but plantation areas nonetheless led white opposition to reform. Nor was the success of that revolution an inevitable byproduct of economic progress in the cities. On all the major frontiers, the postwar white South moved forward entertaining a vision of progress in which segregation and white supremacy would not be disturbed in any fundamental way. Because economic and educational gaps between the races had widened, integration was seen not as an opportunity but as an economic threat.

One might have thought that profit-seeking employers would take the lead in breaking down racial barriers. But in one industry after another, patterns of occupational segregation proved remarkably persistent. In the paper industry, the extraordinary conditions of World War II brought no permanent change. Labor economist Herbert Northrup wrote, "If anything, by 1950, segregation of job facilities had become more rigid."[79] His observation is consistent with that of economic historian Robert Margo, who finds that blacks were underrepresented in the growth of southern nonfarm employment between 1900 and 1950 and that this gap cannot be explained by differences in education.[80] Donald Dewey, virtually the only white economist at a southern university to devote research to the race issue, reported in the mid-1950s that in most plants, "the racial division of labor . . . remained fixed as far back as anyone can remember."[81]

One might attribute this rigidity to the power of tradition, but essentially similar segregation systems were readily adopted in new industries such as petroleum and in plants managed by outside firms. One company with "Yankee" management "right down to the personnel level" assigned black workers solely to janitorial and laborer jobs. The personnel manager explained, "I don't believe [company name] as a corporation gave a damn one way or another. . . . Local situation dictates and that is probably how it was done here."[82] Even in 1961 company

guards at General Motors' Fisher Body plant in Atlanta barred
blacks from entering the grounds to apply for production jobs
that had been advertised.[83] Evidently, discriminatory segregation
was not inconsistent with the profit motive in the postwar South.

To be sure, blacks also experienced severe discrimination in
northern cities, in employment, housing, schooling, even at times
in public accommodations. But because the North never institutionalized Jim Crow segregation, the two regions were on different evolutionary paths. When the Supreme Court declared the
Civil Rights Act unconstitutional in 1883, many northern states
quickly adopted their own public accommodations laws. Almost
all nonsouthern states (and virtually all cities) had such laws by
1964, but no southern state came close to doing so.[84] Economic
historian William Collins finds that the establishment in 1941 of
the Fair Employment Practices Committee led to significant gains
for black workers, but not in the South.[85]

However inevitable the revolution may appear in retrospect,
as of the late 1950s neither Civil Rights activists nor segregationists had reason to believe that fundamental change in the
South was imminent or even likely in the near future. Civil Rights
forces won a famous victory in 1956 in Montgomery, Alabama,
when the Supreme Court upheld a lower court ruling ending the
city's bus boycott and declaring the bus segregation laws unconstitutional. But the dispute was marked by bombings both before
and after the ruling, and the culprits were quickly acquitted, with
little public objection from the white community. Like many
other southern cities, Montgomery subsequently sold or leased
its parks rather than submit to court-ordered desegregation.[86] So
it seemed at the time that the Montgomery victory would join a
long list of victories in the courts—most prominently *Brown v.
Board of Education*—that generated little real change on the
ground. As John Hope Franklin wrote in 1956, "The wall of segregation had become so formidable, so impenetrable, apparently,
that the entire weight of the American tradition of equality and
all the strength of the American constitutional system had to be

brought to bear in order to make the slightest crack in it."[87] Five years later, the eminent southern historian C. Vann Woodward wrote, "The modern South rests on those very foundations and is continuous in its economic, political and racial institutions and doctrines with the order established in 1877. In racial policy, political institutions and industrial philosophy, there has been no break with the founding fathers of the New South."[88] With the aid of hindsight, we can see that these perceptions and implicit predictions were shortsighted. But the barriers to change described by Franklin and Woodward were very real, and proving them wrong over the next half-century was not easy.

CHAPTER 3

SOUTHERN BUSINESS AND
PUBLIC ACCOMMODATIONS

An Economic-Historical Paradox

With the aid of hindsight, the landmark Civil Rights legislation of 1964 and 1965, which shattered the system of racial segregation dating back to the nineteenth century in the southern states, is clearly identifiable as a positive stimulus to regional economic development. Although the South's convergence toward national per capita income levels began earlier, any number of economic indicators—personal income, business investment, retail sales—show a positive acceleration from the mid-1960s onward, after a hiatus during the previous decade. Surveying the record, journalist Peter Applebome marveled at "the utterly unexpected way the Civil Rights revolution turned out to be the best thing that ever happened to the white South, paving the way for the region's newfound prosperity."[1]

But this observation poses a paradox for business and economic history. Normally we presume that business groups take political positions in order to promote their own economic interests, albeit at times shortsightedly. But here we have a case in which regional businesses and businessmen, with few exceptions, supported segregation and opposed state and national efforts at racial integration, a policy that subsequently emerged as "the best thing that ever happened to the white South." In effect southern business had to be coerced by the federal government to act in its own economic self-interest! Such a paradox in business behavior surely calls for explanation, yet the case has yet to be analyzed explicitly by business and economic historians.

This chapter concentrates on public accommodations, a surprisingly neglected topic in Civil Rights history. In retrospect, desegregation of restaurants, motels, and movie theaters may seem to have been relatively easy and perhaps of secondary historical and economic significance. But this perception emerged only after the fact. In the early 1960s denial of equal service by private firms catering to the public was the single most prominent source of racial protest in the South, and this part of the Civil Rights Act was "more passionately and extensively debated both in and out of Congress than any other section."[2] So strong was the opposition that early forecasts by knowledgeable observers gave Title II (Public Accommodations) virtually no chance of approval. Yet by the end of the decade, this once burning issue had all but disappeared from the national agenda.

Was the opening of public accommodations merely social change, or was it an economic issue as well? It certainly had economic consequences. Black people who lived through that era recall the *hardship* of traveling when there was no certainty of finding a place to eat or sleep overnight. Those who owned a car could avoid exposure to humiliation on buses and trains, but because they were not accommodated in any hotel in the South patronized by whites, black travelers usually stayed in private homes.[3] John Lewis describes his family's preparations for a trip in 1951:

> There would be no restaurant for us to stop at until we were well out of the South, so we carried our restaurant right in the car with us. . . . Stopping for gas and to use the bathroom took careful planning. Uncle Otis had made this trip before, and he knew which places along the way offered "colored" bathrooms and which were better just to pass on by. Our map was marked and our route was

planned that way, by the distances between service stations where it would be safe for us to stop.[4]

Black travelers could buy guidebooks listing hotels and restaurants that were open to them. The best-known of these, *The Negro Travelers' Green Book,* makes interesting reading. The foreword to the 1956 edition stated, "The White traveler has had no difficulty in getting accommodations, but with the Negro it has been different. He, before the advent of a Negro travel guide, had to depend on word of mouth, and many times accommodations were not available." Recommended establishments were indicated by a star, though a parenthetical remark was careful to note that omission of the star "does not necessarily mean inferior accommodations."[5] The *Green Book* continued publication through 1963, but even at that late date, listings for national chains were not to be found.

SOUTHERN BUSINESS AND DESEGREGATION

The starting point for understanding the public accommodations conflict is recognition that racial segregation was fundamentally a business policy by profit-seeking firms. One often hears that the Civil Rights Movement mainly succeeded in breaking down Jim Crow laws or de jure segregation. But segregation in such facilities as lunch counters, restaurants, and hotels was rarely required by law, and when statutes or municipal ordinances did exist, enforcement was generally at the discretion of proprietors.[6] Indeed because the federal courts after *Brown* ruled consistently that state-enforced racial discrimination was illegal, most laws *requiring* segregation had been repealed by the 1960s.[7] By then the strongest legal defense of segregation was the argument that in the absence of state action, private establishments had the right to determine their own clientele. This was in essence the basis on which the Civil Rights Act of 1875 was declared unconstitutional in 1883. Although the Warren Court often overturned sit-in convictions on narrow grounds, it never ruled that exclusion on the basis of race by private businesses was unconstitutional.[8]

Nor for the most part were segregated restaurants and hotels intimidated by threats of retaliation if they were to serve black customers, by "gangs bent on violence if they break the dominant norm."[9] To be sure, issues could become politicized as the sit-in movement persisted, and at that stage business efforts at compromise were sometimes stymied by politics. During the 1961–1962 boycott of white stores in Albany, Georgia, for example, when several businessmen expressed a willingness to negotiate with the boycotters, their reward was to be censured by a majority of the city commission! But this was a tactical move during a time of political crisis. There were certainly ugly threats and incidents associated with public accommodations, though the worst of these occurred *after* the Civil Rights Act, when desegregation came as a shock to small towns and outlying areas. But in most times and places during the protracted struggle, from the sit-in at Greensboro, North Carolina, in February 1960 to passage of the Act in July 1964, firms and business groups were free to make their own decisions on racial policies. Overwhelmingly they chose segregation. Where segregation was practiced, there seem to be virtually no examples of voluntary desegregation initiated by business in the absence of economic pressures such as sit-ins or boycotts.

Businessmen feared that serving blacks, particularly in socially sensitive activities such as eating and sleeping, would result in the loss of white customers. From the beginning and throughout the controversy, this fear was repeatedly expressed. When asked in late 1959 by James Lawson and others to begin serving African Americans at lunch counters voluntarily, Nashville department store owners Fred Harvey and John Sloan declined, saying they would lose more business than they would gain. After two months of sit-ins, an interracial seven-man committee appointed by the mayor recommended that merchants divide their lunch counters into two sections: one for whites and one for those who wanted to eat in an integrated setting. Even on a ninety-day trial basis, this modest proposal was rejected by both sides.[10]

After weeks of consultation with affected businesses, the chairman of a committee to resolve the sit-in crisis in Greensboro—where the mayor actively favored desegregation—reported:

> The managers are extremely sensitive to public reaction, and merchants engaged in general merchandising businesses who also have food departments are fearful that if they served all races on an integrated basis in the food department, they will lose a sufficient percentage of their present patronage to the nonintegrated eating establishments in our city to cause a presently profitable food department to operate at a loss.[11]

Often the fear was framed as a prediction that patronage would quickly tip from all-white to all-black. One southern manager complained, "Managers are defenseless against this situation. We are being singled out as tyrants who are being unfair to Negroes, when our duty and that of all business firms is to do the best job they can for the majority, and whites comprise the majority of our trade. *Is it democratic for a minority to rule a majority?*"[12] His clear assumption was that black customers would make his shop unacceptable to white patrons.

The complaint that particular establishments were being "singled out" may suggest that the problem was essentially a matter of coordination or incomplete coverage, arising only because white customers could readily switch to "nonintegrated" alternatives. Eventually the issue did take this form in many municipalities, once business leaders came to believe that desegregation was inevitable. But from the perspective of 1960, fears of a "tipping" phenomenon operated at the level of the shopping district as well as the level of the individual firm. As urban historian Alison Isenberg suggests, desegregation was a threat to the downtown area as a whole. If anything, downtown merchant groups in the South saw their "coordination problem" in terms of *maintaining* segregation collectively. Thus the owner of Martin's Department Store in Greensboro predicted that desegregation would make "a kind of ghetto out of this section of the city."[13]

Perhaps the clearest indication that segregation was a business decision is the fact that, at least initially, none of the national chains took active steps to change the policy in their southern franchises, even when they came under pressure beginning in 1960. The executives of Woolworth, Kress, Kresge, W. T. Grant, and other chains were not themselves subject to the social pressures of southern communities toward racial conformity. Yet virtually without exception, their initial response was to defer to the judgment of local managers. This April 1960 statement by a Woolworth vice president in response to a letter from a Baptist minister was typical:

> Our company has always considered itself a guest in any community in which it is located. As such, we endeavor to be good neighbors and to abide by local customs established by local people for the conduct of business in their towns. As you undoubtedly know, the customs to which you take exception had been in vogue for many years before our stores were established. In our opinion, under these circumstances it is unrealistic to expect that Woolworth would take the initiative in endeavoring to change them.[14]

Although such policy statements were generally couched in terms of deference to local customs, one can hardly doubt that the response would have been different if the companies believed that segregation entailed a sacrifice of profits. Only when sit-ins and boycotts inflicted heavy losses on local franchises and it became clear that these campaigns would continue indefinitely did national chains reluctantly begin to encourage accommodation to pressures for change.[15]

THE DYNAMICS OF QUASI-VOLUNTARY SOCIAL CHANGE

February 1, 1960, when four black students from the Agricultural and Technical College sat down and ordered coffee at Woolworth's lunch counter in Greensboro, North Carolina, now stands as one of the iconic dates of Civil Rights history. It is commonly known as the first sit-in, though this label is not quite right. A round of sit-ins took place in Kansas and Oklahoma two years before, with some success, though the Greensboro Four knew nothing of them. They also were unaware of sit-ins organized in various cities by the Congress of Racial Equality during the 1940s, nor the 1939 sit-in by Samuel Wilbert Tucker at the segregated library in Alexandria, Virginia. In Nashville test sit-ins took place in November and December 1959. But Greensboro was the sit-in that took off, as hundreds of fellow students joined in the days to come, and the tactic quickly spread to towns and cities throughout the upper South states of North Carolina, Virginia, and Tennessee.[16]

It is probably best not to overanalyze the motivations of the early sit-in participants. The Greensboro students were not seeking a specific economic objective, and they were not planning a test case on constitutional grounds. But they were angry at the symbolic injustice of lunch counter exclusion and frustrated at the lack of progress since the *Brown* decision six years before. The fact that most older Civil Rights leaders initially opposed the sit-ins was no deterrent, but added an element of intergenerational resentment to the youthful zeal. Sociologists track the process of diffusion through media news and activist organizations, including the newly formed Student Nonviolent Coordinating Committee (SNCC), which grew directly out of the sit-in movement.[17]

In almost every case, the initial response of both local managers and chain executives was to wait out the demonstrators, in the belief that their energies would soon fade. Governor Luther Hodges of North Carolina, owner of many segregated Howard Johnson restaurants, likened the protest to hula hoops, the latest youthful fad.[18] The only debate was whether to allow the sit-inners to remain in their places indefinitely (unserved), to close the lunch counters, or to request eviction by the police under trespass laws. All three tactics were deployed in cities throughout the South, often with remarkable success. Only in retrospect does the outcome appear inevitable.

Little Rock, Arkansas, is a case in point. Proud of its progressive, cosmopolitan image, the city voluntarily desegregated its libraries, public transportation, and some parks in the 1950s.[19] After the city was badly burned by the school integration crisis of 1957, a moderate pro-business group took control of the school board and city government in 1959, engineering a compromise to reopen the high schools. Despite this lesson on the costs of uncompromising resistance, when the first student sit-ins at downtown lunch counters took place in March 1960, Woolworth officials immediately called city police. Subsequent harsh fines and sentences "swiftly ground the movement to a standstill." An effort by the NAACP to organize a boycott collapsed within a week. When sit-ins were resumed the following year by the Arkansas branch of SNCC, downtown business leaders still refused to budge, apparently hoping to outlast the demonstrators with a combination of intimidation and solidarity in resisting change. The white business attitude in 1961 was summarized by Everett Tucker, incoming school board president and director of industrial development for the Chamber of Commerce: "The best thing for Little Rock to do now is nothing."[20]

In his detailed micro-study of political dynamics in three Alabama cities, historian J. Mills Thornton reports that well into the early 1960s, segregationists felt they were winning the struggle, and they had good reason for this belief. In Birmingham, after negotiations over lunch counters and fitting rooms broke down, an Easter 1962 boycott of downtown stores was an utter failure. As one prominent Birmingham moderate put it, "Most businessmen felt that the demonstrations would fizzle in time."[21] In Rock Hill, South Carolina, more than a year of sit-ins, mass arrests, and national publicity resulted only in closure of lunch counters at Woolworth's and McCrory's, the two chief targets.[22] In Durham, North Carolina, a 1961 campaign to integrate local movie theaters was successfully resisted and died out.[23] In Albany,

Georgia, the boycott of white stores during 1961–1962 attracted national attention but ultimately failed. In Greenwood, Mississippi, as late as December 1963, Jane Stembridge of SNCC saw "not one scrap of evidence that we are overcoming. No lunch counter in downtown Greenwood has opened to Negroes, no public school desegregation has occurred, no jobs have opened up and very few people have been successful in their attempts to become registered voters."[24]

A particularly chilling example of failure was the campaign to desegregate Chapel Hill, North Carolina, a university town long considered an oasis of cosmopolitanism and tolerance. Despite early successes at some restaurants, as late as 1964 three of Chapel Hill's five motels did not accept Negro lodgers, and 32 percent of the local restaurants maintained discriminatory policies of some type. Local activists protested through sit-ins and other forms of civil disobedience, but opponents—including many business owners—successfully blocked a proposed local public accommodations ordinance. Because the Chapel Hill story received little media attention and the presiding judge was ruthless in prosecuting offenders, the movement achieved virtually none of its goals prior to the federal Civil Rights Act of 1964.[25]

If private-sector desegregation was up for grabs in the early 1960s, when did the tide turn, and what was the cause? A perusal of the pages of national retail trade periodicals such as *Women's Wear Daily* tells a central part of the story: sit-ins and boycotts did real damage to retail businesses, especially in the downtown shopping districts of southern cities. The losses had at least two components: denial of black patronage for political reasons and diversion of white customers deterred by disruption and turmoil. The Woolworth manager in Greensboro estimated that only 5 percent of his trade was from black customers, yet sales fell by 20 percent in 1960 and profits by 50 percent.[26] In many cases, when businesses were resistant to sit-ins, local Civil Rights groups announced boycotts of some or all businesses. In Nashville, where blacks represented 30 percent of downtown customers, a black boycott in support of the sit-ins was believed to be around 98 percent effective.[27]

After Greensboro the business press seemed fixated on the threat; hardly a week went by without coverage of the issue, often with a series of brief updates on events in various cities. Precise quantification of the impact is beyond reach, but the major headlines speak for themselves: "Negro Protests Plague Chains, No End in Sight"; "Retail Losses Cited in Negro Sitdowns, Spread Is Feared"; "Segregation Issue Still Disturbing Retail Scene"; "Boycott Hurts in Nashville."[28] As one Washington source put it, "Merchants aren't saying much about this, but they're scared to death, because they are afraid they will lose business either way."[29]

Although many dismissive statements were issued by both national and local spokesmen—indeed there is no evidence that southern protests had detectable effects on national chain-store profits, even when supplemented by pickets in northern cities—their underlying apprehensiveness was not hard to detect. In one anonymous interview, the manager of a variety store "afflicted by the spreading sitdown controversy over segregated eating facilities" reported that sales fell between 20 and 30 percent during protests. The manager worried that the problem would hurt future expansion plans because some would stay out "until this thing blows over—and the end doesn't show the slightest inkling of being in sight."[30] More potent than current losses were fears for the future. According to *New York Times* interviews, the paramount concern voiced by urban merchants was "a fear that prolonged racial tensions might drive customers of both races into the suburban shopping centers never to return. . . . Downtown stores in all [southern cities] have felt the keen knife of competition from the suburbs."[31]

Thus when the demonstrators showed their persistence by returning for new rounds of protest, business and civic leaders in many cities were ready to acquiesce, especially in the border states. The earliest major cities to announce plans to desegregate public accommodations were San Antonio and Galveston, Texas, and Baltimore, Maryland, in March and April 1960. In Dallas, lunch counters were desegregated in June 1960, and a committee of business and civic leaders coordinated full downtown integration as of July 26, 1961.[32] In Nashville an agreement to desegregate lunch counters was reached in May 1960, after weeks of secret negotiations, providing the first success at a major southern city outside of Texas. In Richmond, Virginia, the two largest department stores desegregated their eating places in January 1961, and a lengthy boycott ended in August of that year when agreement was reached with seven downtown stores.[33] All told, lunch counters in over a hundred cities dropped race barriers within a year of the first sit-ins, and the number continued to rise over the next two years.[34]

Effects of Desegregation on Sales

Given the dire expectations of retailers, many southerners were surprised by the relative lack of adverse reaction on the part of white customers. A woman in Winston-Salem, North Carolina, with many years' experience at a food counter remarked, "I wouldn't have believed it. There's not been one word said between a white customer and a Negro in my hearing. Not one!" A manager who had absorbed heavy losses during four months of protest observed, "If I'd known it could have been done this easily, I'd have been for it right from the start."[35] In Charlotte, North Carolina, *Women's Wear Daily* reported that within a short time, "merchants and the public have come to take the presence of Negroes [at department and variety store lunch counters] as a matter of course."[36] The president of Harvey's Department Store in Nashville remarked, "The biggest surprise I ever had was the apparent 'so-what' attitude of white customers."[37] In May 1961 the *New York Times* reported, "Almost without exception, desegregation of lunch counters has been accomplished peacefully and without any significant loss of white customers."[38] Two years later businessmen questioned by the *Wall Street Journal* reported "no grave economic dislocations from integration and they leave no doubt that desegregation of commercial facilities has been less painful than expected."[39]

Such testimonials should not necessarily be taken at face value, because desegregation was often carried out under a blanket of nonpublicity, by agreement with local newspapers. Having agreed to accept black customers, however grudgingly, business groups were determined to put the best possible face on the outcome, often freely rewriting their own history in the process. Can the favorable impact of desegregation on commerce be confirmed by more objective evidence?

One of the few local economic indicators continuously monitored across the 1950s and 1960s is department store sales, tracked by the Federal Reserve since the 1920s and by the Census Bureau beginning in 1966. These figures are by no means a comprehensive index of economic activity, but department stores were central to downtown shopping areas, and it happens that they were also at the center of the early sit-ins and desegregation conflicts. The Federal Reserve data were in fact widely discussed during times of severe crisis, in debates over the cost of racial turmoil. Although coverage was far more limited in the 1950s than later, continuous series can be assembled from the early 1950s to the 1970s for about fifteen southern cities.[40]

It must be acknowledged that such sales data do not necessarily provide a clean before-and-after test of the hypothesis that desegregation was good for business. In some cities, such as Dallas and Little Rock, initial integration of lunch counters was extended relatively smoothly to hotels, restaurants, and theaters. But in others, such as Nashville, Atlanta, and Memphis, a promising start on lunch counters was followed by continued demonstrations, directed at noncooperating merchants but very likely disruptive to downtown shopping nonetheless. Thus there is an unavoidable subjective element in the choice of a desegregation turning point in particular cities.[41]

The best available example of an early desegregating city is Dallas. There civic leaders responded to picketing by arranging for blacks to be served at forty-nine downtown restaurants on July 26, 1961, followed by removal of white-only signs throughout the area. Strong "no-nonsense" tactics were applied to foot-draggers. For example, when it was reported that a state fair concessionaire had denied service to a Negro family, the mayor himself called the party in question and told him that his license would be revoked immediately if it happened again.[42] The Dallas data clearly suggest an acceleration of sales after the sweeping desegregation of 1961 (Figure 3.1).

Later entrants enjoyed a similar reward. An example is Little Rock, where a "secret committee" of leading merchants, bankers, and Chamber of Commerce representatives took charge, reversing the original resistance and quietly initiating a desegregation process beginning in January 1963.[43] An indication of the trepidation with which businessmen approached the matter is

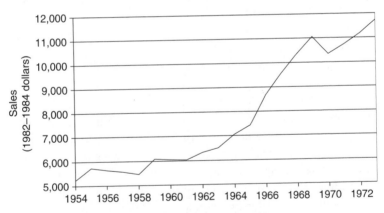

Figure 3.1 Dallas department store sales, 1954–1973.
Sources: Compiled from monthly reports collected by the Federal Reserve System ("Monthly Department Store Sales—Selected Cities and Areas"), on microfilm supplied by the Minneapolis Federal Reserve Library. Beginning in 1966, the series is compiled from the U.S. Bureau of the Census, *Monthly Department Store Sales in Selected Areas.*

that white negotiators initially tried to persuade blacks to agree not to patronize the newly integrated dining rooms when the Arkansas Razorbacks football team was playing in Little Rock.[44] But by April James Forman of SNCC called Little Rock "just about the most integrated city in the South."[45] Figure 3.2 illustrates the dramatic results. The decline of 1956–1962 reflects the schools crisis and its discouragement to new industrial investment rather than disputes over public accommodations. But the same moderate businessmen played leading roles in resolving both crises, and the timing evidence points to the 1963 desegregation as a turning point.

In Atlanta, famously self-styled as "the city too busy to hate," sit-ins began with the first wave in early 1960, but the path to desegregation was far from smooth. Sit-ins were suspended after one day pending negotiations with the business community. But little progress was made; one business representative told the students, "We are not even thinking about thinking about doing

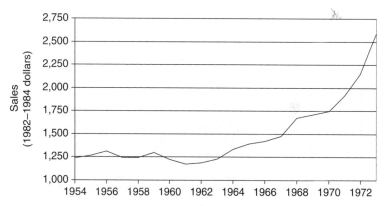

Figure 3.2 Little Rock department store sales, 1954–1973.
Sources: Compiled from monthly reports collected by the Federal Reserve System ("Monthly Department Store Sales—Selected Cities and Areas"), on microfilm supplied by the Minneapolis Federal Reserve Library. Beginning in 1966, the series is compiled from the U.S. Bureau of the Census, *Monthly Department Store Sales in Selected Areas.*

away with segregation." Protests resumed in June, targeting Rich's Department Store, the largest retailer. Although Richard Rich himself was the very epitome of the southern business moderate, the store's employees refused service and turned out the lights. At a meeting with the students the next day, Rich angrily exclaimed, that he did not care if another Negro ever came into his store again. The store's board was equally intransigent, even seriously discussing the possibility of becoming an all-white store. A group of senior business, political, and Civil Rights leaders finally reached agreement (without student representatives) in March 1961 to desegregate lunch counters, but only as of the following October, after court-ordered school desegregation. Figure 3.3 confirms that retail sales were flat or declining from 1959 through 1961, with limited growth in 1962 and 1963, as desegregation remained partial, contested, and uncertain. Full de-

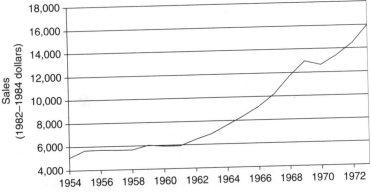

Figure 3.3 Atlanta department store sales, 1954–1973.
Sources: Compiled from monthly reports collected by the Federal Reserve System ("Monthly Department Store Sales—Selected Cities and Areas"), on microfilm supplied by the Minneapolis Federal Reserve Library. Beginning in 1966, the series is compiled from the U.S. Bureau of the Census, *Monthly Department Store Sales in Selected Areas.*

segregation was achieved only with the Civil Rights Act of 1964, at which time sales growth accelerated.[46]

These relatively progressive examples contrast with the notorious case of Birmingham, Alabama, where in 1962 the City Commission closed all public parks in response to court-ordered desegregation. Negotiations at that time over lunch counters and fitting rooms came to nothing, and the business community held firm against concessions even in the face of a massive and highly effective boycott of downtown stores in 1963. Police Commissioner "Bull" Conner's violent response to demonstrations inflicted lasting damage on the city's reputation, prompting intervention by the federal government in favor of a negotiated settlement. Figure 3.4 shows that department store sales in Birmingham hit bottom in 1963, after seven years of decline. Even in Birmingham, the belated desegregation agreement evidently reversed the downward slide, and growth resumed after passage of the Civil Rights Act of 1964.[47]

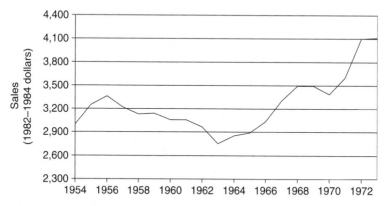

Figure 3.4 Birmingham department store sales, 1954–1973.
Sources: Compiled from monthly reports collected by the Federal Reserve System ("Monthly Department Store Sales—Selected Cities and Areas"), on microfilm supplied by the Minneapolis Federal Reserve Library. Beginning in 1966, the series is compiled from the U.S. Bureau of the Census, *Monthly Department Store Sales in Selected Areas.*

SOLVING THE COORDINATION PROBLEM: FROM
QUASI-VOLUNTARY TO FEDERAL LEGISLATION

These apparent business success stories inspired the Kennedy administration to promote and mediate voluntary local settlements. Advisors such as Robert Rankin and Benjamin Muse of the Southern Regional Council maintained extensive business contacts in the South and favored an appeal to enlightened self-interest. In light of later developments, it may seem surprising that the Kennedy administration's "running tallies of progress" were initially developed to bolster its case *against* a comprehensive federally imposed policy.[48]

As seen by business moderates, the resurgence of prosperity in cities that reached settlements on public accommodations served both as a model for emulation and as a form of business competition relative to cities in the deep South, while the 1963 breakdown of law and order in Birmingham vividly demonstrated the dangers of failure to compromise. But to suggest that from 1963 onward the process of desegregation was driven by the enlightened self-interest of national chains and southern business elites would be to drastically oversimplify the historical record. As the political leadership in Washington learned, voluntary desegregation agreements could go only so far in the absence of mechanisms to enforce compliance and in the presence (current or anticipated) of competition for white customers from still-segregated establishments.

Although the administration heard repeatedly from southern businessmen that voluntary agreements were much preferred over coercive legal measures, by the summer of 1963 it had become evident that the voluntary approach was sputtering to a standstill, well short of full desegregation. Figure 3.5 shows the running tallies through July of that year. In November a memo from Assistant Attorney General Louis Oberdorfer acknowledged, "Reports of progress in desegregation of privately owned public facilities show virtually no breakthroughs since the middle of October. We are receiving only occasional status reports from businessmen and our monthly reports from United States Attorneys show very little change is now taking place."[49]

Worse yet, partial desegregation often seemed only to make things worse. In a follow-up memo Oberdorfer noted the "curious patchwork pattern" that had emerged from the voluntary process, in which most lunch counters were integrated but most restaurants were not. In a number of towns, theaters were desegregated but drive-ins were not. The unevenness of outcomes generated strong feelings of inequity on the part of businesses and threatened to unravel existing agreements. Numerous reports appeared in late 1963 and early 1964 of firms that reinstituted segregation after initially signing a quasi-voluntary agreement.[50] Perhaps worst of all from the administration's perspective, segregation holdouts prolonged black grievances and failed to end demonstrations.

This lack of clarity prevailed even in Atlanta, the best-known example of enlightened business-led desegregation. True enough,

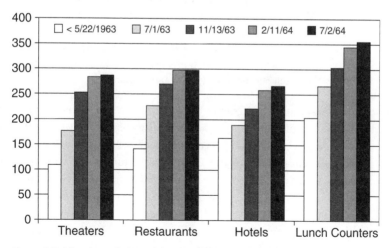

Figure 3.5 Number of cities desegregated 5/22/63–7/2/64.
Source: Compiled from Oberdorfer File on Southern Business, Burke Marshall Papers, John F. Kennedy Library, Box 30.

Atlanta mayors openly appealed to economic self-interest in re-
forming racial policies. The Atlanta Chamber of Commerce was
the only major business group in the state to speak out in favor
of desegregating the public schools, and the Chamber's 1961 letter to the governor to this effect was signed by prominent bankers,
furniture dealers, and utility executives. Historian Alton Hornsby
notes the irony that the same business leaders who were in the
forefront of the schools issue were "steadfast in their opposition
to desegregation of their own lunch counters." Mayor Ivan Allen
was the only prominent official from the South to testify in support of the public accommodations provisions of the Civil Rights
Act. On closer inspection, however, one learns that Allen supported federal legislation only because he had been unsuccessful
in persuading Atlanta hotels and restaurants to desegregate voluntarily. Allen wrote:

> Everything I had tried in those areas [hotels and restaurants] had
> failed. There had been endless meetings with the hotel and restau-
> rant people over the past three or four years, and no matter what
> agreement was reached everyone involved would be split in every
> direction. The hotel and restaurant associations would not even re-
> spond to the pragmatic argument that unless they opened their doors
> to everyone, Atlanta's convention and tourist business—not to men-
> tion its favorable national image—would plummet.

Allen's testimony was reluctant, a response to a personal appeal
from the President. But the accuracy of his assessment is amply
confirmed in confidential surveys conducted by local interracial
groups. In August 1963 the Council on Human Relations of
Greater Atlanta found that there were fewer than twelve restaurants "which can be said with any reasonable degree of certainty
to be desegregated, and only half of these are in the downtown
area. . . . Arrangements for a recent group of Negro guests required hours of interviews with several hotels."[51]
    Awareness of the uneven and uncertain record of the volun-
tary approach helps to account for the rapid, late-breaking shift

in Washington toward a more comprehensive public accommodations law. President Kennedy's Civil Rights message early in
1963 pledged only to "continue to encourage and support action
by state and local communities, and private entrepreneurs, to assure all members of the public equal access to all public accommodations."[52] As late as June the plan was to limit coverage to
"business establishments having significant interstate commerce,
including chain stores, large department stores, restaurants and
hotels along interstate highways, but not to the smaller local
stores."[53] When the president invited about a hundred businessmen to the White House to promote his plan, one chain-store
board chairman "had the distinct impression that few of those at
the White House today desired a public accommodations law."[54]
But on June 11 the president called for legislation "giving all
Americans the right to be served in facilities which are open to
the public—hotels, restaurants, theaters, retail stores, and similar establishments."[55]

Once the major chains decided to acquiesce in desegregation
as the lesser evil, and as they were on their way to deciding that
acquiescence was a positive good that they had secretly favored
all along, the strategic situation changed dramatically. Although
the early results were favorable in many places, both the chains
and downtown merchant groups still harbored fears of being un-
dercut by still-segregated rivals in competition for affluent white
customers. Hence many formerly resistant firms became reformers themselves, calling not only for federal legislation but for the
most comprehensive coverage that was legally possible. The adjustment process was by no means smooth, however, and opinion within the business community was divided throughout the
period.

Behind the scenes, however, the administration was hearing
much more cooperative sentiment from national drug and variety store chains.[56] A turning point of sorts was marked in July
1963, with the appearance of an editorial in the trade publication *Chain Store Age*. The key passage read:

That a federal law prohibiting racial discrimination in retail outlets would be helpful to retailers in localities where segregation is still required by local law or local custom would seem to be rather obvious. . . . One possible feature of the proposed new legislation which the chains will have to oppose with the utmost vigor is a suggested provision limiting its coverage to large-scale retailers or those operating stores or restaurants in more than one State. Not only would any such ill-conceived limitation be basically unfair to those covered by the law, but it would to a large extent defeat the law's only purpose—to give all Americans equal service in all "places of public accommodation whether privately or publicly owned." To emancipate the Negro in some stores and restaurants but to permit discrimination against him in others would be to perpetuate what we must continue to regard as our national shame until it is wiped out altogether.

The editorial was quickly and eagerly circulated within the Justice Department. Later that month the *Kiplinger Washington Letter* reported that although most businessmen are opposed to intrusion on the rights of private property, "more and more you hear this said: 'May be better to have federal law to force everyone to drop the color bars and get it over with fast. Better than piecemeal, some doing it, others not.' This feeling now is not widespread, but it's gaining support gradually."[57]

This changing business sentiment undoubtedly contributed to the greatly strengthened public accommodations provisions of the bill submitted to Congress on June 19, 1963. The initial consensus among observers was that the section had been submitted as a gesture to the movement but that it had little realistic chance of passage. For the better part of the subsequent year-long debate, this assessment was repeatedly heard, both by supporters and by opponents of the measure. On June 28, for example, Adam Clayton Powell said, "Idealistically, I'd have liked to have seen a public accommodations bill yesterday, but knowing the political realities, I'd have to say that, as it looks now, it doesn't have a chance."[58] Even in January 1964 observers doubted that the administration could gain passage without surrendering public accommodations.[59] Unexpectedly, however, the House of Representatives fended off all attempts to water down the section. Contributing to the strength of supporters was, as reported by the *Wall Street Journal,* a virtual absence of organized business opposition to the bill. One conservative midwestern Republican remarked, "There's been a lot of talk about the bill infringing on property rights, but as far as I can tell the people who own the property don't seem to think so."[60]

In May Republican Senate leader Everett Dirksen, who had long harbored grave doubts about mandatory desegregation of public accommodations, announced his support for a modified but not fundamentally weakened version of the bill. Armed with Dirksen's endorsement, the Senate voted cloture on June 10, and the bill itself was passed and signed by President Johnson on July 2, 1964. Although it would be a significant overstatement to say that a national chain-store coalition instigated and directed the entire legislative campaign, their relief at the bill's passage was evident. A Woolworth official pledged immediate compliance, saying, "Woolworth will now be able to serve all its customers in all its stores on a desegregated basis," adding that most of its stores had already desegregated.[61]

The clarity of the new rules spread the commercial benefits throughout the region. Figure 3.6 tracks the real value of retail sales of general merchandise in the South between 1953 and 1973, clearly showing growth acceleration as of 1964. One might wonder whether this apparent turning point merely reflects the swing of the national business cycle. However, Figure 3.7 graphs the same retail sales figures as a share of the U.S. total over the same historical period; the figure offers even more powerful evidence of a Civil Rights effect. By this indicator, southern retail business lagged the nation throughout the years of sit-ins and mass boycotts, turning the corner only in 1965.

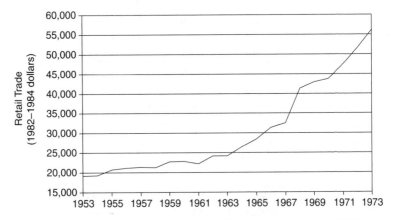

Figure 3.6 Retail sales in the South: general merchandise, 1953–1973.
Source: Compiled from U.S. Bureau of the Census, *Monthly Retail Trade Report.*

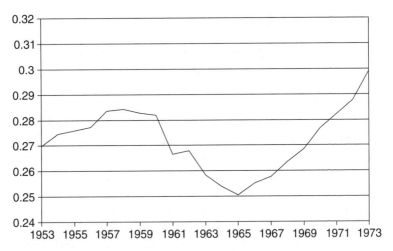

Figure 3.7 Retail sales in the South as share of U.S. total: general merchandise, 1953–1973.
Source: Compiled from U.S. Bureau of the Census, *Monthly Retail Trade Report.*

ENFORCEMENT AND COMPLIANCE UNDER TITLE II

In light of the vociferous debate over public accommodations, the Johnson administration anticipated massive backlash and perhaps violent resistance. In the end, the results were anticlimactic. *Time* magazine reported, "From Charleston to Dallas, from Memphis to Tallahassee, segregation walls that had stood for several generations began to tumble in the first week under the new civil rights law."[62] According to an October 1964 survey of fifty-three cities in nineteen states, desegregation had been accomplished in more than two-thirds of the hotels, motels, chain restaurants, theaters, and sports facilities, as well as public bars and libraries. A few well-publicized enforcement cases aroused intense interest for a relatively brief period, but then, as Muse reported, "as a matter of active national concern it receded into history."[63]

Such retrospectively dismissive accounts exaggerate the overall ease and inexorability of the process, and even the certainty of the outcome. Many small towns and rural areas had been virtually untouched by the Civil Rights Movement, and dozens of complaints poured into the Justice Department in the first month (July 1964) as Civil Rights groups launched systematic testing campaigns throughout the South.

In many localities, the first reaction of proprietors was often open defiance. At Farr's Café in Bessemer, Alabama, the owner-manager turned away a group organized by the West Jefferson County Coordinating Council, saying, "Get out. We don't serve niggers here." Described in the FBI report as "quick tempered, very outspoken," Farr admitted the refusal (his own version of his statement was "Get out. We serve Negroes, not niggers"), and he reiterated his intention to continue this policy at a second FBI interview. The case was closed on October 12, 1965, after a court injunction against the defendant. At Montalas Restaurant in Montgomery, Alabama, on April 12, 1965, the owner made threatening gestures with a knife and told a black customer not to come back. On June, 1966, the owner of Bek's Frostop in

Prattville, Alabama, told an interracial couple, "The restaurant is closed as of this minute." At Virginia's Drive-In Restaurant in Anniston, Alabama, on June 5, 1967, an army major was refused service at the front door and told to go to the back. Many of these proprietors were quite candid in their first FBI interviews, often saying that they believed segregation was necessary for the survival of their businesses. In a few cases, establishments claimed to have converted into private clubs exempt from the law. This was the tactic in one protracted and controversial dispute at Whit's Café in Little Rock, against which private suits were brought by local Civil Rights leaders Daisy Bates and Ometa Jewell.[64]

Within two or three years, the overwhelming majority of establishments were committed to compliance. The Justice Department case reports do not provide many specifics on the precise social and financial processes at work, but generally the defiant tune had changed by the second or third interview. Realization that both Civil Rights forces and the Justice Department were serious about enforcement undoubtedly played a role. Only a small fraction of complaints actually went to court, but the number of lawsuits brought by the Justice Department in the first three years (ninety-three, augmented by many private suits) was enough to make clear the implications of continued outright noncooperation. From the lameness of the excuses offered—the waitress did not know store policy, that section was closed for cleaning, the refusal was not really because of race—one might well question the sincerity of many of the compliance pledges extracted by Justice Department investigators. But undeniably, the volume of complaints diminished over time. Figure 3.8 displays the time line of complaints under the law in Alabama and the dates on which the files were closed. After early peaks in the second half of 1964 and 1965, new allegations of discrimination dwindled to a trickle by 1968. Alabama seems to have been somewhat ahead of the region as a whole, since the overall volume of public accommodations complaints did not peak until 1971.[65]

Although the largest absolute number of cases arose in cities (Birmingham, Mobile, and Montgomery), on a per capita basis the volume of litigation was far higher in smaller Alabama towns such as Marion, Prattville, Russellville, Selma, and Thomasville (Figure 3.9). Most of these were small businesses: drug stores, gas stations, truck stops, drive-ins. Legal rulings soon extended coverage to virtually every lodging place and restaurant, and by the early 1970s litigation had moved on to socially sensitive areas such as bowling alleys and skating rinks. Ultimately most such activities also came under coverage, as the courts eroded the somewhat academic distinction between "places of entertainment" and "places of enjoyment." The last attorney general's report with a section devoted explicitly to public accommodations appeared in 1977.[66]

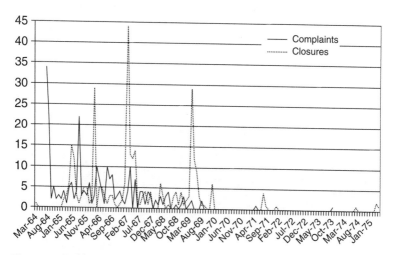

Figure 3.8 Public accommodations complaints and case closures: Alabama, 1964–1975.

Source: Compiled from the records of the Department of Justice. Civil Rights Division. Class 167 (Desegregation of Public Accommodations). Litigation Case Files, Boxes 1–15. Located in the National Archives at College Park, Maryland.

The Supreme Court arguments on public accommodations were particularly interesting in light of this discussion. The Justice Department expected to initiate enforcement actions, but in fact the key test cases were brought by two businesses seeking injunctions against the Act: the Heart of Atlanta motel in Atlanta and Ollie's Barbecue in Birmingham. Solicitor General Archibald Cox chose to defend the law on the basis of the Commerce Clause of the Constitution. Although this decision was probably made to avoid the need for outright reversal of the 1883 decision overturning the Civil Rights Act of 1875, Cox was able to present considerable evidence that discrimination was damaging to commerce, most immediately by discouraging interstate travel by blacks, but even more substantially by generating racial unrest and protest, thus curtailing business activities, tourism, and the convention trade.[67] Furthermore the Court's majority opinion (drafted by Justice Clark) explicitly adopted the foregoing

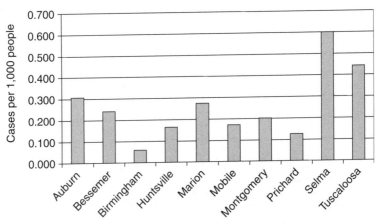

Figure 3.9 Public accommodations cases in Alabama relative to city population.
Source: Compiled from the records of the Department of Justice. Civil Rights Division. Class 167 (Desegregation of Public Accommodations). Litigation Case Files, Boxes 1–15. Located in the National Archives at College Park, Maryland.

analysis of competitive externality to justify the Act's application to smaller concerns with little direct involvement in interstate commerce, such as Ollie's Barbecue. Citing testimony before congressional committees, Clark wrote:

> Racial discrimination by one restaurant in a city encouraged the practice throughout the area because of the other proprietors' fear of the competitive advantage gained by the segregated restaurant in increased white trade. Thus if Congress had limited coverage of the Act to those large restaurants which clearly cater to interstate patrons there would have existed a very real danger of injury to interstate commerce resulting from this competitive disadvantage.

As if in confirmation of Clark's analysis, the owner of Ollie's Barbecue, Ollie McClung—after declaring "I'm shocked" to the press—served five black customers within two hours of the Court's decision on December 14 and subsequently thrived for the next thirty-five years.[68]

AFTERMATH

The interpretation advanced in this chapter is that southern businessmen were locked into a low-level equilibrium, the stability of which was bolstered by the fact that they did not see it that way themselves. Both as firms and as downtown collectivities, businesses balanced the loss of black consumer spending against anticipated losses of white patronage. When their hand was forced by economic pressures, southern businesses learned in most cases that the adverse white reaction was not nearly as severe as they had feared. But white customers also learned that desegregation was not as bad as they had feared, a process no doubt facilitated by the absence of alternatives when desegregation was in effect a public choice. Thus we have a remarkable example of collective coevolutionary learning toward a better economic outcome.

The fact that white business interests gained along with black customers gives this reading some resemblance to the

interest-convergence theory advanced by legal scholar and former Civil Rights attorney Derrick Bell, which holds that vindica-
tion of "even the most basic rights for blacks requires a perceived
benefit for whites."[69] But Bell's thesis emphasizes white interests
as a limitation or constraint on black progress. What it misses in
the present example is the possibility that perceptions of costs
and benefits can change over time and that these changes can be
impelled by the exercise of political and economic pressure, as
well as persuasion. Ultimately the public accommodations issue
boiled down to a coordination problem in many places, where
the end-point was accepted, but no one wanted to make the first
move; arriving at that point required extensive learning by doing
on the part of both business and customers.

A window on the businessman's view of this transition was
offered by Julius Manger Jr., the hotel chain owner recruited by
the Johnson administration to help convert southern businessmen to the new outlook. Reflecting in September 1964 on the
success of the campaign, Manger listed these as his most persuasive arguments:

> 1) I was able to point out the experience of other public accom-
> modations' owners in desegregating their facilities and show that
> when desegregation took place jointly, there was no economic loss
> and there was no trouble between the races.
>
> 2) I was able to say with conviction that Negroes did not crowd
> into public accommodations once they were given the right to use
> them but quite to the contrary used public accommodations much
> less than would be expected. I pointed out that the main reason for
> this was that the Negro just did not have the money necessary to pay
> the bill.
>
> 3) In Charlotte and Savannah we had a larger investment in our
> hotel and motel properties than anyone else. In both of those cities,
> therefore, I was able to say to other hotel and motel owners that I
> was not just asking them to do something and then going to walk
> away, but that actually we had a bigger investment to lose than they
> did. . . .

4) The moral justice of allowing Negroes to use public accommodations facilities was always recognized by the thinking people in the communities I visited, and I am sure this played a large part in their decisions to comply with the new law.

5) In case everything else failed, I was always able to point out that trouble was almost inevitable if nothing was done. I found again and again, that the last thing people want in their communities is trouble.[70]

An issue not directly addressed here is how desegregation in public accommodations related to longer-term change in racial attitudes. Survey evidence shows a trend toward increased tolerance of desegregation among whites dating from the 1940s, in the South as well as the North.[71] It is difficult to believe, however, that the dramatic decline in southern white support for strict segregation between 1961 and 1968 was unrelated to the observed correlation between desegregation and economic progress during those years.[72]

As in many historical cases of unanticipated radical change, after the revolution almost everyone who has anything to say about the past recalls that they themselves were early advocates of reform. The process of retrospective historical revisionism applies to business history as well. In his case study of desegregation in Norfolk, Virginia, Carl Abbott commented astutely, "Indeed, the image of a mobilized business leadership which could take the city's problems in hand was a sophisticated form of boosterism, as much as it was a description of political realities." According to Abbott, Norfolk's business-oriented Committee of 100 "did not serve as a major force for change in Norfolk," but "by openly ratifying the inevitable, the city's business leaders helped to make desegregation respectable."[73]

In some cases the reorientation began almost immediately after passage of the Civil Rights Act. When Andrew Young returned to the motel in St. Augustine, Florida, where five days earlier coffee was thrown on him and acid dropped into the pool, "those people were just wonderful, explaining that they had been afraid of losing business and 'didn't want to be the only ones to integrate.'"[74] Of Chapel Hill, John Ehle wrote in 1965, "I know of few leaders in Chapel Hill, in either the liberal or conservative camps, who don't admit privately that the passage of the bill was helpful. . . . Mrs. Agnes Merritt run[s] the Pines, and she said recently she was certainly grateful for that law, for she now had her old friends and customers back."[75] Perhaps the champion revisionist city was Greensboro. Hal Sieber of the Greensboro Chamber of Commerce gave this account:

> When I first got to Greensboro I heard the white power structure condemning the sit-in demonstrators as if they were subversives. . . . Five years later I heard the Mayor of the city brag about the fact that we were the home of the first sit-in, as if we had invented the electric light bulb.[76]

Franklin McCain, one of the original Greensboro Four, found it "rather amusing" that civic leaders used the sit-ins to support the city's status as the "Gateway to the New South." McCain acknowledged, however, that that tactic was "only smart": "I'm sure if I were the chamber of commerce, I'd do the same thing."[77]

CHAPTER 4

DESEGREGATING
SOUTHERN LABOR MARKETS

By the 1930s labor markets in the South had come to display a distinct "racial wage gap," supported by systems of *vertical* workplace segregation. Not only were job categories classified by race, but black wage rates typically peaked about where white pay grades began. These structures persisted through World War II and the 1950s, showing few signs of softening even in the presence of rapid urbanization and industrial employment growth. During this period, federal efforts to mitigate labor market discrimination were largely ineffective in the South, fostering the widespread impression that substantive changes in this area were virtually impossible.

Nonetheless access to well-paying "responsible jobs" was a core part of the Civil Rights agenda all along—contrary to the belief that the movement's focus shifted from *rights* to *economics* only after the legislative successes of the mid-1960s. In response to these demands, Title VII of the Civil Rights Act had a dramatic effect on regional labor markets, breaking down segregation barriers and opening a wide range of job opportunities to blacks for the first time. The most extreme case of segregation and the most discontinuous break with historical practice was the textiles industry. Opening southern textiles to black workers was a true accomplishment of the Civil Rights campaign, though it is missing from most historical narratives of the movement. Sustained progress in a broader range of industries and occupations required decades of pressure and often litigation, also parts of the ongoing struggle. As later sections of this chapter will show, these gains also had a pronounced regional dimension that is often missed. Both parts of the story deserve a more prominent place in Civil Rights history.

INTEGRATING SOUTHERN TEXTILES

The operative labor force of the southern textiles industry was virtually all white for more than a century, a pattern dating back to antebellum times. Slaves were successfully used in textile mills during the depressed 1840s, but they were pulled out in favor of agriculture during the booming 1850s, and when the regional industry began its postbellum resurgence, it drew first upon whites for reasons of both experience and racial favoritism. Although the ascendancy of the southern branch relative to New England was based on the cheapness of its labor, southern blacks were not utilized, and this exclusion was persistent in the face of advocacy and experimentation with alternatives. Economists have referred to this as an "ideal textbook example of Kenneth Arrow's model of discrimination,"[1] in which an initial racial exclusion became perpetuated by fixed costs of employment policies coupled with racial hostility on the part of white employees.

Economists often distinguish models of discrimination based on *employer prejudice* from those driven by *worker prejudice*. But both mechanisms are needed to comprehend the exclusionary segregation that came to prevail in southern textiles. If employers could have quietly added a few black workers to an all-white mill, the extreme contrast in racial experience profiles might gradually have faded. But such efforts in the 1890s met with violent rebellion by white workers. A series of experiments with all-black cotton mills between 1895 and 1905 were watched with genuine curiosity within the industry, but all of them failed. With hindsight these failures may be attributed to a lack of worker experience and impatience on the part of capital, but the perverse effect was to confirm the prevailing belief that blacks could not handle factory work. The family-based character of the mill village added a social dimension to racial exclusion.[2]

This long-entrenched industry tradition changed abruptly following enactment of the Civil Rights Act of 1964. Figure 4.1 displays the share of black workers in the textile mills of South Carolina from 1918 to 1981. As of 1964, the black female share was virtually zero, while the black male share was barely 5 percent—almost entirely "outside" laboring jobs such as carrying and opening cotton crates or janitorial work. The black share jumped to 25 percent in 1970 and to 34 percent by 1980. The South Carolina figures are displayed because of that state's unique annual labor reports, but the trends in all the southern textile states were similar: a century of rigidity followed by rapid change beginning in 1965. In oral histories collected in the early 1980s, black workers in textile areas referred to integration as "the change" and associated it with the reversal of black regional migration between the 1960s and 1980s.[3]

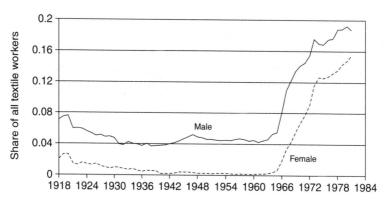

Figure 4.1 Black share of textile workers: South Carolina, 1918–1981.
Source: South Carolina Department of Labor, *Annual Reports.*

How should we understand this historic transformation? From the 1960s to the present, observers have dismissed the significance of "the change" on the grounds that textile employers turned to blacks only because of the pressures of the labor market during the boom years of the 1960s, offering them low-status, low-paying positions that whites would no longer accept. Thus labor economist Richard Rowan wrote in 1970 that "Negroes would have been hired in textile mills without government pressure in the 1960s. The labor market brought the major change." Historian Mary Fredrickson maintained in 1983 that "when 'the change' occurred it was both carefully planned and swiftly implemented. . . . The relative ease with which Southern employers, generally a group intransigent in the face of federal mandates, responded to the regulations of the Equal Employment Opportunity Commission (EEOC) and the Office of Federal Contract Compliance reflected the industry's need for new workers and a growing reliance on black labor."[4]

Every careful empirical study, however, rejects the proposition that the racial revolution in southern textiles can be explained away as a self-interested employer response to labor market conditions. Earlier episodes of labor market tightness, including both world wars, brought no such lasting changes. On the basis of EEOC reports filed by employers in North and South Carolina, Alice Kidder and colleagues found that measures of county-level labor market pressures (unemployment and the ratio of employment to population) were not correlated with increases in black textile employment. This finding was replicated in later research by James J. Heckman and his coauthors, who found that the break in demand for black labor occurred almost simultaneously in the textile counties of South Carolina, regardless of local demographic or economic conditions. It is true that wages and turnover rates for white workers increased during the 1960s, but few mill workers were actually transferring to newer, higher-skill industries, and many textile firms reported far more applicants than positions throughout the period. The evidence thus confirms Kidder's summary statement, "It is clear that the textile industry could have found white workers to take the 20,000 jobs added in the mid-sixties in textiles had it been determined to do so."[5]

These findings do not refute the idea that employers did indeed have an economic interest in expanding the pool of available labor. Echoing a common refrain, one textile executive wrote that the Civil Rights Act was a "blessing in disguise" for them, because it facilitated their efforts to overcome white resistance to "the changing social mores of our times." In the same year the *Winston-Salem Journal* reported, "If anyone complains, management can blame the government." Some years later, the personnel manager of Burlington Mills recalled, "The government gave us a nice way to facilitate [desegregation] and if anybody wanted to complain about it, white people who would say 'hey why are you hiring all of these black people,' you'd say 'because the government forces us to do this,' you could place the blame on the government."[6]

But these recollections were after the fact. Southern employers did not speak out in favor of Title VII during the debate over the Civil Rights Act, and the voting on this section was as regional as on other parts of the bill. When the EEOC held hearings in Charlotte on employment discrimination in southern textiles in 1967, employers declined to participate, and several were bitterly critical of the proceedings. The pioneering black workers hired in the first wave after 1965 certainly had no doubt that federal legislation was critical in changing company policies. Corine Lytle Cannon, one of the first black employees hired at Cannon Mills in Kannapolis, North Carolina, told an interviewer, "That was the whole thing. It would never have been if it had not been for the Civil Rights Act. It would still be like it were." Interestingly, most white workers interviewed shared this view, though not necessarily with the same positive sentiments.[7]

The mobilization of black job applicants asserting their rights helps to explain a challenge that has puzzled researchers in this area: namely, how could small, underfunded enforcement agencies such as the EEOC and the Office of Federal Contract Compliance have had such a dramatic impact on the industry? Observers often cite President Johnson's Executive Order 11246 of 1965, which prohibited discrimination in firms with federal contracts, and some studies do find a positive correlation between such contracts and expanded black employment. But these effects explain only a small part of the overall shift. EEOC procedures were complex and time-consuming, so that the share of complaints leading to court action was minuscule. Yet the effect of the law was large and immediate. The direct reason was that many potential black applicants were following the legislation closely and acted accordingly. Floyd Harris, one of the first black textile workers in West Point, Georgia, recalled:

> I was active in the social revolution that went on from the fifties through the sixties and early seventies, so I was aware of what the black leaders were talking about. We wrote the laws and they passed the Civil Rights bill, and I knew that if the federal government made it a law it'd have to be followed. Our management here is smart and they knew it too.[8]

Such assertiveness was actively fostered by the EEOC. Figure 4.2 displays a brochure issued in 1967 shortly after the Charlotte hearings, calling attention to the change in the industry's racial climate and virtually urging blacks to apply for textile jobs. One could easily have mistaken the flyer for an industry recruitment ad, but in fact it was a government document, complete with information on whom to contact if you were turned away or mistreated. Confronted with such raised expectations on the part of applicants, it is not surprising that management felt it had little choice but to comply.

Thus we have another example, with some parallels to public accommodations, where southern business was compelled or at least impelled by outside authority to take actions serving its own best economic interest, as became clear shortly after the event.

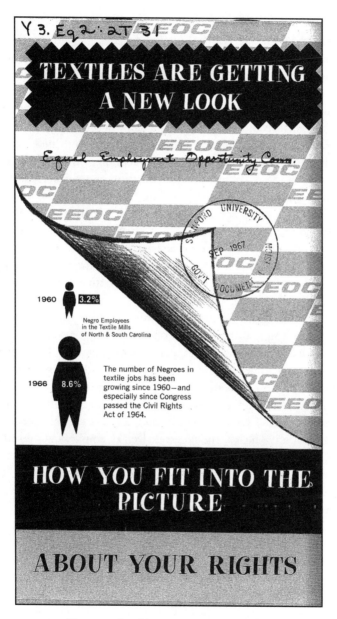

Figure 4.2 Flyer circulated by Equal Employment Opportunity Commission, 1967.
Source: Equal Employment Opportunity Commission. *Textiles Are Getting a New Look.* Washington DC, 1967.

Management shared many of the same racial prejudices that were held by white workers, and their "enlightened" views on integration emerged only after a learning process based on experience and observation at their own firms. The first black hires were approached with extreme caution in an effort to identify "safe Negroes" through detailed screening and perhaps the personal recommendation of someone at the firm. New black workers were often placed in the most menial and undesirable positions, reflecting management's perception of their limited capacities. In these circumstances, evaluation of a worker's performance could easily be contaminated by hostility and doubts about his or her competence on the part of supervisors. Relatively soon, however, management learned that the first black hires were actually better qualified and more motivated than the average white worker. In many cases, race relations on the shop floor improved over time, as stereotypes on both sides were undermined by experience.

Labor historian Timothy Minchin recounts a particularly striking example of managerial opinions changing on the basis of evidence. Robert Gardiner, personnel manager at Dan River Mills, was genuinely astonished in 1969 to read a newspaper article in which a textile executive claimed that blacks had proven themselves to be good textile workers. Gardiner wrote to a colleague, "When I read this comment . . . I was curious because, from all I have heard, the Negroes we are employing are shiftless, lazy, don't want to work and leave as soon as they are hired." So a Dan River team undertook a systematic study of comparative worker performance in their own company, the results of which showed conclusively that blacks had lower rates of absenteeism and turnover than whites and "no discernible difference in productivity," except that black workers scored marginally higher than whites in some job classifications. The same absence of difference was reported by the manager of Erwin Mills, a division of Burlington Industries: "On turnover, absenteeism, and job performance, we can't tell the difference, really.

Their work record and performance are comparable with those of any other group." In light of these assessments, perhaps we should not be surprised by a 1969 *New York Times* report: "Virtually all of the large companies have begun to preach a doctrine of equal, color-blind employment."[9]

Was the Textiles Industry a "Hollow Prize"?

A common response to this account of breaking an industrial color line is to say that the gains were hardly worth the effort because the American textiles industry was in decline. On this view, the textiles jobs opened to black workers were only a fleeting mirage, as these jobs were soon eliminated by labor-saving technologies and foreign competition. Thus famed Civil Rights attorney Jack Greenberg writes, "Textiles turned out to be a mistake, because the industry was declining and technology was replacing a growing share of labor."[10]

This dismissive assessment is itself both anachronistic and shortsighted. The first generation of black textile workers had no doubt that their new employment opportunities constituted a major step forward economically. EEOC records show that mill jobs paid around $90 per week, compared to $25 per week for domestic work. For struggling semisubsistence farmers, the desegregated industry offered the same escape route from poverty for many blacks that it had for earlier generations of white hill people. Speaking to an interviewer years later, retired mill worker William "Sport" Suggs was emphatic: "The mill job was definitely something that made my living better. The wages were much higher. . . . I was glad, and a whole lot of black people were pulled up, made their living a whole lot better. I bought this old house here. . . . I sent three of my children to college."[11]

Because textiles was the South's largest industry, its desegregation was the single largest contributor to the sharp increase in relative black incomes between 1965 and 1975. According to economists John Donohue and James Heckman, this jump was an exclusively southern regional phenomenon. Thus the textiles example stands in sharp contrast to the much stouter resistance to black entry mounted by white construction workers in the northern states.[12]

Nor is it true that the textiles industry was in decline at the time of the Civil Rights revolution. Employment grew rapidly throughout the 1960s, both in textiles and the closely related apparel industries. It is true that total national employment in these industries peaked in the mid-1970s, but the pace of decline was moderate until the 1990s. Total black employment in southern textiles increased from fewer than 100,000 in 1970 to more than 220,000 in the early 1990s, so that the industry continued to provide an escape route from poverty for a full generation of African Americans. A notable feature of this experience is that the gains were realized by a generation whose educational opportunities had been severely restricted. These economic advances cannot be seen as a result of *Brown v. Board of Education* because progress in school desegregation was quantitatively insignificant before 1968—though they might be considered a delayed return to the longer-term improvement in the quality of segregated black schools. A second important feature is that these relative gains were sustained over time, even after the industry began to decline and the political climate had changed. Perhaps one channel for this persistence was that mill workers like Sport Suggs were able to transmit some of their own economic gains to the next generation, in the form of better opportunities for education and access to new, growing sectors of the economy.

If textiles employment declined over time mainly because younger, better-educated workers were pulled out of the industry in favor of higher-skill, better-paying positions in other sectors, as the nation's comparative advantage shifted, this would not be considered a major economic or social concern. This is not quite what we see from the mid-1970s to the mid-1990s, however, when wage gains largely came to an end for both black and white workers in textiles and elsewhere. In light of this transition to slower growth, it is understandable that some observers became disillusioned about the economic benefits of the Civil Rights revolution. But this shift reflected broader changes in national labor markets and labor market policies rather than inherent weaknesses or strategic mistakes by the Civil Rights generation.

BEYOND TEXTILES

In other southern industries, the impact of the Civil Rights Act on racial employment patterns was not as dramatic as in textiles. Figure 4.3 displays the South Carolina data for all manufacturing other than textiles. The immediate effect of the act itself is barely visible, but black employment doubled between 1966 and 1972, and then continued to rise across the 1970s. Notably, fluctuations in black employment paralleled those for whites. Although the black share was rising, there was no span of years where blacks were hired at the direct expense of white jobs.

There were two main reasons for this gradualism. The textiles industry was extreme in its policy of virtually complete exclusion

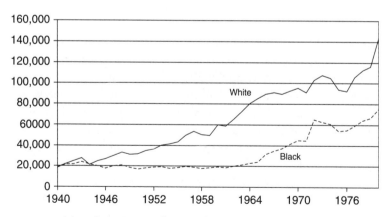

Figure 4.3 Manufacturing employment by race: South Carolina industries other than textiles, 1940–1980.
Source: South Carolina Department of Labor, *Annual Reports.*

of blacks from operative positions. Other industries employed at least a moderate number of black workers, but only in jobs governed by segregated "lines of progression." In terms of pay, the white trajectory typically began at about the point where black wages peaked. In these industries, the progress of desegregation was not well measured by black employment per se but by access to the higher-paying job classifications. The second reason for the slower pace is that these issues played out through an accelerating blizzard of complaints and litigation made possible by Title VII of the Civil Rights Act.

Within the first five years of the Act and for some time after that, it was by no means obvious to observers that a revolution had occurred in southern labor markets. Studies conducted in the late 1960s and early 1970s emphasized instead the stubborn persistence of barriers to progress: recalcitrant employers skeptical about the aptitude and qualifications of black workers; hostility on the part of white coworkers, who also shared these beliefs about low black ability; ignorance of job opportunities on the part of blacks or an unwillingness to apply for jobs because they anticipated rejection; and the relatively limited work experience and educational background that most southern blacks actually had at that point, providing an aura of credence to white prejudicial beliefs. Writing in 1968, sociologist Louis Ferman reported "no large-scale movement of Negroes into jobs from which they had been traditionally barred." A study directed by labor economist Ray Marshall using EEOC data for 1966 and 1969 stressed the large North-South gap in black employment and occupational status and the very limited progress in closing the gap to that point. Reports from southern cities informed and confirmed this sense of pessimism, especially for black men. For example, the director of a new Apprenticeship Information Center in Houston reported that young black men refused to believe counselors who tried to recruit them into the program by claiming that "times have changed." When the study was published in 1978 (though still based mainly on 1960s data), editors Marshall and Christian wrote that racial exclusions and educational deficiencies were generating "a widening of the gap between black and white incomes in the South."[13]

With the aid of hindsight, we can say with confidence that these assessments were mistaken and that this was in fact a uniquely favorable period for black progress in southern labor markets. But the pace was very uneven. It seems accurate to associate the historical break with the passage of the Civil Rights Act, because in the cases that have been closely studied, no significant change was under way prior to that point. But utilization of Title VII often required years of litigation. The enforcement powers of the EEOC had been severely weakened during the legislative process, as the political price for Republican support. It was not until 1972 that the EEOC gained authority to seek judicial enforcement and the provisions of Title VII were extended to federal, state, and local governments.[14] Perhaps most important were court decisions confirming that the Act would indeed require major changes in southern employer behavior.

The paper industry paid substantially higher wages than textiles, a consideration that may help to explain why it soon became "perhaps the most litigated industry in the south," according to a Civil Rights lawyer speaking in 1977. As industry executives later acknowledged, they had no plans to employ blacks in any but menial positions before the Civil Rights Act.[15] But as in textiles, black paper workers were keenly aware of the passage of the Act and filed for job transfers almost immediately after it came into effect on July 2, 1965. When the transfers were not approved, workers filed suit under Title VII, often with the support of the NAACP Legal Defense Fund. In a landmark 1968 case, the Justice Department sued Crown-Zellerbach, a major paper employer based in Bogalusa, Louisiana, along with its leading union. The outcome was a court determination that even a superficially neutral seniority system could be illegal if it hindered rectification of long-standing restrictions on the advancement opportunities of black workers. This decision led in turn to the Jackson Memorandum of 1968, negotiated by the Office of Federal Contract Compliance, in which International Paper and its southern unions accepted the principle that blacks could advance to their "rightful place" on the companywide seniority ladder. This agreement certainly did not end litigation, and many black workers (as well as the EEOC) were deeply dissatisfied with the resulting system. But black representation in industry blue-collar jobs gradually increased from 15 to nearly 30 percent by the 1990s, including many of the higher-paying machine-tending jobs they had previously been denied.[16]

Another landmark Supreme Court decision was *Griggs v. Duke Power* (1971), which established the "disparate impact" test for discrimination in promotion criteria. The case itself nicely illustrates the wide range of uncertainty about the meaning and significance of Title VII and why it ultimately had a major impact as interpreted by the courts. At its Dan River plant in North Carolina (opened in the 1950s), Duke Power followed a standard practice of hiring blacks only into a segregated Labor Department, in which the highest wage was lower than the lowest wage paid in the all-white departments. When the Civil Rights Act was passed, the company instituted a number of changes that to its black employees seemed merely cosmetic. Explicit racial job categories were eliminated (though facilities were not desegregated), but in their place, minimum scores on IQ-type tests were imposed for transfers into all jobs other than the Labor Department. This was in addition to the requirement of a high school diploma, which had been added—again excepting the Labor Department—in 1955. Workers already in these positions (exclusively white) were exempt from these requirements. The company clearly felt that it could achieve compliance by phasing in merit criteria in place of race and that consequent changes would be gradual and modest.[17]

On March 1, 1966, fourteen Duke Power janitors signed a letter of complaint, placing it on the plant manager's desk. This was a worker-initiated action. The instigator, a former tobacco share-cropper named Willie Boyd, had been active in the NAACP for many years and closely followed the passage of the Civil Rights Act. The company responded by informing the men that standards were being raised and that they were welcome to take the test.[18] Four days later, the group forwarded their complaint to the EEOC, which tried to resolve the matter through conciliation. The company did indeed promote the first black worker (a high school graduate) to the Coal Department in August of that year, but it refused all other changes in job practices, essentially snubbing the EEOC. Only then did the workers turn to the NAACP Legal Defense Fund, which assisted them in filing suit on September 9, 1966. Duke's resistance was initially rewarded when the district court judge refused to allow testimony on the company's explicitly racial pre–Title VII system and rejected the case on the basis of the Tower Amendment, allowing the use of professionally developed tests in employment decisions. The court of appeals reversed this decision in part in 1970, rejecting the argument that prior practices were insulated from remedial action but agreeing that there was no showing of discriminatory intent in the diploma and test requirements. Ultimately, however, the U.S. Supreme Court ruled unanimously—five years after the initial complaint—that tests having a "disparate impact" on minorities could be invalid regardless of intent, unless shown to be demonstrably a reasonable measure of job performance. As a result of the decision, the high school graduates in Duke's Labor Department were promoted, and the education and testing requirements were waived for the others. Willie Boyd ultimately became the first black supervisor over white men at the Dan River plant.[19]

More fundamentally, *Griggs* and related rulings gave new credibility to EEOC guidelines and impelled a much more thoroughgoing change than firms had anticipated. One legal scholar writes, "*Griggs* infused Title VII with extraordinary power. . . . Without *Griggs*, the statute might have warranted little more than a text note in law case courts." Citations to the case in federal courts rose steadily through the 1970s, reaching a peak in 1980 before declining in the next decade.[20]

THE REGIONAL CHARACTER OF
LABOR MARKET CHANGE

Numerous studies have identified a positive statistical effect of federal enforcement on black employment during this era, either by comparing covered and uncovered firms or by finding evidence of discontinuity when the law changed.[21] These estimated effects are typically small and account for only a fraction of the overall change in black employment. An additional channel was private litigation, as in *Griggs*. Between 1964 and 1981 more than five thousand Title VII cases were decided in federal courts, many of them private. More than seventeen hundred were class-action suits. Impressive as they are, these numbers do not include cases settled out of court or decided in state courts. Sometimes merely initiating litigation could generate a desired response. Even in textiles, an industry that seemed to have quickly learned the advantages of desegregation, positions were often opened to blacks only after legal action was taken or threatened. Thus at the J. P. Stevens plant in Abbeville, South Carolina, the share of blacks assigned to the position of utility man jumped from 10.3 to 20.5 percent immediately after the filing of a lawsuit on March 16, 1972. At the same juncture, the share of doffers who were black jumped from 3.8 to 28.6 percent, and spinners from 9.6 to 24.5 percent, and blacks were assigned for the first time to the position of warper and creel tender.[22] Further—and this may have been the most important long-term channel—in the wake of *Griggs*, many large corporations hired EEO specialists and implemented equal-employment policies without direct government intervention.[23]

Although precise figures are lacking, the great majority of early Title VII cases were from the South, and the employment and income effects were greatest in that region. The long-standing explicitly racial structures in southern firms provided an inviting target for litigation, in contrast to the northern states, the majority of which had enacted fair-employment legislation in the decades prior to the Civil Rights Act.[24] Desegregating bathroom facilities and cafeterias was especially difficult, resisted by many southern employers until compelled by federal agencies. Even after compliance, firms often had to deal with objections and threats from disgruntled white workers.[25]

From a quantitative standpoint, the reason that Title VII had its greatest impact in the South is that discrimination in that region took the form of vertical segregation, the virtual exclusion of blacks from whole job categories above the lowest. Thus employment policy could have rapid effects on relative black occupational status and earnings simply by removing these barriers. Butler, Heckman, and Payner find that most relative wage growth for blacks between 1960 and 1970 was due to the shift from "laborer" positions into higher-paying "production" operative and craftsman jobs, plus relative wage increases within these categories.[26] This conclusion is consistent with that of sociologists Mark Fossett, Omer Galle, and William Kelly. Using an ordinal measure of occupational segregation with decennial census data, the authors find that changes in occupational inequality during the 1950s favored whites in the South but blacks in the non-South; in contrast, shifts in southern occupational inequality during the 1960s and 1970s favored blacks.[27]

Another feature of labor markets with regional implications is the preference of consumers to deal with someone of their own race, sometimes seen as the most difficult form of discrimination to overcome. Surveys of department stores and drug stores during the late 1960s found that southern establishments were well behind northern in employing black sales personnel, citing fear of lost patronage as the primary reason. As in public accommodations, national chains showed little leadership in the matter and indeed were the slowest to promote in response to Civil Rights pressures. When policies began to change, however, most of the chains adopted full-blown affirmative action plans between 1968 and 1970. Using data from reports to the EEOC, a study by Timothy Hyde compared hiring trends in "consumer-exposed" and "non-exposed" industries between 1966 and 1973. Hyde found that exposed industries were indeed slower to change, but only in northern cities! In the South no difference was observed between the two types of industries. Some of the divergence may be attributable to the larger share of black customers and the more extreme exclusion in the South. But it is also possible that southern white customers found the transition easier than their northern counterparts.[28]

A very southern counterexample is provided by the Shoney's Big Boy restaurants, whose owner, Ray Danner, developed a coded system (blackening the "o" in "Shoney's" on black job applications) in an effort to "lighten up" their stores. Shoney's was one of the last southern chains to accept integration in the 1960s, and Danner firmly believed that too many black employees (the unwritten limit being two black waitresses at any one time) was bad for business. Egregious as it is, however, Shoney's is in some ways the exception that proves the rule. By the time the case came to court in 1989, Danner was considered a dinosaur and his associates were already maneuvering to have him replaced as CEO. The new management extracted a substantial portion of the court-ordered payment from Danner's personal fortune, and the 1992 settlement was followed by a sharp increase in black employment at the firm.[29]

Was It Management or Labor Unions?

In trying to explain continuing resistance to workplace desegregation and black occupational advancement, economists find it far easier to understand the perspective of labor than of management. The overlap between emotional motives for racial separation and economic interests in exclusion is an old story in the history of labor unions.[30] Indeed most southern craft unions, like their counterparts elsewhere in the country, were strictly segregated, severely limiting opportunities for black workers. Even when national industrial unions emerged from the 1930s with a racially inclusive organizing message, they typically found that their southern branches were stoutly opposed to integration. When Philip Murray, president of the Congress of Industrial Organizations (CIO), ordered in 1950 that all forms of segregation be ended in Steelworkers Union meeting halls, he was firmly rebuffed in Birmingham. Into the 1960s, the overwhelming majority of southern steelworkers were in "racially identifiable departments" governed by segregated (and highly unequal) seniority lists.[31] This was the prevailing pattern throughout the South. For a combination of racial and economic motives, white workers objected to the presence of blacks on equal terms; employers acquiesced in this prejudice for fear of alienating or losing experienced incumbent workers, especially if these workers were represented by a union.

The problem with this simple narrative is that in case after case, unionized or not, southern management showed no interest in resisting or undermining segregation. Southern textile firms were unconstrained by unions yet virtually all white prior to the Civil Rights Act. Where labor and management jointly agreed on a plan of racial separation, as in steel, paper, and rubber, it is often difficult to discern which side was the initiator and which the protector of the resulting system. At the Hughes Tool Company in Houston, racial discrimination was so entrenched in union tradition that the NAACP succeeded in having the Independent Metal Workers decertified as a bargaining agent by the National Labor Relations Board in 1964. But only after signing a Plans for Progress memorandum in 1961 as a federal contractor did Hughes Tool "abandon its longtime segregationist allies" by blaming the union for its racial practices. And even then the company proved to be in no hurry to desegregate restrooms, dining areas, drinking fountains, or jobs.[32]

In Alabama, with one of the longest industrial histories in the region, a survey of firms in all major branches of the economy found not a single case before the 1960s where management

> drawing on cost calculations, business norms, or some abstract concept of justice, chose to desegregate the work place or break down job discrimination. . . . Even in retrospect, off the record, within the confines of their own offices, businessmen did not recall that the racial order created any "impediments" or "difficulties" for their enterprises.[33]

The conclusion is inescapable that, with rare exceptions, southern management shared the perception that blacks were inferior candidates for advanced positions and found it all but impossible to contemplate a genuinely desegregated future for their firms.

Thus southern management did not jump at the opportunity to use Title VII as a means of escape from the constraints of white prejudice or unions. Instead they found ways to rationalize their racially exclusive choices. A producer of fabricated metals told an interviewer in 1966, "Negroes don't want to be promoted."[34] Citing blacks' poor educational background, a paper executive asserted in 1971 that they were "not good prospects for skilled jobs."[35] Faced with pressure from federal agencies to abolish explicitly racial criteria for hiring and promotion, the employer's first reaction in numerous cases was to institute formal test-taking as an alternative.[36] Exactly what management's thinking was is often difficult to determine. No doubt they were genuinely concerned about the dilution of quality in skilled positions. But the fact remains that the tests were imposed only after Title VII was enacted, and there was little doubt about their implications for the race issue. In the circumstances, the Supreme Court had reason to view testing requirements as a vehicle for preserving de facto segregation and therefore to insist that tests for promotion had to be specifically related to the jobs in question.

The overall record of organized labor in the Civil Rights revolution is decidedly mixed. As segregated organizations whose members had a vested interest in privileged positions in the labor market, unions were clearly part of the problem. Despite the liberal position of the national United Auto Workers on the race issue, a survey in the mid-1950s showed that over 80 percent of the members of the UAW local in Memphis (representing workers at an International Harvester plant) belonged to white Citizens' Councils; in Alabama, 83 percent of white union members voted for George Wallace in 1968.[37] Yet, as labor historian Alan Draper points out, the labor movement did at least offer an alternative vision of shared interests that was helpful in facilitating change in the 1960s, albeit under heavy federal pressure. The national labor federations and many southern state labor councils maintained steady pressure toward racial liberalization on their reluctant white southern members. The Virginia AFL-CIO supported black voter registration as early as 1959, while the 1960 North Carolina AFL-CIO convention passed a resolution applauding the student sit-ins at lunch counters. In Mississippi, the AFL-CIO Industrial Unions Department contributed $5,000 to the Congress of Racial Equality (CORE) to help defray expenses incurred by the Freedom Rides. Claude Ramsay, president of the Mississippi AFL-CIO for twenty-six years, received Civil Rights awards from the NAACP and the A. Philip Randolph Institute in the 1980s.[38]

To be sure, many of these gestures of support for Civil Rights were vehemently protested by white union members. But in the post–Civil Rights era, organized labor has been a leading force in efforts to build biracial political coalitions in the South. For labor as well as management, desegregation was a learning experience.

COMPLEMENTARITY BETWEEN EDUCATION AND OCCUPATIONAL ADVANCE

The entry of southern black workers into previously closed blue-collar occupations constituted a significant step forward for a generation whose educational opportunities were severely limited. But it would have been a one-time breakthrough rather than an enduring revolution if these gains could not be transmitted to the next generation through access to education that opened the door to skilled and white-collar jobs. For those interested in documenting the effects of the Civil Rights Act, a standard approach in economics is to control for schooling to demonstrate that gains in black employment were not merely responses to improved education. Although the Act passes such a test, to leave the matter at that misses the larger process by which new employment opportunities and schooling were historical complements.

The trend toward better-quality black schools predates the Civil Rights Act and even the *Brown* decision. From the disastrous setback associated with disfranchisement at the turn of the twentieth century, there was a long, slow improvement in the relative quality of black schools, propelled by agitation, litigation, and private philanthropy—in short, by the forerunners of the modern Civil Rights Movement.[39] For the era in which we can clearly assign resources to students by race—the era of segregated schools—using such indicators as pupil-teacher ratios, term length, and teacher salaries, black schools had progressed to near equality with white schools by the late 1950s.[40] The black high school graduation rate in the South increased from 18 percent (of twenty- to twenty-four-year-olds) in 1950 to 35 percent in 1960. Some economists attribute virtually the entire gain in relative black incomes to this long-term increase in black human capital.[41]

This reductionist economic perspective neglects the feedback from the labor market to the value of black schooling. Prior to mechanization, planters had a clear economic incentive to discourage black education. Why educate the black, they asked, "when as soon as one of the younger class gets so he can read and write and cipher, he wants to go to town. It is rare to find one who can read and write and cipher in the field at work."[42] Ostensibly sympathetic whites, even northerners, believed "that it is a crime for any teacher, white or black, to educate the negro for positions that are not open to him," and that the purpose of black schools should be to "educate [blacks] for their environment and not out of it."[43] Thus black schools typically did not offer training in such subjects as stenography, accounting, bookkeeping, printing, or typing. The Rosenwald Fund's curriculum expert acknowledged, "If commercial courses were offered in the negro school there would no doubt be tremendous pressure to get into them and the only result would be keen disappointment for almost everyone." The black high school in the textile center of Greenville, South Carolina, excluded textiles from its curriculum.[44]

In the face of such disincentives, it is remarkable how much progress was achieved in black schools through sheer effort and willpower on the part of the NAACP. But persistent black students who overcame discouragements to complete high school sometimes found that they had to conceal this fact to gain employment. James Field was hired as a laborer at Union Bag in Savannah in the 1940s and was told "they didn't want no smart black man." Field recounts, "When I filled my application out . . . I put ninth grade instead of twelfth, because I figured they didn't want . . . no smart black man, in order to get hired. I was hired."[45]

Despite the apparent improvement in quality, surveys by the Southern Regional Council (SRC) found that glaring gaps in curricula between black and white schools were still present in 1961 and 1962. In Houston, the all-white vocational school offered training in air-conditioning and refrigerator mechanics, drafting, machine shop, photography, printing, radio, television, and welding—none of which were taught at any of the five Negro high schools. By that time training in auto mechanics was one of the more popular options in vocational education, but with a few exceptions, these courses were offered only at white high schools. Negroes were excluded from modeling schools and hospitals with nurses' training. Similar differences were found in Chattanooga and Atlanta. In every case, high school officials defended their programs by saying that their curriculum was a rational response to job availability.[46] After telling of a Negro supermarket checker with a college degree, the SRC report concluded, "Education may get you nowhere."[47]

Economists David Card and Alan Krueger show that the rate of return to black education increased sharply for the cohort born between 1940 and 1949 (i.e., those coming into the labor force in the late 1960s and 1970s). Because the return for southern-born blacks increased relative to whites and northern-born blacks, Card and Krueger argue that the rise was driven by prior improvements in the quality of black schools, and not simply by "economywide" reduction in discrimination. But if structural change in the labor market was highly region-specific, as argued here, then a simple identification of labor market returns and school quality does not hold. Indeed the highest rate of return estimated by Card and Krueger is for northern-born blacks residing in the South in 1980, strongly suggesting that by that date, regional changes in the labor market were more important than prior gains in southern black schools.[48] Expanding black job opportunities, in turn, fostered rising (derived) demand for education.

Thus we find that the labor market breakthroughs of the mid-1960s coincided with an accelerated increase in the black high school graduation rate in the South, from 35 percent in 1960 to 57 percent in 1970—a period prior to any major progress in school desegregation—and a further increase to 71 percent by 1977. Black enrollment in higher education grew even more dramatically, from 84,000 in 1960 (overwhelmingly in historically black institutions) to 426,000 in 1976 (the majority at predominantly white institutions).[49] Complementarity between higher education and labor market desegregation is suggested by the simultaneous upsurge in recruitment visits by corporate representatives to historically black colleges, from an average of just four per school in 1960 to nearly three hundred per school in 1970.[50]

Occupational Status: Moving Up in the Labor Market

This complementary progress in education and desegregation was reflected in advances in black occupational status throughout the urban South. Tables 4.1–4.3 display census figures for middle-class occupational categories in three economically diverse southern cities: Atlanta, Birmingham, and Charlotte. The patterns are similar in all three: little to no progress in the 1950s in either shares or numbers; positive trends beginning in the 1960s, both in absolute numbers and in the black share of the total, especially in clerical and skilled labor positions; strong positive growth by the end of the century, especially in Charlotte and Birmingham. The 1950 starting point for the "professional" column may be misleading, in that this category includes both ministers and schoolteachers. But in every other case, the advances reflect the desegregation of occupations and accelerated progress in black education, both consequences of the Civil Rights revolution of the 1960s. Similar patterns are observed in cities throughout the South.

Comparisons with northern cities are difficult because the published census did not report occupational totals for nonwhites outside the South in 1950. But Table 4.4 draws on the census samples of the Integrated Public Use Microdata Series to compare the black occupational distribution for the entire South with that of the rest of the country. Aggregation on this scale is risky, but the table clearly shows that progress in the South began only after 1960, and the subsequent increases in employment shares (for all categories except professional) were far greater in the South than elsewhere. Table 4.5 repeats the exercise, dividing the employment shares by the black share of the

Table 4.1 Black Occupational Distribution, Atlanta 1950–2000

	Professional		Managerial		Clerical		Sales		Skilled Labor	
	Number	% of Total	Number	% of Total	Number	% of Total	Number	% of Total	Number	% of Total
1950	1,995	15.8	934	7.9	1,971	7.0	704	5.8	3,056	19.4
1960	3,275	16.6	696	4.3	3,938	11.0	761	5.0	3,315	18.8
1970	8,610	32.0	2,408	15.6	16,596	36.1	2,387	17.0	7,808	38.5
1980	9,285	37.6	5,862	33.4	19,290	60.6	6,839	41.2	7,992	60.5
1990	8,463	30.1	7,396	33.1	19,280	67.9	8,511	42.1	8,185	68.3
2000	10,217	25.7	7,527	23.9	17,360	68.4	8,116	37.8	6,544	59.4

Sources: U.S. Census of Population 1950, vol. 2: *Characteristics of the Population*, Tables 35 and 36; Census of Population 1960, vol. 1: *Characteristics of the Population*, Tables 74 and 78; Census of Population 1970, volume 1: *Characteristics of the Population*, Tables 86 and 93; Census of Population 1980, *General Social and Economic Characteristics*, Tables 121 and 135; Census of Population 1990, *Social and Economic Characteristics*, Tables 174 and 185; American Fact Finder, DP3, *Profile of Selected Economic Characteristics*; Census 2000 Summary File 3 (SF3).

Table 4.2 Black Occupational Distribution, Charlotte 1950–2000

| | Professional | | Managerial | | Clerical | | Sales | | Skilled Labor | |
	Number	% of Total	Number	% of Total	Number	% of Total	Number	% of Total	Number	% of Total
1950	755	13.2	288	4.3	415	4.2	172	2.7	1,291	18.8
1960	1,115	12.9	343	4.0	700	5.2	212	2.5	1,268	14.9
1970	1,908	13.2	555	5.3	3,299	14.2	535	4.9	3,299	22.1
1980	3,664	17.6	1,788	8.8	6,847	21.2	1,990	9.5	3,878	25.2
1990	5,081	17.1	3,855	11.9	11,142	29.0	4,888	15.0	5,293	27.8
2000	10,089	19.0	8,314	16.2	17,540	39.6	7,805	20.0	5,111	22.0

Source: U.S. Census of Population 1950, vol. 2: *Characteristics of the Population,* Tables 35 and 36; Census of Population 1960, vol. 1: *Characteristics of the Population,* Tables 74 and 78; Census of Population 1970, volume 1: *Characteristics of the Population,* Tables 86 and 93; Census of Population 1980, *General Social and Economic Characteristics,* Tables 121 and 135; Census of Population 1990, *Social and Economic Characteristics,* Tables 174 and 185; American Fact Finder, DP3, *Profile of Selected Economic Characteristics;* Census 2000 Summary File 3 (SF3).

Table 4.3 Black Occupational Distribution, Birmingham 1950–2000

	Professional		Managerial		Clerical		Sales		Skilled Labor	
	Number	% of Total	Number	% of Total	Number	% of Total	Number	% of Total	Number	% of Total
1950	1,961	17.7	890	8.1	907	5.1	700	6.6	2,914	15.7
1960	2,431	19.2	668	7.0	1,462	7.2	514	5.1	2,533	15.6
1970	2,968	21.0	729	9.2	3,576	16.1	826	9.2	3,497	23.3
1980	4,729	35.3	2,265	24.2	8,362	37.7	2,930	26.7	5,002	41.8
1990	5,939	39.8	3,463	34.0	10,809	56.2	5,620	44.8	4,866	51.5
2000	9,643	52.5	4,635	50.3	13,532	71.6	6,493	62.0	4,121	56.6

Source: U.S. Census of Population 1950, vol. 2: *Characteristics of the Population*, Tables 35 and 36; Census of Population 1960, vol. 1: *Characteristics of the Population*, Tables 74 and 78; Census of Population 1970, volume 1: *Characteristics of the Population*, Tables 86 and 93; Census of Population 1980, *General Social and Economic Characteristics*, Tables 121 and 135; Census of Population 1990, *Social and Economic Characteristics*, Tables 174 and 185; American Fact Finder, DP3, *Profile of Selected Economic Characteristics*; Census 2000 Summary File 3 (SF3).

Table 4.4 Black Occupational Distributions, North vs. South 1950–2000 (% of regional occupation total)

	Professional		Managerial		Clerical		Sales		Skilled Labor	
	North & West	South	North & West	South	North & West	South	North & West	South	North & West	South
1950	1.9	11.1	1.2	4.1	2.3	4.4	1.2	3.1	2.3	8.5
1960	2.3	10.1	1.2	2.7	3.0	4.0	1.5	2.6	3.0	8.1
1970	3.7	10.0	2.6	4.8	6.2	8.5	3.1	5.1	4.3	11.1
1980	5.2	11.6	4.1	7.0	8.1	12.6	4.1	7.9	4.8	11.7
1990	5.7	10.9	5.0	8.9	9.6	15.0	5.7	11.1	5.3	12.4
2000	5.8	12.6	5.3	10.5	9.5	18.2	6.5	14.4	5.5	13.4

Source: Integrated Public Use Micro Series samples.

Table 4.5 Relative Black Occupational Distributions, North vs. South 1950–2000 (% of regional occupation / % black in population)

	Professional		Managerial		Clerical		Sales		Skilled Labor	
	North & West	South	North & West	South	North & West	South	North & West	South	North & West	South
1950	.41	.51	.26	.19	.50	.20	.26	.14	.50	.39
1960	.38	.49	.20	.13	.49	.19	.25	.13	.49	.39
1970	.49	.53	.34	.25	.82	.45	.41	.27	.57	.58
1980	.63	.62	.49	.38	.98	.68	.49	.42	.58	.63
1990	.66	.59	.57	.48	1.10	.81	.66	.60	.61	.67
2000	.67	.67	.62	.56	1.10	.96	.76	.76	.64	.71

Source: Integrated Public Use Micro Series samples.

regional population. This approach shows that in 1950, blacks were severely underrepresented in all of these occupations throughout the country, but even more so in the South than elsewhere. The regional underrepresentation differential in skilled labor had disappeared by 1970, while in managerial, clerical, and sales jobs the gap closed only over several decades. The table confirms that the potential for black progress was greater in the South in part because the pre–Civil Rights black occupational starting point was so low. But contrary to what a pure convergence model would predict, regional progress, once under way, seemed to gain momentum over time.

COMPULSION VERSUS VOLUNTARISM

In seeking to understand the persistence of change, it helps to go back to an early 1960s debate about the best way to foster black employment gains. When President Kennedy issued his executive order in 1961, requiring firms with federal contracts to take "affirmative action" to end discrimination, he also created the President's Commission on Equal Employment Opportunity, headed by Vice President Lyndon Johnson, to oversee compliance. Great hopes were placed on a subcommittee called Plans for Progress, created to promote voluntary fair-employment practices among federal contractors. The initiator and first head of Plans for Progress was Atlanta lawyer and businessmen Robert Troutman, who also happened to have been a classmate of Robert Kennedy's at Harvard. Within a year, eighty-five firms had signed on to the program, often with great fanfare and a White House ceremony. Troutman argued forcefully for the virtues of this approach in promoting lasting change: "Compulsion is not the thing. I'm a lawyer. I can show you how to get around the executive order. It's got to be voluntary."[51]

Troutman and Plans for Progress came under intense criticism. Herbert Hill Jr., labor secretary of the NAACP, charged that the plans resulted in "more publicity than progress" and that firms had signed on "as a way of securing immunity from real compliance with the anti-discrimination provision of their government contract." As moderate a figure as Whitney M. Young Jr., the new executive director of the National Urban League, commented, "We've tried the voluntary approach for years, and nothing's happened." A report by former Urban League president Theodore W. Kheel, prepared at the request of Vice President Johnson, urged the administration to give priority to compulsory approaches by using the leverage inherent in its power to cancel contracts with private companies. "Purely voluntary approaches," he wrote, "are not likely to produce lasting results." Under heavy pressure, Troutman resigned in August 1962.[52]

Perhaps most devastating of all, a survey completed in January 1963 by the Southern Regional Council of twenty-four Atlanta employers, all of whom had approved Plans for Progress more than a year before, found that except for a handful, the plans were "largely meaningless." Many regional managers were unaware of the plan or believed that it did not apply to "regional divisions like us." Others knew of the plan and the executive order but "said their work was extremely technical, implying it was too technical for a Negro. Few appeared to have considered the hiring of Negroes as secretaries and clerical workers." The SRC interviewers reported that many companies reflected the statement of one regional manager of a national firm: "We signed it because practically all of our major manufacturing is in the northern part of the country. When [we] signed this Plans for Progress thing we signed it as a corporation as a whole. It doesn't mean that down here in Atlanta we have to hire them. This is a sales office." Although some firms later disputed the SRC characterization, the undeniable quantitative truth was conveyed in a March 2, 1963, memo from Burke Marshall to Robert Kennedy: despite reports of progress, "the numerical gains are slight."[53]

The verdict of history has clearly come down on the compulsory side. As recounted earlier, throughout the South it is difficult to find moves toward serious workplace desegregation prior to passage of the Civil Rights Act; even then, most employers resisted, delayed, and tried to minimize change, abandoning this position only as a kind of capitulation to the looming enforcement of Title VII by the courts. Despite the decisiveness of this historical assessment, one may still ask whether the voluntarist side may have had something to contribute after all. If employers had persisted in doing only the bare minimum required by law, would the progress of desegregation have been anywhere near as far-reaching and persistent as in fact it was?

Virtually all of the early surveys of firms' experience with desegregation reported that the key to success was concerted determination by management to accomplish its goal, combined with explicit, no-nonsense communication of the goal to all employees. When management was half-hearted and reluctant, white workers often compounded the problem by complaining loudly and making life miserable for new black hires. But where company leadership made it clear that desegregation would happen and had their support, the widely predicted departures of white workers almost never occurred.[54] Sometimes this new initiative entailed real soul-searching by executives, especially at companies that had regarded themselves as progressive on racial matters. At a 1965 conference, the manager of employee relations at International Harvester asserted that his firm was an early leader in race relations but acknowledged that segregated facilities had not been removed "until a few years ago." He went on to say, "There are a few operations where, while Negroes are employed in substantial numbers, yet, somewhat inexplicably, they are not employed in certain work areas or departments. More importantly, their absence cannot be easily explained away solely by such as the obvious lack of qualified candidates." He attributed these patterns to the background of the decision makers and the absence of concerted momentum from the top.[55]

No doubt most personnel managers were not this introspective. But sociologist Frank Dobbin argues that once the determination of the federal government and the courts became clear, laggard employers began a desperate search for practical desegregation policies that they could adopt and for metrics to use in their legal defense. The most readily available models were none other than the Plans for Progress, beginning with the celebrated plan adopted in 1961 by Lockheed Aircraft for its plant in Marietta, Georgia. Drawing upon an infrastructure they already possessed, large national companies turned to their human relations personnel to formalize hiring criteria and promotion procedures, with the explicit objective of taking these decisions out of the hands of foremen and lower-level managers who were likely to discriminate. When the courts adopted similar metrics for compliance in the wake of the *Griggs* decision, in effect the Plans for Progress were enacted into law in the 1970s.[56]

From this perspective, the Civil Rights Act and Title VII enforcement initiated a process of institutional adaptation within American corporations, which subsequently developed a life of its own. Its momentum and survival power were enhanced when Title VII cases were extended to women in the 1970s. By the end of that decade, the majority of U.S. firms had adopted explicit antidiscrimination policies, personnel offices, job postings, and centralized hiring, promotion, and discharge practices. "By the early 1980s," according to Dobbin, "leading firms had troops on hand who were fighting for equal opportunity programs. They had internalized the civil rights movement."[57]

So entrenched had these programs become, that when the Reagan administration proposed to abolish the Office of Federal Contract Compliance Programs and dismantle affirmative action in the 1980s, business groups successfully opposed these measures, reversing their position of two decades earlier. Surveys of major employers found that the great majority planned to maintain or extend their affirmative action programs, despite cutbacks in government enforcement.[58]

Mainly in the South?

Accounts of the bureaucratization of equal employment pay almost no attention to its regional dimension. This is understand-

able, since the firms involved were national and standardizing
their personnel practices on a national basis was part of the process. Yet these programs had their greatest impact in the South.
Until the late 1960s, both government and management believed
that employment discrimination was primarily a regional problem. One northern personnel manager later remarked, "We were
the good guys. We never dreamed they meant us. The major thrust
of the law seemed to be aimed at 'the other fellow'—at smaller, or
less enlightened, or regional employers and at certain obviously
discriminatory unions—but only occasionally or very indirectly
at important national employers like us." Of course this compla-
cency proved to be mistaken. But in their formative phase, Plans
for Progress and their affirmative action descendants did indeed
have a regional focus.

The prototype Plan for Progress, at Lockheed-Marietta, was
very much a southern phenomenon. The director of personnel
and architect of the plan, Hugh Gordon, was a southerner, born
in Norfolk, Virginia, and educated at Virginia Tech and Georgia
Tech. When the California-based company first came to Georgia
in 1951, its adoption of a segregated job system may have been
somewhat reluctant, but it was nonetheless relatively firm
throughout the 1950s. But Lockheed came in for heavy criticism
when it was awarded a contract worth more than $1 billion to
build the C-141 Starlifter in March 1961, just one week after
President Kennedy's executive order banning discrimination in
contractor firms. In response, Lockheed drew up and adopted the
first Plan for Progress, announced at a White House ceremony on
May 25. The plan committed Lockheed not just to nondiscrimination but also to "aggressively seek out more qualified minority
group candidates in order to increase the number of employees
in many job categories." Unlike many early signers, Lockheed
was serious. Gordon well understood the need for outreach in
order to achieve these goals, and so he launched an unprecedented series of recruiting visits to black high schools and colleges. The ready availability of these institutions and networks

was distinctive to the South. Realizing that many potential black applicants were poorly prepared—more so in the South than elsewhere—Gordon took pains to assure that black hires were included in training classes offered to employees on company time. Later he extended the outreach beyond Lockheed, organizing the Merit Employment Association for the Atlanta region and enlisting other leading firms in the effort. According to Dobbin, Lockheed's plan embodied all of the core principles that became standard in affirmative action plans during the 1970s.[59]

Many observers believe that progress toward racial equality in the labor market largely came to an end during the 1980s, when "the contract compliance program virtually ceased to exist in all but name" under the Reagan administration.[60] Resources available to the EEOC were drastically cut, and the Supreme Court moved to restrict race-conscious affirmative action measures. Dobbin writes, "In the 1980s, change slowed to a standstill. Blacks no longer gained more ground in industries subject to affirmative action. Their gains slowed in other industries as well."[61] To this, one may only respond: Perhaps so, but not in the South. In most southern cities, both numbers and black occupational shares grew impressively throughout the 1980s and 1990s. Figure 4.4 tracks black occupational shares by region in firms reporting to the EEOC. The most striking feature of the graph is the steady growth of black white-collar employment in the South.[62]

There are many possible reasons for the divergence in regional trends. No doubt it was easier to maintain black occupational gains where economic growth was still strong, in contrast to the industrial decline that enveloped the Midwest during the 1980s.[63] Perhaps too there was an element of "regional convergence" at work, in that black representation in key occupations in the South was still well below the rest of the nation. But in light of the foregoing discussion, a likely contributor to ongoing southern progress was the fact that in that region, black shares in these occupations were substantially higher than elsewhere.[64]

The greater black presence in management helped to maintain awareness of the race issue, while more black clerical and sales employees facilitated recruitment through word-of-mouth channels. Studies consistently find that the variable most strongly related to new black employment is the percentage of job applicants who are African American. Additional contributors are the black share of the city population and customer base, the hiring officer's race, and the presence of blacks already employed. All of these factors favored the South throughout the historical period under study. Indeed one study of personnel data from a large retail firm finds not only that black managers were more likely to hire blacks than nonblack managers, but that these differential effects were most pronounced in the South.[65]

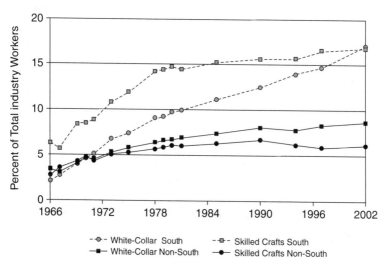

Figure 4.4 Black occupational shares by region: large employers, 1966–2002.

Source: Equal Employment Opportunity Commission. *Job Patterns for Minorities and Women in Private Industry*, various years.

REVERSING REGIONAL MIGRATION

Perhaps the most decisive evidence of desegregation's profound effect on regional labor markets is the reversal of migration patterns that had prevailed for more than half a century. The timing was directly related to new job opportunities. Blacks began to move into textile areas almost immediately after passage of the Civil Rights Act. On the basis of her interviews with textile workers, Mary Fredrickson attributed the shift to "the fact that black children no longer have to leave the region to become successful, that a decent education in an integrated public school is attainable for both black and white, and that black workers are not denied jobs on the basis of their race." She quotes a black employment manager for a major textile firm: "There is a marked difference now, and people who couldn't get away from here fast enough are coming back comfortably."[66] During 1965–1970 these inflows were outweighed by ongoing out-migration from other parts of the South. But since 1970 net black migration has been persistently southward, increasingly so over time. Between 1985 and 2010 more than 1.5 million African Americans moved south from all other regions of the country (Table 4.6).

This "reverse" black migration is remarkable not just for its direction but also for the reversal in educational selectivity. During most of the pre–Civil Rights era, additional years of schooling greatly increased the probability of black out-migration from the South.[67] Some of this differential reflected the effect of literacy on awareness of and ability to take advantage of job opportunities in distant cities. But especially in later years, out-migration primarily reflected the bleakness of job prospects for educated black southerners in their native region. Thus the SRC employment report for Chattanooga found an out-migration rate of 65 percent among local black high school graduates.[68]

A paper by Jacob Vigdor demonstrates that while black income gains in the 1960s and 1970s reflected both labor market

Table 4.6 Net Migration into South, 1870–1880 to 2005–2010 (in thousands)

Decade	White	Black
1870–1880	91	68
1880–1890	–271	88
1890–1900	–30	–185
1900–1910	–69	–194
1910–1920	–663	–555
1920–1930	–704	–903
1930–1940	–558	–408
1940–1950	–866	–1,581
1950–1960	–234	–1,202
1960–1970	1,807	–1,380
1970–1980	3,556	206
1980–1985	1,808	83
1985–1990	971	325
1990–1995	1,344*	358
1995–2000	1,127*	347
2000–2005	1,027*	318
2005–2010	731*	267

*Non-Hispanic White

Sources: Eldridge and Thomas, *Population Redistribution and Economic Growth* 3, p. 90; U.S. Bureau of the Census, *Historical Statistics of the United States to 1970,* pp. 94–95; Kasarda, Irwin, and Hughes, "The South Is Still Rising," p. 35; Isaac Robinson, "Blacks Move Back to the South," p. 43; U.S. Bureau of the Census, *Current Population Reports: Geographic Mobility: Special Studies; Domestic Migration across Regions, Divisions, and States, 1980 to 1985; Geographical Mobility: Special Studies, 1990 to 1995; Migration by Race and Hispanic Origin, 1995 to 2000; Current Population Survey: Annual Social and Economic* Supplement, 2005–2010. Figures for 1985–1990 are the sums of the annual figures for 1985–1986 and 1986–1987, plus those for 1987–1990.

breakthroughs and educational advances, the southern rise of black relative income after 1980 was largely attributable to the selective in-migration of highly educated individuals.[69] By the 1990s the typical black migrant was a young, educated person pursuing opportunity in the booming metropolitan areas of the New South. Table 4.7 lists the metropolitan areas with the largest

Table 4.7   Metropolitan Areas with Largest Black Gains
1985–1990 and 1995–2000

1985–1990		1995–2000	
Atlanta	74,705	Atlanta	114,478
Washington-Baltimore	29,904	Dallas	39,360
Norfolk–Virginia Beach	27,645	Charlotte	23,313
Raleigh-Durham	17,611	Orlando	20,222
Dallas	16,097	Las Vegas	18,912
Orlando	13,368	Norfolk–Virginia Beach	16,660
Richmond	12,508	Raleigh-Durham	16,144
San Diego	12,482	Washington-Baltimore	16,139
Minneapolis–St. Paul	11,765	Memphis	12,507
Sacramento	10,848	Columbia	10,899

Source: Frey. "The New Great Migration," p. 94.

black gains for 1985–1990 and 1995–2000. Atlanta tops both lists. For 1995–2000 nine of the top ten areas are southern. Demographic studies show that although the South attracted a larger absolute number of white migrants, blacks were substantially more likely than whites to choose the South as their destination. The highest black migration rate into the region was among the college-educated.[70]

Decisions to migrate and the choice of destination have many bases besides economics. In interviews with reporters, many black migrants emphasized their desire to return to family and cultural roots in the South. Others mentioned climate and cities friendly to families, especially black families. But in nearly all cases, at least for working-age migrants, a precondition for enjoying any of these amenities was a well-paying job. Elizabeth Little, a middle-aged woman from Peoria, Illinois, was initially apprehensive about moving to Memphis, where her husband enjoyed playing winter golf, to take a job as an administrative assistant in an architectural firm. She told a reporter in 1998, "Now I am truly glad I came. The southern hospitality is incredible, and I really feel as an African-American that I have a chance to make a better life here. In fact, I can see owning my own business someday."[71] Jacqueline Dowdell explained that her choice to move from New York to North Carolina in 2005 to work as a communications coordinator for a health care company was definitely a financial decision, while adding that "the move also gave her time to research her family's roots in Virginia."[72] Sometimes new employment opportunities enabled native southerners to stay in the region rather than migrate out like previous generations. A story about the spread of affluent suburbanites into rural areas such as Newton County, Georgia, reported, "Many well-educated natives of the county who once assumed they would have to leave to find a good job, like Michael Davis, the plant scheduler at SKC, now say they are thrilled to be able to work where they grew up."[73] Typically reverse migrants to the South were not choosing cultural identity over real income; they were attracted by an appealing combination of both, and the emerging middle-class black communities generated additional economic opportunities in turn. When *Black Enterprise* magazine named its best cities for African Americans in 2004, the top eight spots were all in the South.[74]

Confirming the complementarities among income, employment, and community, Figure 4.5 shows that median black male income grew faster in the South than in any other region during the 1990s. By the end of the decade, the southern median virtually equaled that in the Northeast and Midwest, eliminating a regional income gap as old as the nation itself.[75] Racial equality was still a remote prospect, but black incomes relative to whites in 2000 were as high or higher in the South than anywhere else in the country.

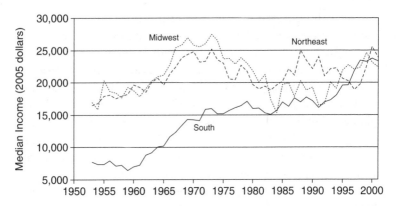

Figure 4.5 Median black male income by region, 1953–2000.
   Source: U.S. Bureau of the Census. Current Population Survey. Annual Social and Economic Supplements. Historical Income Data. Table P-5.

WERE WHITE SOUTHERNERS HURT BY BLACK GAINS?

Having shown the reality and persistence of black economic progress in the South dating from the Civil Rights revolution of the 1960s, we may now go on to ask whether these gains were won at the expense of southern whites or instead were part of an economic restructuring in which all, or at least most, parties shared the gains. In posing this question, it must be acknowledged at the outset that it is not possible to compare the true historical record with all possible counterfactual alternatives. One can easily construct hypothetical scenarios in which maintaining white exclusivity over major occupations and job progressions might have raised the incomes of white incumbents compared to what they actually earned. For those who had already invested the fixed costs of committing to a career path, merging racial seniority ladders may have meant that some white promotions were delayed compared to when they would otherwise have occurred. It would be pointless to deny that some southern whites experienced some (presumably short-term) setbacks in this opportunity-cost sense of the concept.

But if we ask the question in more straightforward historical rather than hypothetical terms, the broad answer is clear: southern black employment gains did not come at the expense of white employment, and southern black income gains did not cause southern white incomes to fall. Figure 4.6 displays median male income in the South by race from 1953 to 2000. The black relative gains are dramatic—from less than 40 percent of the white median in 1960 to nearly 60 percent between 1960 and 1972, and from 60 to 75 percent between 1990 and 2000—but at no time did white incomes fall as black incomes rose. When southern incomes stagnated between 1973 and 1990, reflecting broad trends in national labor market conditions, they did so for both races. When the white median ticked downward because of cyclical fluctuations in the economy, the same was true for the black median. What we see, in other words, is not a redistribution of income in the name of historical justice but an integration of black workers into the regional economy. When we add the consideration (as argued elsewhere) that the Civil Rights revolution invigorated the regional economy by opening it to

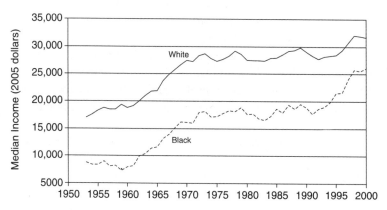

Figure 4.6 Median male income in the South by race, 1953–2000.
Source: U.S. Bureau of the Census. Current Population Survey. Annual Social and Economic Supplements. Historical Income Data. Table P-5.

inflows of capital, creativity, and new enterprises from around the world, it becomes clear that most white southerners were long-term beneficiaries of this historical change.

A related question, distinctive to economics, is whether desegregation was economically efficient. Jim Crow segregation was certainly discriminatory, and in the economic tradition descended from Gary Becker, discrimination based on employer or worker prejudice is inherently inefficient. So it might seem, prima facie, that government actions to eliminate or reduce discrimination would constitute a gain in efficiency. But many economists have great difficulty accepting this conclusion, even in the extreme case of the Jim Crow South, because they start from a presumption that profit-seeking employers take full advantage of all available knowledge concerning the productive attributes and potential of their employees. In the context of "the market's endless search for efficiency" (in the words of Senator Orrin Hatch), government actions to compel and constrain these employers can only reduce efficiency, unless the employers have been somehow constrained by legal barriers or discriminatory unions. No doubt it is this strong presumption that inclines so many economists to locate the problem not in the labor market but in "pre-market" discrimination, primarily in public schools shaped by political forces. The strongest counterargument from an economic standpoint has been that if the discriminatory setting constitutes a disequilibrium phenomenon, then government policies may improve efficiency by eliminating discriminatory firms more rapidly than would have happened through competitive market processes.[76]

But if instead aggressive desegregation of the southern workplace gave rise to a collective learning process on the part of employers, constituting a genuine improvement in their knowledge of the productive potential of black employees (as well as of the adaptive capacities of their white workers), then the premise of most efficiency discussions is mistaken. No such adaptation was under way prior to the Civil Rights Act, and for most southern employers, it did not begin until aggressive enforcement gave them little choice but to make the best of a fundamentally new situation. Changes in the demand for black labor in turn encouraged and facilitated investments in African American human capital, pushing the system out of its long-standing low-level equilibrium. This is not to deny that the mechanisms for accomplishing these goals were often cumbersome and costly, and it is not to claim that the process was in any way optimal. But the change itself was an unambiguous improvement in economic efficiency as well as equity. The evidence in this chapter argues that this is indeed the correct reading of the historical record in the South.

CHAPTER 5

THE ECONOMICS OF SOUTHERN

SCHOOL DESEGREGATION

Of all the settings for the epic Civil Rights revolution, the most difficult to analyze economically is the struggle for racially integrated schools. *Brown v. Board of Education* in 1954 was a landmark decision, overturning the "separate but equal" nostrum and thus preparing the way for toppling most other forms of state-mandated segregation across the next decade. But progress in school desegregation itself was negligible during that same time span. Only with new enforcement tools provided by Title VI of the Civil Rights Act, combined with increasingly stringent federal court decisions, were school districts compelled to accept desegregation in a quantitatively meaningful form. Between 1968 and 1980 the public schools of the South moved from the least to the most racially integrated in the nation. Long-term studies show that this breakthrough led to substantial gains in educational attainment and earnings for black southerners, with no measurable adverse educational effects on white students.

Unlike public accommodations and the labor market, however, desegregation of schools did not gather momentum and become embedded in the expectations and behavior of white southerners over time. In many urban areas, whites responded by leaving desegregated school systems in large numbers, either for all-white private schools or for suburban districts with few black students. When the Supreme Court sharply restricted cross-district busing in 1974 (in *Milliken v. Bradley,* a case arising in metropolitan Detroit), the result was to replace de jure with a high degree of de facto segregation between predominantly black urban and predominantly white suburban districts, on the northern model. As courts withdrew from enforcing integration, many southern school districts drifted toward resegregation after 1990.

Despite all of these setbacks and disappointments, the larger historical accomplishment stands out: Desegregation of southern public schools facilitated a major upward step in the educational attainment and economic status of African Americans. Here again, the regional dimension of the process is often missed. By the first decade of the twenty-first century, relative black test scores were higher in the South than in most other regions of the country, reversing the pattern of more than a century. These gains did not come at the expense of southern whites, whose scores also improved. Whereas interracial exposure and black educational attainment proved vulnerable to the end of court-ordered desegregation elsewhere, these adverse effects were less common in the South. Debarred from using race as a basis for school placement, many southern districts have tried integration by socioeconomic level as an alternative, often with favorable results. These developments have emerged from the same educated middle-class communities that have attracted so many black migrants to the metropolitan areas of the South, a legacy of the Civil Rights revolution.

THE TRAJECTORY OF SCHOOL DESEGREGATION

By the 1950s, legally segregated schools were distinctive to the South (see Map 5.1). But efforts to raise the quality of southern black education began much earlier. A gradual recovery from the low point after disfranchisement was initiated by private philanthropies. By far the largest of these was the Rosenwald Fund,

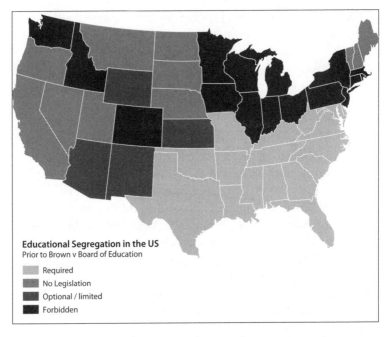

Map 5.1 Educational segregation in the United States prior to *Brown v. Board of Education.*

Source: Wikimedia Commons, with permission to copy freely granted under the terms of the GNU Free Documentation License.

established in 1917 by Julius Rosenwald, then president of Sears, Roebuck and Co. By 1932 the Fund had supported construction of nearly five thousand black schools in the South and estimated that more than one-third of black students attended one of these schools. Economists John Donohue, James Heckman, and Petra Todd conclude that philanthropic funding allowed southern black school quality to keep pace with improvements in white schools during this period, though not to close the gap between them. The funds all required substantial matching contributions from local residents and public school systems, so black southerners them-selves also deserve much credit for this educational progress.[1]

Closing the racial gap in school spending began only in the mid-1930s, largely as the result of a concerted campaign by the NAACP to enforce the "equal" part of *Plessy v. Ferguson.* Known as the Mangold Plan after the New York attorney who devised it, the NAACP strategy targeted the seven southern states with the most unequal school allocations, which also happened to be states whose education laws failed to mandate equal funding for black and white schools. Donohue, Heckman, and Todd show a close correspondence in most states between NAACP litigation and the beginning of the shift toward more equal teachers' salaries. Although there were wide differences among the states, Figures 5.1a and 5.1b display trends in two school quality indicators for the South as a whole, based on data compiled from state education reports by David Card and Alan Krueger. Black and white teachers' salaries were close to equal by the time of the *Brown* decision. The pupil-teacher ratio was lower in white schools, but progress on this score continued during the decade between *Brown* and the Civil Rights Act. What was said of Hyde County, North Carolina—"By 1964 . . . black schools had improved enormously"—was true in many other localities across the South.[2]

These observations have led many to question the NAACP's decision in 1950 to turn from demanding enforcement of *Plessy* to calling for its overthrow. Opinion within the organization was by no means unanimous on the change of strategy, but mainly because some thought the time was not yet right for such a dramatic move, not because of disagreement on the objective of overturning state-sponsored segregation. The lead case at that point was *Briggs v. Elliot,* coming out of Clarendon County, South Carolina, where black and white schools were far from equal. In 1951 the county spent $166.45 on each white student but only $44.32 on each black student. Indeed the state's main defense was to acknowledge the inequalities and ask for time to correct them. Although the plaintiffs lost in district court in a 2–1 vote, their argument was accepted by Judge J. Waties Waring

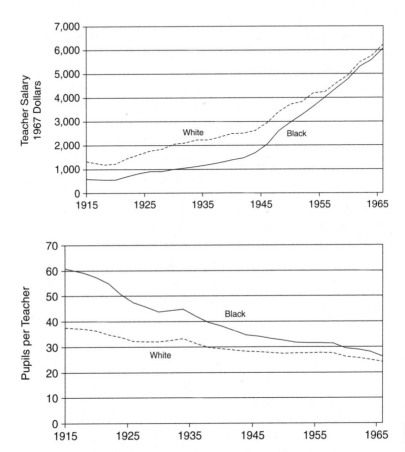

Figure 5.1 Comparison of teacher salaries with pupils per teacher in eighteen segregated states, 1915–1966.

Source: David Card and Alan Krueger. "School Quality and Black-White Relative Earnings: A Direct Assessment." National Bureau of Economic Research, Working Paper No. 3713, 1991. Table 6.

of South Carolina in his dissent, which concluded, *"Segregation is per se inequality."* Although the case from Topeka, Kansas, was given lead billing to lessen the impression that the issue was purely regional, the principle that segregation was inherently unequal prevailed in the case known as *Brown v. Board of Education.*[3]

But was the principle correct? The psychological evidence invoked by the Supreme Court came in for withering criticism, and it seems doubtful that any robust generalizations are possible about the effects of racial segregation on self-esteem per se.[4] But it is evident that the NAACP and the Supreme Court understood the impact of segregated schools within the context of a deeply segregated southern society, in which black schools, even with improved funding, served largely to prepare students for their restricted "place" in that society, and blacks had no effective political channels to change the situation. Thurgood Marshall, in his rebuttal to South Carolina's case, argued that the most important factor "is that for some reason, which is still unexplained, Negroes are taken out of the mainstream of American life in these states." In response to the suggestion that school segregation statutes may have been intended to reduce racial friction, Marshall pointed out that blacks played no role in any such determination, noting that no black legislator then served in any of the segregating states. Although his language was intentionally spare, Chief Justice Earl Warren also made clear that the issue was a matter of principle: "To separate them from others of similar age and qualifications solely because of their race *generates a feeling of inferiority as to their status in the community* that may affect their hearts and minds in a way unlikely ever to be undone." For these reasons, the apparent trend toward equalization in terms of "tangible" factors could not be taken at face value.[5]

In ruling against segregation in principle, however, the Court gave almost no attention to the question of implementation. When the time came for specifics in May 1955 (the case that became known as *Brown II*), signs of defiance in the white South were such that the Court set no time limits but instructed local authorities to desegregate "with all deliberate speed" and "as soon as practicable." Since the southern efforts to circumvent *Brown* through such measures as (ostensibly nonracial) "pupil placement laws," *Brown II* seemed to be a victory for the strategy of indefinite delay. The crisis at Little Rock Central High School in 1957 prompted a show of federal authority, but the near-term result was closure of the city's public high schools for an entire year (1958–1959). When schools reopened in September 1959, only two of the original nine black students were then enrolled. Thus, although several border states quickly desegregated after *Brown*, between 1955 and 1964 the overall percentage of southern black students attending schools with whites rose only from zero to 2.1 percent.[6]

The 1964 Watershed

Why, then, did school districts all over the South acquiesce in desegregation in the late 1960s, after resisting it so stoutly for more than a decade? Once again, the proximate impetus was the Civil Rights Act of 1964. Title IV authorized the U.S. Attorney General to file suits against school districts to enforce desegregation, while Title VI allowed federal agencies to withhold funding from any institution that failed to comply with the agency's antidiscrimination requirements. The latter title gained added force with passage the following year (after the 1964 Johnson landslide) of the Elementary and Secondary Education Act (ESEA) of 1965, which dramatically increased federal funding for public schools. Nearly all the opposition to ESEA came from the South, concerned that funding might be used to force desegregation—a fear that proved accurate in subsequent years.[7] Many districts submitted desegregation plans for the first time after passage of the ESEA, though many of these were token measures under "freedom of choice" plans. Such plans were invalidated by the Supreme Court in its 1968 *Green v. New Kent County* decision, which ordered districts to take positive steps to achieve realistic desegregation. In 1969 the Court intensified the pressure still further, ordering school districts "to terminate dual school systems at once and to operate now and hereafter only unitary schools."[8]

The combined force of these pressures and incentives broke the South's resolve to maintain segregated public schools. Figure 5.2 displays the time path of change, based on district-level data compiled by economists Elizabeth Cascio, Nora Gordon, Ethan Lewis, and Sarah Reber. The dotted line indicates that roughly half of southern school districts were ultimately under court order. But there was also a sharp uptick in "voluntary" desegregation after 1964, which the authors show was systematically related to a district's financial stake in federal funding. By 1966 the Department of Health, Education, and Welfare (HEW) reported that more than 20 percent of southern school districts had funds either deferred or terminated, so the threat was by no

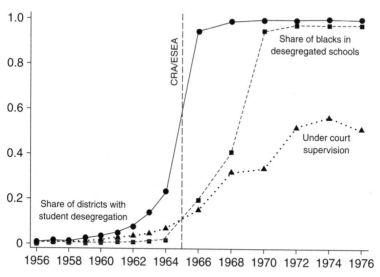

Figure 5.2 Desegregation in the former Confederacy, 1956–1976.
Source: Elizabeth Cascio, Nora Gordon, Ethan Lewis, and Sarah Reber. "Paying for Progress: Conditional Grants and the Desegregation of Southern Schools," *Quarterly Journal of Economics* 125 (2010): Figure 1. Reproduced by permission of Oxford University Press.

means empty. The two modes of enforcement reinforced each other, however, as the *Green* decision essentially gave judicial force to HEW guidelines. Many districts complied in order to avoid court orders, but the role of court supervision nonetheless increased over time. As the figure shows, the major decline in all-black schools came only after *Green*. The process was largely complete by 1970, so that the Court's 1971 decision in *Swann v. Charlotte-Mecklenburg Board of Education* (approving Charlotte-Mecklenburg's busing plan as a means of desegregating) did not play a fundamental role in most of the South.[9]

Uncompromising federal enforcement was the proximate cause of southern acquiescence, but behind the scenes one may detect a gradual change over time in the priorities of the region's business and political leadership. Despite the best efforts of the Southern Regional Council over many years, business leaders rarely if ever played a leading role in school desegregation. In Little Rock, only after closure of the public schools led to a complete cessation of new industrial investment did members of the Chamber of Commerce form a "secret committee" to support a moderate school board slate and compromise on desegregation.[10] The "lesson of Little Rock" was not lost on other communities in the South, especially after the SRC report on the economic impact gained wide circulation. A 1960 survey of eighty white leaders in five business communities found that virtually all of them favored segregation but opposed extreme measures (such as school closing and violence) to preserve it, for fear of the effects on industrial recruitment. In Atlanta the mayor commissioned a study of Little Rock's business losses and solicited advice from that city's Chamber of Commerce. In 1961 the Atlanta Chamber became the only major business group in Georgia openly in favor of desegregated public education—at a time when its members were still resisting desegregation of lunch counters! Elsewhere the timing of the issue was often the reverse. Not until 1969 did the Chamber of Commerce in Greensboro, North Carolina, come out in favor of school desegregation, and at that point the school board accomplished within two months "what for almost twenty years it had said would be educationally impossible."[11]

Court orders and HEW guidelines dramatically changed the racial composition of the public schools, but these changes were almost always followed by "white flight," either to private schools or to whiter suburban districts. One study estimates that within ten years, lower white enrollment typically offset about one-third of the reduction in segregation.[12] Private school enrollments in Mississippi tripled between 1966 and 1973. Many studies describe a "tipping point" phenomenon, whereby whites departed en masse once a threshold percentage of blacks was reached. For Mississippi in 1970 Charles Clotfelter estimated a tipping point just over 50 percent, a figure that was essentially unchanged thirty years later.[13] Figure 5.3 shows that while private school enrollments were falling elsewhere in the country (primarily because of the decline of Catholic schools), those in the South grew rapidly between 1960 and 1980.

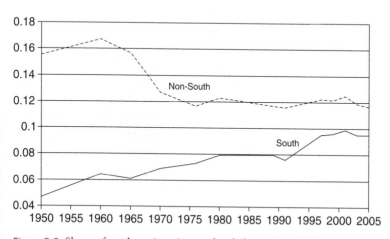

Figure 5.3 Share of students in private schools by region, 1950–2008.
Source: Compiled from National Center for Education Statistics. *Digest of Education Statistics*, various years.

Either private schooling or migration to the suburbs required financial resources not available to many white families. Perhaps for this reason, desegregation of southern schools had a distinct class dimension. In Mississippi families with annual incomes of more than $25,000 were significantly more likely to enroll in private schools. In Nashville the white departure rate in response to court-ordered busing in the 1970s was nearly four times higher in neighborhoods with median incomes above $12,000 than in those with median incomes below $9,000.[14]

Despite this slippage, by 1972 the South had the most racially mixed public schools in the nation, a distinction held for the rest of the century. Table 5.1 shows that the percentage of southern black students attending schools that were 90 to 100 percent black fell from 77.8 in 1968 to 24.7 in 1972, compared to 46.9 percent in the Northeast and 57.4 percent in the Midwest. In parallel, the percentage of southern white students attending schools that were 90 to 100 percent white fell from 70.6 in 1968 to 38.0 in 1972, compared to 82.9 percent in the Northeast and 87.5 percent in the Midwest.

Desegregation was intensely analyzed by social scientists during this period, but remarkably, the literature largely overlooked the most prominent historical feature of the matter: quantitative school desegregation was overwhelmingly a southern regional phenomenon. In the Northeast, desegregation essentially never happened. In the Midwest, rates of extreme segregation did fall between 1972 and 1989 but never reached the low levels of the South and border states. Yet studies and surveys of studies often failed to find a North-South difference and pronounced the issue "inconclusive."[15]

Several reasons for regional divergence stand out. Nearly all of the early desegregation cases pertained to the South. In the 1970s an increasing number of suits were brought in districts outside the South, despite the absence of explicit segregation statutes in these states. Yet regional differences in racial balance continued. One contributing factor for this persistence was the

Table 5.1 Percentage of Black Students in 90 to 100 Percent Nonwhite and Majority Nonwhite Schools by Region, 1960–2005

Region	1960	1968	1972	1976	1980	1988	1991	1999	2005
				Percentage in 90–100% nonwhite schools					
SOUTH	100	78	25	22	33	24	26	31	32
Border	59	60	55	43	37	35	35	40	42
Northeast	40	43	47	51	49	48	50	50	51
Midwest	56	58	57	51	44	42	40	45	46
West	27	51	43	36	34	29	27	30	30
U.S. Total		64	39	36	33	32	34	37	38

Region	1960	1968	1972	1976	1980	1988	1991	1999	2005
				Percentage in 50–100% nonwhite schools					
SOUTH	100	81	55	55	57	57	60	67	72
Border	69	72	67	60	59	60	59	65	70
Northeast	62	67	70	73	80	77	75	78	78
Midwest	80	77	75	70	70	70	70	68	72
West	69	72	68	67	67	67	69	77	77
U.S. Total		77	64	62	63	63	66	70	73

Sources: Clotfelter, *After Brown*, p. 56; Orfield and Lee, *Historic Reversals*, pp. 28, 33.

prevalence of larger school districts in the South, a feature of regional economic geography going back to antebellum times.[16] Larger districts made it more difficult for white families to depart for whiter suburbs. The difficulty of escape was further aggravated by the absence of established networks of private schools in most of the region. Figure 5.3 shows that the region's overall private school enrollment never exceeded 10 percent of the total. An additional contributing factor was the presence of large numbers of low-income whites, often with strong local attachments, for whom the private school or migration options were simply too costly.

Thus the distinctive southern pattern was observed primarily in smaller cities and rural areas. Some of the largest southern central-city districts, such as Atlanta, New Orleans, Birmingham, and Memphis, became predominantly black within a few years of desegregation, following the example of northern cities.[17]

The Supreme Court's press for intensified desegregation reached its peak with the *Swann* decision of 1971, striking down "racially neutral" assignment plans that reproduced segregation based on residential patterns and approving busing as a means of overcoming this problem. The Court's reversal of direction began just three years later and grew directly out of the extension of desegregation enforcement outside the South. In *Milliken v. Bradley* (1974), the Court by a 5–4 vote overturned a district court ruling that called for cross-district busing as a means of overcoming de facto segregation in metropolitan Detroit. Although within-district desegregation continued to be enforced through the 1970s, a series of rulings in the next decade made it progressively easier for districts to be declared "unitary" (i.e., in compliance with *Brown*'s proscription of dual systems) and hence to dismantle plans to achieve racial balance. Thus the specter of "resegregation" was looming in the South well before the *Parents Involved in Community Schools v. Seattle School District No. 1* decision of 2007, which virtually ruled out the use of race in assigning students to schools. The Supreme Court applied this principle to strike down voluntary busing plans not only in Seattle but also in Louisville, Kentucky, a slave-state district with a long history of legal segregation, having abandoned the practice only under court order. The irony of the federal courts prohibiting a locally developed integration plan in the name of racial equity was not lost on veteran Civil Rights observers.[18]

THE EFFECTS OF SCHOOL DESEGREGATION IN THE SOUTH

Despite the unevenness of the record, we can now say with some assurance that southern school desegregation fostered substantial educational and economic gains for African Americans. A series of recent studies, utilizing longer-term data available through the passage of time, has confirmed as well as clarified this contention. Exasperatingly, the studies often fail to analyze regional dimensions of the process explicitly. But a careful reading makes it clear that the gains from desegregation were primarily realized in the South.

Jonathan Guryan finds that in school districts that desegregated between 1970 and 1980, the high school dropout rate for black students declined by two to three percentage points, with no significant impact on the white dropout rate. This finding is robust to controls for family income, parental education, and state- and region-specific trends, as well as to tests for selective migration. Although Guryan finds no difference in the size of the effect between the South and the non-South, he also reports that the declines in black dropout rates were substantially larger in districts where the change in the degree of segregation (as measured by the dissimilarity index or exposure indices) was larger.[19] Because the decline in segregation by these measures was much greater in the South than elsewhere in the country during the 1970s, these results imply that the effect on black dropout rates was greatest in the South.

In a study of Louisiana, Sarah Reber also finds that desegregation led to a substantial increase in black high school graduation rates.[20] An important factor in this case was the sharp increase in per pupil spending on black students, associated with desegregation between 1965 and 1971, because of a change in the formula for allocation of state aid: a 42 percent increase in funding led to a 15 percent increase in black graduation rates. Because of data limitations, Reber was unable to identify an impact on white graduation rates. However, her research provides insight into why desegregation became politically acceptable during this period: because the state legislature directed significant new funding to districts where whites were particularly affected, allowing quality to be "leveled up" to that previously experienced only in white schools.

An earlier study by Michael A. Boozer, Alan B. Krueger, and Shari Wolkon, using data from the National Survey of Black Americans, found that southern black cohorts who began schooling after the transition to desegregation not only completed more years of education but also earned higher weekly wages as of 1990.[21] A more recent analysis by Orley Ashenfelter, William Collins, and Albert Yoon focuses more precisely on region as well as date of birth and confirms that the "desegregation cohorts" in the South experienced dramatic gains in both educational attainment and earnings relative to whites. Although the authors acknowledge that other historical forces may have been at work (such as antidiscrimination policies), their procedure identifies the black southern-born post-desegregation generation with great precision. It seems implausible that labor market changes alone would have had such disproportionate effects on this one demographic group.[22]

Analysis of data from the National Assessment of Educational Progress (NAEP) and the Armed Forces Qualifying Test (AFQT) by Kenneth Y. Chay, Jonathan Guryan, and Bhashkar Mazumder shows that the black-white test score gap declined markedly during the 1980s and that this decline was concentrated in cohorts born in the South between 1963 and the early 1970s.[23] The study shows a steady gain in relative southern black scores on the Armed Forces Qualifying Test, surpassing those for the Rust Belt for the birth cohorts of 1966–1967. The authors do not attribute the decline primarily to school desegregation but point to improved infant health, specifically a dramatic decline in the southern black postnatal mortality rate, associated with access to desegregated hospitals in the 1960s. Their case for a health care effect is strong, but the cohorts in question also correspond closely to those whose first educational experience was in desegregated elementary schools. Improved access to health care alone would not predict that the southern test score gap would actually become smaller than that in other regions, which is what the authors find for both the AFQT and the NAEP. School desegregation, which was much greater in the South, would account for precisely such a pattern. It seems justifiable, therefore, to conclude that school desegregation also made a substantial contribution to closing the black-white test score gap in the South.

The most comprehensive recent study, by Rucker C. Johnson, investigates the long-term impact of court-ordered desegregation during the 1960s, 1970s, and 1980s and finds that exposure to such plans significantly increased educational attainment and adult earnings of black students, while reducing the probability of incarceration and improving adult health status. Johnson attributes these changes primarily to improvements in school quality, measured by changes in per pupil spending levels, which increased with desegregation through mechanisms similar to those described by Reber for Louisiana. As in the Guryan article, Johnson does not identify a regional difference in the estimated effects. But because exposure to court-ordered desegregation was greatest in the South during the period in question, it would seem that these results also contribute to explaining the strong gains for black southerners at this time.[24]

All of these studies imply significant gains from desegregation, but the authors are often not able to identify the precise channels through which the effects were achieved. In Louisiana desegregation was accompanied by a substantial infusion of new resources into newly integrated schools, and Johnson's study suggests that this effect may have occurred more widely. Despite the apparent prior trend toward equalization of expenditures per pupil, it is likely that less tangible aspects of school quality (such as the educational background of teachers) were not effectively equalized before desegregation. It is also plausible that exposure to higher academic standards of a white student peer group (because of wealth, family background, and prior educational attainment) raised the achievement levels of black students, though the value of this channel is uncertain. Or it could be that the fact of integration itself, and the success of the Civil Rights Movement in expanding opportunities, increased the confidence of black students that education would have a positive payoff.[25] Ideally we could decompose the gains into portions explained by each of these factors, but because most of them changed simultaneously, such a calculation is probably not possible. Our inability to do so, however, does not diminish the magnitude or import of this historic development.

Were White Southerners Hurt by School Desegregation?

In public accommodations and labor markets, it is relatively straightforward to show that no substantial segment of the southern white population was economically harmed by desegregation. With respect to public schools, the issue is more difficult. Testifying in 1981, Civil Rights advocate Gary Orfield summarized the state of research on the question: "There are no losses for white children in the desegregation process . . . [and] substantial gains for minority children."[26] Raymond Wolters sharply challenges this statement, citing his own review of districts in which the effort to integrate public schools was clearly a failure. In two of the most embattled cases, however, Wolters's summary suggests that the net educational outcome as of the 1980s may actually have been positive. In Prince Edward County, Virginia, the former school board chairman told an interviewer:

The blacks lost five years of school, and they were hurt immensely by that, but now, they're probably getting a better education. The Academy [Prince Edward Academy, a set of eight private schools opened in 1959] was hard pressed to begin with, but whites have also ended up getting a better education than before. In a way, you could say we've got pretty much what we had before, only better.[27]

Similarly, in Clarendon County, South Carolina, where the *Briggs* case originated, whites generally thought that the new private academy "was as good as the old Summerton Elementary and High School, and blacks recognized that facilities in the public schools were much improved since the 1940s."[28] None of this suggests that the outcomes were ideal, only that the net educational balance may well have been positive for both whites and blacks, even in these cases of early, almost complete resegregation.

The larger issue turns on one's assessment of the motivation and costs of white flight from desegregated schools. Mere distaste for association with blacks may not deserve great weight in the appraisal, and indeed part of the case for desegregation was the idea that racial prejudices would diminish over time with increased contact. But one cannot simply dismiss white fears that an influx of black students with very different educational and family backgrounds would increase classroom disruptions, fighting, and other forms of racial hostility, to say nothing of concerns that academic standards would decline. These fears were not mere fantasies. When Murphy High School in Montgomery, Alabama, was desegregated in 1970, numerous racial incidents were reported, leading the faculty to request that federal marshals and armed guards be posted at the school. When Louisiana schools were integrated between 1969 and 1972, few of them escaped racial conflict over such issues as discipline, hairstyle, dress, language, and homecoming activities.[29] Racial violence typically subsided over time. But when desegregation plans called for white students to be transported to formerly black schools, white parents often anticipated that the facilities would be older and poorer and that the neighborhoods would be less safe.[30] Thus the desegregation debate in many localities was whether the transfers would be one-way or two-way, the latter being far less acceptable to white families. White reassignments to formerly black schools during the 1970s resulted in two to three times more white enrollment loss than black reassignment to white schools.[31]

Because departing white families paid private school tuition, one cannot deny that desegregation imposed financial costs on some white southerners. In their early years, these "segregation academies" were tax-exempt as charitable institutions, implying that the financial costs were shared broadly with the tax-paying public. They were also harshly criticized for low academic standards, reflecting both cost constraints and the strong religious orientation that characterized many of the schools.[32] To the extent that these schools raised costs while lowering educational quality, the losses are undeniable.

In partial mitigation, one may note that the worst features of the new situation receded over time. Hundreds of segregated southern academies were denied tax exemption by the Internal Revenue Service in the 1970s, an interpretation that was upheld by the Supreme Court in 1983. By the 1990s virtually all of the surviving academies had adopted policies prohibiting racial discrimination, and at least some of these were sincere commitments to diversity in the student body. In the Birmingham area as of 2010, for example, the large private schools founded during the desegregation era maintained African American enrollment shares ranging from 3 to 27 percent and averaging about 10 percent. The headmaster of the Montgomery Academy, a school that was sued in 1984 for its racially exclusive policies, was quoted in 2004 as follows: "I am sure that those who resented the civil rights movement or sought to get away from it took refuge in the academy. But it's not 1959 anymore and the Montgomery Academy has a philosophy today that reflects the openness . . . and utter lack of discrimination with regard to race or religion that was evident in prior decades."[33]

As hopeful as this change of private school sentiment may be for the long term, the great majority of southern white students have continued to attend public schools, and these schools have long been more racially mixed than elsewhere in the country. Although the greatest academic and economic gains have accrued to southern blacks, there is no evidence that these gains have come at the expense of white public school students. Janet Schofield's comprehensive 1995 review of research found remarkable unanimity on the conclusion that desegregation has had no adverse effects on test scores or academic attainment for white students.[34] Erica Frankenberg writes, "The evidence was so clear that this issue was rarely raised in court battles by desegregation opponents, in spite of Whites' fears that White achievement would suffer."[35] Consistent with this conclusion, the studies by Guryan and Johnson that identify major black gains from desegregation find no significant effect on white attainment or achievement.

A complicating factor is the fact that by the 1970s, a majority of southern schools had adopted some form of ability grouping or academic tracking, most frequently in secondary schools but often even at the elementary level. In many cases, these systems were adopted as direct responses to desegregation orders, a transparent attempt to avoid racial mixing in classrooms. In Charleston, South Carolina, school officials expanded testing and tracking in public schools immediately after the 1955 *Briggs* ruling, arguing, "This difference in achievement between the races may be our last line of defense."[36] Because they typically led to "racially identifiable classrooms," tracking and ability grouping were frequently challenged in the courts during desegregation litigation, and nearly half were rejected during the 1970s.[37] But such systems were never ruled unconstitutional per se, and many continue to the present day. Studies often suggest that within-school grouping serves as a substitute for between-school segregation.[38]

Whether one interprets these practices as thinly disguised devices to evade integration or more sympathetically as attempts to retain high-aspiration families in the public schools, their prevalence underscores the conclusion that southern white students in general have not suffered educationally from desegregation. True, some of this outcome reflects positive effort on the part of white families, through migration to suburbs, private schools, or lobbying for academically advanced tracks within public schools; hence it has not been costless. But the drive for educational status is central to what we classify as middle-class American behavior. A notable achievement of the Civil Rights Movement is that many black families are now also in position to pursue these goals.

SCHOOLS AND SCHOOL DISTRICTS: THE SUSTAINABILITY OF DESEGREGATION

If southern school desegregation brought great educational and economic gains to African Americans at little cost to white southerners, the obvious question arises: Why has desegregation in this realm been so much more difficult to sustain than in public accommodations or labor markets? To be sure, there were significant costs of adjustment borne in large part by whites, either by paying for private schools or by contriving to maintain high-achievement tracks in public schools. But these costs ought to have diminished over time, as racial attitudes have moderated. As we have seen, private schools that were once racially exclusive now compete for top black students and take pride in their (albeit somewhat limited) diversity. The changes in national political and legal thinking regarding judicial enforcement of racial balance are well known. But whereas the same retreat from active enforcement has had relatively little effect on gains in public accommodations and labor markets, the tendency toward resegregation in schools seems much more powerful, when the law allows it. Why should this be so?

The difference is that the educational sector lacks organizations with sufficient scope to internalize the gains from desegregation. In public accommodations, national chains came to welcome customers of all types—once they determined that most white customers would not be deterred—and local merchant communities also learned to value their reputation for openness. Similarly, firms that had greatly expanded minority employment, however reluctantly, soon discovered a strong self-interest in improved racial tolerance and teamwork. Greater black representation in companies, workplaces, and departments then tends to perpetuate and extend itself through informal channels of communication and support. One might hope that the same self-interest in racial understanding and cooperation would apply to schools, and at times it does, particularly on athletic teams. But in general, the capacity of schools and school districts to internalize these gains is much more limited. A central aspect of the difficulty is that public schools are essentially open systems: the costs of switching between districts is low, especially for the affluent, achievement-oriented families whose children supply the peer effects that are so crucial for educational outcomes.

Behind this diagnosis lies the deeper truth that true racial integration, as opposed to tolerance and desegregation, remains a remote goal in all of these spheres, perhaps more so in education than elsewhere. There seems little doubt of this observation. Charles Clotfelter studied participation in extracurricular activities in racially mixed high schools in the South and non-South from a sample of yearbooks for the 1997–1998 school year. He found a high degree of de facto or self-segregation in both.[39] Most strikingly, although black representation was substantially higher in the South, the degree of membership segregation was sharply higher in schools with higher percentages of nonwhites. Although nonwhites were often members of groups in which they were outnumbered by whites by three to one or more, such a situation almost never occurred for white students. Thus the data are consistent with a "tipping point" process within school organizations, whereby whites tend to abandon an organization once they find themselves outnumbered. Racially segregated proms and homecoming courts were reported to be common throughout the South even in the twenty-first century.[40] These observations do not necessarily imply that racial hostilities were higher than in earlier historical times. But they do tend to confirm the conclusion of historian J. Michael McElreath that "desegregation—the mixing of different races within the same school buildings—was achieved in many places, but real integration happened almost nowhere."[41]

Perhaps the best way to illustrate both the potential and the limitations of internalizing school desegregation is with the district that came closest to doing so: the Charlotte-Mecklenburg School District in western North Carolina. Having long prided itself as a progressive city in a moderate state, Charlotte was one of the first in the South to approve token black transfers in the 1950s and was inching its way toward fuller school integration in the early 1960s, even before the Civil Rights Act. But unlike many southern cities, Charlotte was characterized by a high level of residential segregation, a condition that began in its days as a mill town and continued through the 1950s under the influence of Federal Housing Administration policies and local zoning plans. As a result, extensive desegregation of Charlotte schools was possible only with extensive busing, which made the issue even more contentious than in cities with less concern for their reputation.[42]

Ultimately Judge James McMillan of the federal district court imposed a sweeping desegregation plan in February 1970, busing both white and black students with the goal of desegregating every school in the district. Initially the plan had little local support from any side. But when it was upheld by the Supreme Court in its unanimous *Swann* decision of 1971, subsequent debates made it clear that all parties would have to compromise. Eager to restore stability, the Chamber of Commerce at that point threw its weight firmly behind compliance. Remarkably, a comprehensive busing plan was developed that met with approval from all major political factions. Using the slogan "The City That Makes It Work," corporate boosters "incorporated the achievement . . . into the national marketing of Charlotte as the prosperous and progressive embodiment of the New South." *New York Times* reporter Peter Applebome wrote that the commitment to busing "became as much a part of the civic mythos as the new glass towers sprouting on the streets of downtown." In what became a climactic moment for the city's self-image, when Ronald Reagan denounced busing during a campaign stop in 1984, he was roundly rebuked the next day by the *Charlotte Observer*. Under the headline "You Were Wrong, Mr. President," the *Observer* wrote that Charlotte's "proudest achievement" was "its fully integrated school system."[43]

The busing program generated much favorable national publicity and thus enhanced the Chamber of Commerce goal of fostering Charlotte's ongoing economic growth as a business, transportation, and financial center.[44] But the success was not merely in public relations. Even before busing, achievement test scores indicated that black students in desegregated schools performed better than those in segregated schools, a result noted by Judge McMillan in his ruling. During the 1970s, reading and math scores (at third, sixth, and ninth grades) went from one grade *below* the national average to one grade *above* the national average, a remarkable gain in a brief period. White scores continued to be higher than black scores, but the gap closed over time, and both blacks and whites gained relative to the national average. There may of course have been many factors at work in this performance, but it is difficult to disagree with the school administrator who commented that the rise in test scores "would never have happened . . . absolutely would never have happened without integration."[45]

With the aid of hindsight, it is evident that certain special features of the situation contributed to Charlotte's desegregation experience. A crucial structural factor was the consolidation of city and county school districts in 1960. Large school districts are a distinctive feature of southern economic geography, but the 1960 merger—driven evidently by concern for the educational quality of rural schools, not by the race issue—made Charlotte-Mecklenburg one of the largest systems in the country.[46] As a result, white flight in response to desegregation was minimal, among the lowest of any urban districts in the nation.[47] Some turned to private schools, but these numbers also were relatively small, perhaps a reflection of the working-class character of Charlotte's white population. The demographic structure was also favorable, in that whites constituted two-thirds of the county population, so that a comprehensive busing system did not threaten them with minority status at any school. Even at the peak of the busing program, black students bore a larger share of the transportation burden than did whites. But blacks nonetheless had a strong voice in shaping the details. In the wake of the Voting Rights Act, the first black school board member was elected in 1972, and antibusing candidates were defeated in the elections of 1974 and 1976. But black political ascendancy was not seen as threatening to the white majority, particularly as racial accommodation contributed to economic growth in tangible ways, most directly through support for an airport bond issue in 1978, reversing an earlier ballot defeat. The election of Civil Rights hero Harvey Gantt as mayor in 1981 seemed to symbolize a new "biracial coalition around economic growth."[48]

Why, then, did the Charlotte-Mecklenburg desegregation program not survive? Ultimately the plan fell victim to trends in national politics and judicial rulings, but Charlotte's own economic demography was also at work. The decline of local support was gradual, initiated by newcomers from outside the region who had no sense of commitment to an earlier political bargain but with a strong attachment to the concept of neighborhood schools. Influential as it was, the business elite was unable to control these centrifugal forces or the steady rise in racially identifiable schools. The school board remained steadfast in support of the program through 1991 but changed course in 1992 in an effort to placate the demand for greater choice, adopting a new system of magnet schools in that year. School bond referenda were defeated in 1992 and 1995, in part because black voters were unsure whether the new schools would be racially integrated. The magnet system still targeted racial balance, but a group of white parents (six out of seven of whom were new arrivals) challenged the use of race in pupil assignments, petitioning in 1999 to reopen the *Swann* case. A conservative district judge ruled in their favor, declaring the district "unitary" over the objections of the school board! When the Supreme Court declined to review the case in 2002, Charlotte's business community— more concerned with stability than with racial equity—urged the district to "move on" and adopt an officially nonracial and more decentralized system.[49]

Do these developments mean that the era of educational progress based on desegregation has now come to an end? The only reasonable answer is that it is too early to tell. In Charlotte-Mecklenburg it seems evident that abandonment of mandatory busing and racial balance goals has resulted in increased racial and socioeconomic isolation, and there is evidence that inequality in resources and educational outcomes have also increased.[50] But the district maintains a reputation for quality and has taken steps to address the problems of high-poverty schools.[51] For purposes of the present argument, the events in Charlotte highlight the fragile character of school desegregation on the basis of political consensus within a metropolitan area, even when structural conditions seem favorable. It is also true, however, that local choices in this case were sharply constrained by outside judicial rulings, even before the 2007 Supreme Court decision rejecting desegregation programs in Louisville and Seattle. Judicial restrictions on the use of race thus threaten an effective channel that has generated historically important educational benefits at relatively low cost.

RACE, REGION, AND SCHOOLS

School desegregation led to historic educational and economic gains for African Americans in the South. Whether this record of achievement implies that desegregation provides the best basis for ongoing progress remains hotly disputed.[52] Legal scholar Martha Minow writes, "Scholars agree that desegregation did not fail. . . . The courts lost their nerve."[53] But she acknowledges that the integration ideal has faded among blacks as well as whites. A case can be made that a deeper basis for sustained progress lies in the spread of educational aspirations and values in families and schools, whether racially balanced or not. These types of norms are not free-floating: to be sustained, they have to be linked to a perception that educational achievement will have an economic payoff. But once in place, they offer African Americans access to the tools of mobility and voice that have long given middle-class white families an advantage in education. Many black families now seem to have reached this threshold, especially in the South.

Some studies question whether the end of court-ordered desegregation has actually increased racial isolation in the schools. The standard indicators do show such a rise, in the South and elsewhere, after 1990 (see Table 5.1). Both measurement and policy issues are complicated during this period by demographic change, primarily the rise of Hispanics in the school-age population and the associated decline in the percentage of whites. A report issued in 2007 by the U.S. Commission on Civil Rights examined districts that had been under court order in seven southern states, concluding that although "a cursory view of the data . . . suggests that unitary districts [i.e., those whose court desegregation orders have been lifted] have greater levels of racial concentration than districts that remain under court supervision," these differences can be largely be accounted for by such factors as district size and the percentage of enrolled students who are white.[54] Similarly, a study of the hundred largest school districts in the South and border states by Clotfelter, Ladd, and Vigdor found that only one measure of racial isolation actually increased between 1994 and 2004: the percentage of blacks attending schools that are 90 to 100 percent nonwhite. But this rise was largely driven by the overall increase in the share of students who are Hispanic, Asian, or another race.[55]

The most comprehensive analyses show, however, that release from court supervision does lead to a gradual increase in black-white segregation over time. The effects have been greatest in the South, where 80 percent of the districts still under court orders in 1990 were located. The key question is whether these trends have had consequences for educational outcomes. Using a national sample of districts that were under court order as of 1991, economist Byron Lutz finds that dismissal of desegregation plans led to an increase in black dropout rates and black private school attendance—but not in the South! None of the adverse effects was observed in southern districts; instead southern black dropout rates continued their downward trend, in both dismissed and nondismissed districts. White dropout rates were not affected, but white enrollment in public schools increased in response to dismissals, a phenomenon Lutz refers to as "reverse white flight." A possible vehicle for explaining these trends is that districts invested additional resources in minority neighborhoods after dismissal of a desegregation plan in order to mitigate negative consequences for black students. Examples of such expenditures include Nashville, Tennessee, and Lafayette Parish, Louisiana, as well as Charlotte-Mecklenburg.[56]

Evidence of continued southern distinctiveness may be found in scores on national achievement tests. The National Assessment of Educational Progress in reading and mathematics has been conducted by the U.S. Department of Education since 1971.[57] Scores on standardized tests are by no means a comprehensive measure of educational performance, but they provide a means

of assessing broad trends over nearly forty years, across an era
during which regional and racial gaps were initially very large.
The data show that in both reading and mathematics, at each
of the grade levels tested, the gains for southern black students
have exceeded those for any other category. Figures 5.4–5.6
display the record for Reading at age nine. Figure 5.4 shows
that the South as a region made strong gains, moving from 25
points below the national average in 1971 to a position of virtual parity by 2008. Figure 5.5 underscores the dramatic rise in
black test scores between 1971 and the 1980s.[58] Although
black scores remained below white scores in every region, by
the most recent test year, the racial gap was smaller in the
South than in the Midwest, and barely below that of the Northeast.[59] School principals in Wisconsin and Nebraska were said
to be "stunned" to learn that test scores of blacks in their states
were lower in 2008 than anywhere in the old South.[60]

The decline in the southern test gap was not due to low scores
by southern whites. In fact the average scores of southern whites

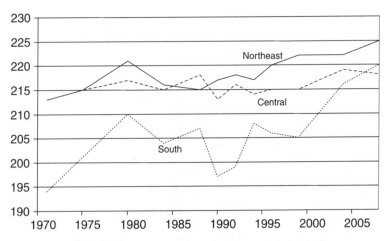

Figure 5.4 NAEP reading scores age nine by region, 1971–2008.
Source: National Center for Education Statistics. *National Assessment
of Educational Progress.* NAEP Data Explorer.

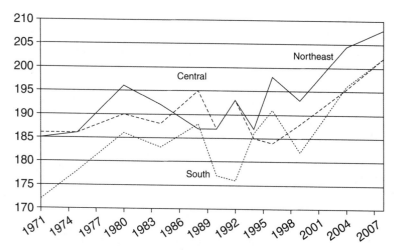

Figure 5.5 NAEP reading scores of black students age nine by region, 1971–2008.

Source: National Center for Education Statistics. *National Assessment of Educational Progress.* NAEP Data Explorer.

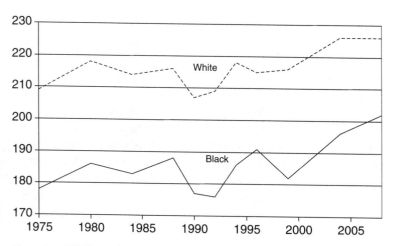

Figure 5.6 NAEP reading scores age nine by race: South, 1975–2008.

Source: National Center for Education Statistics. *National Assessment of Educational Progress.* NAEP Data Explorer.

also grew faster than the national average in both reading and mathematics, at every grade level. Figure 5.6 displays the regional data for reading by race at age nine. Here again, we can safely say that the gains of southern blacks were not achieved at the expense of southern whites.[61]

Intriguing as they are, these results do not tell us the underlying reasons for these test score advances. From the 1970s to the mid-1980s southern black gains reflect the first-generation effects of school desegregation, as previously discussed; since that time, however, continuing long-term improvements for southern blacks are clearly not attributable to ongoing desegregation. If anything, that process has stalled, if not reversed. They may, however, reflect an upgrading of the socioeconomic status of classroom peers, white or black, an effect widely documented in the educational literature.[62] By plausible extension, black test score gains in the South broadly track the progress in income and occupational status documented in the previous chapter, perhaps with a lag of five to ten years. A corollary is that they also reflect a greater black voice in school and school district policies, a legacy of the Civil Rights revolution.

One familiar vehicle for middle-class educational advance is suburbanization. Although it may have appeared in the 1970s that white flight had left blacks confined to resegregated cities, the number of southern black suburbanites grew by 5.5 million between 1960 and 2000, more than in all other parts of the nation combined. Many of these were new in-migrants to the region, in search of quality schools as well as other urban amenities. Although most still lived in racially identifiable (though not segregated) neighborhoods, the suburbs were often economically dynamic and ethnically diverse, attractive to newcomers from around the globe as well as to African Americans. Suburban historian Andrew Wiese writes, "African-Americans' deep cultural roots in the South provided the foundation for the boomerang migration of talented blacks—a southern 'brain drain' that swelled the region's black middle class and encouraged the growth of affluent African-American suburbs as well as growing integration in some of the South's most dynamic suburban areas."[63]

An example of black voice is provided by the school district in Rock Hill, South Carolina, which has persisted in desegregation programs (first by race but more recently by socioeconomic class) that have evidently enhanced rather than threatened its reputation for good schools and high academic standards.[64] Rock Hill is essentially a suburb of Charlotte, and its residents are keenly aware of developments in that city. The district was never under court order but worked out desegregation plans approved by HEW in 1977 and has achieved relatively high levels of racial balance since that time. With a new elementary school scheduled to open in 2002, two newly elected black board members pushed for a greater emphasis on racial balance in upcoming reassignment decisions. Their plan was supported by a biracial coalition and decisively supported by voters in the school board elections of 2002. In subsequent negotiations, race per se was demoted as an assignment criterion in favor of socioeconomic status (proxied by eligibility for free and reduced lunch) and test scores, but by either measure the dissimilarity index fell dramatically between 2001–2002 and 2007–2008. In its years of operation, the program has generated neither massive white flight nor militant political reaction, but instead seems to attract the same sort of broad-based political support that Charlotte enjoyed during the heyday of its busing program.

Clearly Rock Hill's circumstances are unusual: a white majority (54 percent) in an affluent district with a paucity of exit options; a strong middle-class black community; and a local college and newspaper advocating progressive values. Thus the specifics of the Rock Hill experience cannot be neatly packaged for export and use in other localities. But at least some of these elements are found elsewhere in the South—indeed a key precursor for the desegregation plan was the prior reform of the method of electing school board members, prompted by the threat of a lawsuit under the Voting Rights Act. According to political scientist Stephen Samuel Smith, greater black representation facilitated a coalition with working-class whites, who in the end supported a plan in which they too would enjoy some of the benefits of desegregation based on socioeconomic status.

The demographic and political configuration of Rock Hill has some resemblance to other southern districts that have pursued socioeconomic balance as an alternative to race. The best-known examples are Wake County, North Carolina (Raleigh), and Jefferson County, Kentucky (Louisville), both of which reported dramatic gains in test scores at the onset of their programs. Whereas Seattle essentially abandoned integration in the wake of the 2007 *Parents Involved* decision, Louisville—a district with a history of court-ordered merger and desegregation plans—has maintained and if anything strengthened its commitment since the Court's ruling.[65] In these and most similar cases, diversity plans remain locally controversial. But with larger school districts and growing middle-class black communities, the South would seem to have a stronger basis for plans that are both educationally successful and politically viable. Of the districts identified by Richard Kahlenberg as using family income as a basis for assigning students to schools, more than one-third are located in the South.[66]

Nothing in this review offers any easy remedy for inner-city school systems that are isolated both racially and economically. In many respects the exodus of the black middle class to the suburbs aggravates these problems by depriving the schools of articulate advocates and by undermining the commonality of interest based on race. These issues are not distinctive to the South, and it is fair to say that they underscore the limitations of the Civil Rights revolution as economic reform, even in the region where the movement has experienced its greatest success.

CHAPTER 6

THE ECONOMIC CONSEQUENCES
OF VOTING RIGHTS

Barely one year after passage of the Civil Rights Act of 1964, in the wake of violent resistance to black voter registration in Selma, Alabama, the Voting Rights Act was passed by Congress and signed into law by President Johnson. In a rare display of consensus, historians and political scientists agree that the Act revolutionized politics in the South. Bolstered by the presence or threatened presence of federal examiners and observers, black registration rates jumped almost overnight in the targeted areas and were soon comparable to national norms. Within a few years, scores and then hundreds of African Americans were elected to county, municipal, and school board positions throughout the region. Edward Kennedy, who as a member of the Senate voted for the original bill and all four of the subsequent extensions, called the Act "one of the most successful pieces of legislation ever approved by any Congress," and Lyndon Johnson identified it as the most important of his political career.[1]

The effects of the Voting Rights Act on black political representation, however, were not nearly as rapid and immediate as the registration figures would suggest. In public accommodations, employment discrimination, and even school desegregation, a plausible case could be made for an underlying shared economic interest between southern blacks and whites, to be realized with a modicum of tolerance and cooperation. Political power, in contrast, has distributional aspects that are difficult to compromise, for motives driven by economics as well as by a sense of racial status. For these reasons, southern states and jurisdictions responded to the voting rights revolution with a series of measures intended to minimize the impact of black votes. Meaningful representation therefore came only after protracted litigation in federal courts, reflecting an ongoing political mobilization in which the Act of 1965 was only one early step. The number of black elected officials in the South thus continued to rise through the 1980s and 1990s, nearly doubling the non-South figure by the end of the century.

Did this access to the political process actually improve the economic well-being of black southerners? It is difficult and perhaps impossible to establish an objective standard for this question, but the evidence is undeniable that local political participation generated positive change in aspects of life important to these communities and their members, if often modest in economic scale. In many southern cities, black political power has played an important role in improving racial economic equity. By ensuring that gains from economic growth would be more broadly shared, voting rights often facilitated the building of political coalitions that advanced the interests of whites as well as blacks. In this sense, the case confirmed Johnson's entreaty to white southerners that by granting blacks voting rights, whites "would find that a burden has been lifted from [their] shoulders, too."[2]

THE HISTORICAL PATH OF THE SOUTHERN BLACK VOTE

The struggle for black voting rights in the South began long before the Voting Rights Act of 1965. Disfranchisement between 1890 and 1910 was virtually complete, institutionalized by such devices as poll taxes (which typically cumulated each year if unpaid) and literacy tests as conditions for voting but effectively enforced through local control of voter registration. As early as 1915, the NAACP persuaded the U.S. Supreme Court to invalidate Oklahoma's grandfather clause exempting whites from literacy tests if a linear ancestor had been entitled to vote on January 1, 1866. A sustained campaign for legislation against the poll tax during the 1930s and 1940s was unsuccessful, but in 1944 the Supreme Court struck down the Texas white primary after three decades of litigation. Southern black voter registration subsequently began a slow increase, from an estimated 3 percent of the voting-age population in 1940 to 12 percent in 1947 and 20 percent in 1952.[3]

Black registration in this era was primarily in the cities, and under certain conditions it could be politically influential. In Durham, North Carolina, a city with many black-owned businesses and a sizable middle-class population, "Negroes had developed a sizeable, cohesive, and deliverable vote by the end of the 1940s."[4] Historian J. Mills Thornton argues that competition for black votes in Montgomery, Alabama, during the 1950s exacerbated tensions between old-line and modernizing white factions, contributing to political paralysis in the city's response to the bus boycott of 1955–1956.[5] Over most of the region, however, blacks were deterred by a combination of administrative obstacles (primarily the intimidating use of literacy tests), threats of retaliation, and (as a consequence) a sense of fatalism and resignation on the part of potential registrants. Margaret Price of the Southern Regional Council quoted a black resident of Walton County, Georgia: "There is no need to vote, it won't amount to anything anyway. White folks are running things and will keep on doing so."[6]

The slow pace of progress was not greatly changed by the Civil Rights Act of 1957, which authorized the U.S. Attorney General to sue local election officials on behalf of individuals who had been unfairly denied registration. Although the Act was historic as the first federal Civil Rights law since 1875, enforcement powers were watered down in the Senate (a compromise

engineered by Majority Leader Lyndon Johnson) and only weakly
pursued in practice. Between 1958 and 1960 just twenty-three
complaints were received and only five cases were initiated by
the Justice Department.[7] Litigation and registration accelerated
somewhat after the Civil Rights Act of 1960, which expanded
the authority of federal judges and required local authorities to
maintain comprehensive voting records. But there was little reason to expect that this Act alone would do much to change the
long record of merely incremental progress. Between 1960 and
1962 the estimated southern black registration rate barely budged,
from 29.1 to 29.4 percent.[8]

The break in the historical trajectory came in 1962, with the
launching of the Voter Education Project. Encouraged by the
Kennedy administration, five major Civil Rights organizations
joined forces to support local groups in a mass registration effort
throughout the South, coordinated by the Southern Regional
Council. The campaign had considerable success, registering ap-
proximately 700,000 new voters in two and a half years. But it
also served to define the boundary between those areas that were
receptive to registration and those that were stoutly resistant.
Potential registrants frequently faced retaliation, especially in the
Deep South, and organizers often met with violence. Even with a
more sympathetic administration, many activists expressed anger
over what they regarded as the hands-off policy of the Justice
Department. Assistant Attorney General Burke Marshall, head
of the Civil Rights Division, acknowledged in 1964 that the
Deep South results were "not encouraging." Thus the Johnson
administration was preparing more aggressive voting rights legislation even before the bloody showdown at the Edmund Pettus
Bridge in Selma, Alabama, on March 7, 1965.[9]

The Voting Rights Act of 1965 was a drastic measure, targeting a region of the country and essentially preempting state and
local authority over voter qualifications. Sections 2 and 3 are permanent and national, restating the Fifteenth Amendment principle that the right to vote may not be restricted because of race,

and giving federal courts authority to appoint voting examiners or election observers where necessary. Section 4 defines a "trigger" for federal action: that a jurisdiction imposed a literacy test or similar device *and* that voter turnout was less than 50 percent in the 1964 presidential election. These criteria covered six southern states fully (Alabama, Georgia, Louisiana, Mississippi, South Carolina, and Virginia), plus about forty counties in North Carolina. Literacy tests were banned entirely in covered areas, and the U. S. Attorney General was authorized to assign federal examiners to enroll qualified voters. Anticipating state and local countermeasures, Section 5 barred covered jurisdictions from enacting any new voting procedure without prior federal approval. These emergency measures affecting targeted areas were adopted for just five years, but in fact they were renewed with little change five years later (though literacy tests were banned nationwide at that time). Within three months of enactment, Attorney General Nicholas Katzenbach dispatched examiners to thirty-two counties in four states, registering many thousands of new voters in some of the most notorious districts. Although this frenetic early pace soon slowed, by the end of 1967 federal examiners were active in fifty-eight southern counties. In many others, local registrars changed their practices in order to avoid federal intervention.[10]

Figure 6.1 suggests the abruptness and speed of the change. In some states (such as Georgia and North Carolina), registration rates grew fairly steadily from 1940 onward, while others (such as South Carolina and Virginia) showed considerable progress by 1964. But registration increased in all southern states during the late 1960s, and the discontinuity was particularly marked in Alabama, Louisiana, and Mississippi.

Figure 6.1 also shows that black voter registration rates have essentially been maintained since passage of the Voting Rights Act, albeit with fluctuations. Indeed states that were once the worst offenders (Alabama, Louisiana, and Mississippi) have black registration rates notably higher than others. Despite marked swings in state and national politics, no southern state has returned to pre-1960s exclusion practices. Equality in registration between blacks and whites was somewhat longer in coming, in part because white registration rates also increased. But southern black registration rates actually exceeded those of blacks outside the South by the 1980s and were higher than white rates in the same state in many years. Patterns of voter turnout by race were broadly similar.[11]

Black Elected Officials

Dramatic as these breakthroughs were, the path from registration and voting to fair representation in southern politics was far from smooth. There were several striking early successes.

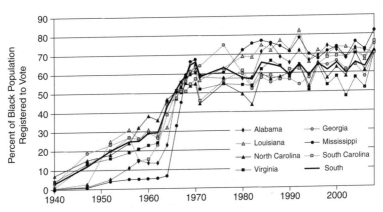

Figure 6.1 Southern black voter registration, 1940–2008. Garrow writes that the decline between 1970 and 1971 is the "wholly artificial" result of changing the population base from 1960 to 1970.

Sources: Voter Education Project, as compiled by Garrow, *Protest at Selma,* pp. 7, 11, 19, 189, 200 (1940–1971); and as compiled by Stanley, *Voter Mobilization,* p. 97 (1976–1980). The figures after 1980 are from the Census Bureau, compiled in Bullock and Gaddie, *Triumph of Voting Rights,* pp. 380–382.

Newly enfranchised voters in Macon County, Alabama, elected a black sheriff for the first time, in 1966. The Freedom Democratic Party of Mississippi successfully backed Robert Clark of Holmes County in his election to the state house of representatives in 1967. And in some cases, black voters influenced electoral contests between white candidates in a favorable direction. A significant example was the defeat of Sheriff Jim Clark, the scourge of Selma, Alabama, by a more moderate opponent in 1966.[12] Refuting pessimistic forecasts, a survey as of the early 1970s reported that "in many areas black southerners have accomplished what many observers thought impossible, that is, to develop effective organization and conduct efficient campaigns." By 1974, in the states covered by the Voting Rights Act, nearly a thousand black officials were serving, compared to just seventy-two in 1965.[13]

Nonetheless a report by the U.S. Commission on Civil Rights on the tenth anniversary of the Voting Rights Act found that black representation was still far below its demographic potential in these states, so that "minorities have not yet gained a foothold on positions of real influence."[14] Although overt barriers to registration and voting had receded (without disappearing entirely), the primary reason for the continued disparity was a series of measures adopted by white-controlled states, counties, and municipalities to alter jurisdictions and voting rules so as to dilute the black vote and minimize its impact. The earliest and most flagrant response was by the state of Mississippi, which in 1966 enacted legislation that (1) allowed counties to appoint rather than elect school superintendents, (2) permitted counties to shift from single-member districts to at-large elections for county commissioners, and (3) substantially increased the number of signatures required for independent candidates to get on the ballot.[15] The intent of these measures was never in doubt. News reports from the legislative session made this clear, one state senator openly stating that countywide balloting would safeguard "a white board and preserve our way of doing business."[16]

Mississippi's actions led to the important Supreme Court decision in *Allen v. State Board of Education* (1969), which held that such changes required federal preclearance. The ruling not only strengthened the hand of the Justice Department but also expanded the interpretation of Section 5 to include a group's power to make its votes effective. The scope of the expansion remained to be worked out over time. In *Mobile v. Bolden* (1980), a divided Court held that vote dilution was actionable only if discriminatory intent could be established. But this severe restriction was promptly reversed by Congress in the 1982 renewal of the Act, which prohibited any voting procedure resulting in members of a protected class having "less opportunity than other members of the electorate to participate in the political process and to elect representatives of their choice," adding that "the extent to which members of a protected class have been elected to office in the State or political subdivision is one circumstance that may be considered" in this determination. The result was a series of judicial rulings and out-of-court settlements in the 1980s, significantly expanding the number of black elected officials in the South. A statistical analysis published in 1994 concluded that the transition was primarily driven by black-majority districts compelled by enforcement of the Voting Rights Act.[17]

Figure 6.2 shows the rise in the number of black elected officials in the South between 1969 and 2001, in comparison with the number in the rest of the nation. Although the increase is continuous, the litigation-driven acceleration in the 1980s is evident. At that point the South surpassed the non-South, where the growth of black elected officials stagnated. The timing thus confirms Congressman Melvin Watt's 2006 statement in support of Voting Rights Act renewal: "Although the successes of the Voting Rights Act have been substantial, they have not been fast and furious. Rather, the successes have been gradual and of recent origin."[18] Watt was first elected to Congress in 1992 after redistricting to create black-majority districts in North Carolina, as one of the first two black representatives from that state in the twentieth century (the other being Eva Clayton).

Table 6.1 presents a statistical summary for 2001, showing that the great majority of these officials were in local government positions, such as county commissioners, city councilors, and school board members. But black candidates also gained seats in southern state legislatures, and these too had their greatest growth spurt in the 1980s and 1990s.[19] Although the Voting Rights Act initiated the process and was central to its success, the results came only after decades of political and judicial struggle.

Table 6.2 presents the same information as an index of proportionate representation, that is, the black share of officeholders relative to the black share of the voting-age population. One can see that blacks were still underrepresented by this measure

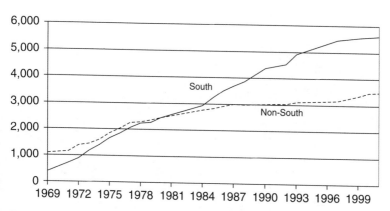

Figure 6.2 Number of black elected officials, 1969–2001.
Source: Joint Center for Political and Economic Studies, *Black Elected Officials*, various issues.

Table 6.1 Number of Black Elected Officials in the South, 2001

State	State Senate	State House	County Commission	Mayor	City Council	Law Enforcement	School Board
Alabama	8	27	80	46	421	57	91
Arkansas	3	12	8	32	231	0	122
Florida	5	17	24	14	120	39	16
Georgia	11	36	95	30	261	43	118
Louisiana	9	22	131	33	219	122	161
Mississippi	10	35	105	54	362	109	124
North Carolina	7	18	57	30	258	29	85
South Carolina	7	24	74	28	219	9	157
Tennessee	3	14	47	3	58	27	27
Texas	2	14	17	34	247	44	87
Virginia	5	10	48	5	72	15	85
SOUTH	70	229	678	309	2,468	494	1073

Source: Joint Center for Political and Economic Studies, *Black Elected Officials: A Statistical Summary 2001*, (2002) Table 2.

in 2001, in most offices in most southern states. The overall index for the South was just 0.375. But as the lower section shows, this level of black representation was much higher than elsewhere in the country, relative to the size of the black population. This regional contrast is surely part of the attractiveness of the South for African Americans.

To be sure, there is no guarantee in the U.S. electoral system that any group will hold offices proportionate to its share of the population. Whether it does so depends on the geographic concentration of its members, as well as the cohesiveness of voting patterns within and between groups. But when a large minority group has been historically excluded from the political process, and voting is still highly polarized by race, there is no way that election rules can be fairly established without considering how the racial composition of officers will be affected. Political scientists debate the extent to which race-conscious voting has diminished in the twenty-first century, but given the historical context, it is difficult to see how these results could have been achieved in any other way. Abigail Thernstrom, who in 1987 was highly critical of the use of the Voting Rights Act to assure fair racial representation, acknowledged in 2009 that she has come "to a greater appreciation of the benefits of race-conscious districting in the South."[20]

An indication that race-conscious voting has persisted is the fact that black southerners have had nowhere near the same success in statewide elections—where no redistricting has occurred. Douglas Wilder's election as governor of Virginia in 1989 stands out as a rare exception. In many ways, it is an exception that proves the rule. Wilder's first successful run for statewide office four years earlier was for lieutenant governor, an official that in Virginia often goes on to contend for the one-term governorship. Not only were both elections extremely close, but the bulk of Wilder's white votes were from northern counties and Hampton Roads, fast-growing areas with large nonnative populations. Elsewhere in the South, few African Americans have held statewide

Table 6.2 Number of Black Elected Officials Relative to Share of Voting-Age Population, 2001

	State Senate	State House	County Commission	Mayor	City Council	School Board	All Elected Offices
Alabama	0.927	1.04	0.979	0.427	0.979	0.427	0.717
Arkansas	0.562	0.85	0.0	0.434	0.0	0.434	0.432
Florida	1.316	1.068	0.503	0.269	0.503	0.269	0.339
Georgia	0.713	0.789	0.512	0.196	0.512	0.196	0.350
Louisiana	0.762	0.723	0.661	0.362	0.661	0.362	0.468
Mississippi	0.62	0.863	0.749	0.539	0.749	0.539	0.565
North Carolina	0.673	0.76	0.913	0.288	0.913	0.288	0.42
South Carolina	0.621	0.721	0.836	0.377	0.836	0.377	0.496
Tennessee	0.607	1.013	0.155	0.06	0.155	0.06	0.176
Texas	0.546	0.782	0.112	0.248	0.112	0.248	0.155
Virginia	0.672	0.591	0.505	0.117	0.505	0.117	0.429
South							0.375

Non-South	0.095
Illinois	0.098
Michigan	0.150
New Jersey	0.213
New York	0.079
Ohio	0.143
Pennsylvania	0.071

Sources: Bullock and Gaddie, *Triumph of Voting Rights*, Table 12.4; Joint Center for Political and Economics Studies, *Black Elected Officials 2001* (2002), Table 3.

office. No black candidate has ever been elected to a state constitutional office in Alabama, Arkansas, Louisiana, Mississippi, South Carolina, or Tennessee. Georgia has been exceptional on this count, electing African Americans to such state offices as attorney general, commissioner of labor, and public service commissioner in 1998, 2002, and 2006.[21]

The essence of the statewide challenge may be seen in Figure 6.3, which compares black and white populations in the four southern states that once had black majorities. Despite robust black in-migration since 1970, the earlier era of racially selective

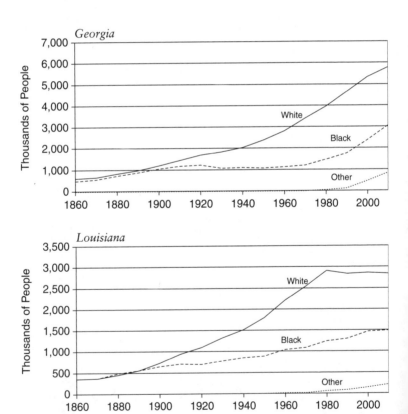

out-migration has left blacks at less than 35 percent of the total in every state except Mississippi (at 37.3 percent in 2010). In order to form a statewide majority, white southerners must join a coalition in which blacks constitute a majority. This has proven to be an uphill struggle in the post–Civil Rights South.

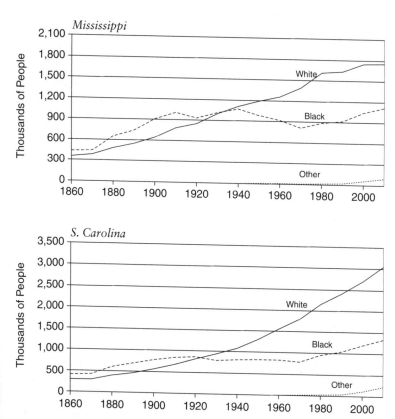

Figure 6.3 Comparison of black and white populations in four southern black majority states, 1860–2010.

Sources: Carter et al. *Historical Statistics of the United States, Millennial Edition.* Vol. 1, Table 2244–2340; U.S. Bureau of the Census. *Statistical Abstract of the United States 2001*, Table 24 (p. 26); *Statistical Abstract 2012*, Table 19 (p. 24).

VOTING AND ECONOMIC GAINS

Did the dramatic rise in black voter registration and elected officials generate tangible gains for the southern black population? It was by no means obvious to participants or observers that electoral politics was the best path to progress. "If Negroes could vote," Martin Luther King told a rally at Selma, "there would be no Jim Clarks, there would be no oppressive poverty directed at Negroes, our children would not be crippled by segregated schools, and the whole community might live together in harmony."[22] But four years earlier, when the Voter Education Project was under discussion, many younger activists argued that the Kennedy administration was trying to stifle direct action protests in its own political interest. Lonnie King of SNCC recalled, "I felt what they were trying to do was kill the Movement, but to kill it by rechanneling its energies."[23] Long after the Voting Rights Act was passed, similar skepticism was often voiced about the efficacy of voting for a group laboring under the weight of extreme poverty, limited education, and determined opponents. As late as 1977 the *New York Times* reported that "the full potential of black political power in Dixie remains unrealized" owing to a lack of political experience, organization, motivation, and economic power.[24]

Despite well-founded grounds for this pessimism, we now have enough historical perspective to confirm that political participation fostered by the Voting Rights Act led to tangible gains over time for black communities in the South. The magnitude of these advances must be understood within limits faced by any local (and even state) economic policies. No individual voter, nor even a large minority group, can reasonably expect that merely electing representatives will reshape national economic policy, much less overthrow the fundamentals of the economic system. Changes of that magnitude require larger political coalitions, and even then may be out of reach in the face of broad technological and economic forces. Within the range of realistic feasibility for local communities, however, the changes wrought by southern voting rights have been real and in many ways fundamental.

An early study by William Keech of the impact of black voting prior to the Voting Rights Act in Tuskegee, Alabama, and Durham, North Carolina, found modest improvements in street paving, garbage collection, recreational facilities, and fire stations in black neighborhoods; new hiring of black firemen; and appointments to boards, commissions, and civil service jobs.[25] Studies undertaken after the Voting Rights Act was passed report gains along similar dimensions in response to increased black political representation: more black police, more paved roads and streetlights, upgraded sanitary conditions, and better access to basic city and county services.[26] In Hancock County, Georgia, pressure from newly enfranchised voters ended racial discrimination in access to Federal Housing Administration (FHA) loans and public assistance.[27] The most systematic effort to track change over time is by political scientist James W. Button, who followed six Florida communities between 1960 and 2000. Table 6.3 displays the percentage of streets paved in black and white subcommunities during this period. The jump in the 1960s is visible, but the continued progress in later decades is nearly as notable. As the white mayor of Titusville explained, "Through the early 1960s the city council was composed of an old-line group of people—rural, southern, here all their lives, and some of whom still carried Civil War memories. Blacks did not receive their fair share of services because they were considered second-, even third-class citizens."[28]

But it would be an error to suppose that a fairer distribution of public services always occurred as a smooth democratic response by elected officials to a new group of voters. There were angry confrontations and threats in every one of Button's Florida communities, in some cases escalating to racial violence. The nearby town of Quincy had a full-scale riot in 1970, when a black policeman shot a crippled black man who allegedly attempted to

Table 6.3   Percentage of Streets Paved in Black and White Subcommunities of Six Florida Cities, 1960–1985

Cities	1960		1970		1980		1985	
	Black	White	Black	White	Black	White	Black	White
Crestview	12	38	30	54	52	70	65	85
Lake City	10	50	20	70	44	87	75	90
Gretna	0	20	53	20	51	40	51	40
Titusville	10	92	40	80	97	91	99	98
Daytona Beach	50	97	70	99	99	100	99	100
Riviera Beach	37	85	40	90	98	100	99	100

Source: Button, *Blacks and Social Change*, Table 5.1.

evade arrest in a local bar. When blacks did achieve positions of power, they did not always act wisely or honestly. In 1977 the black chair of Riviera's housing authority was asked to resign after charges of nepotism, ignoring federal (Department of Housing and Urban Development) guidelines, and hiring and protecting a fugitive felon. The black mayor of Gretna and the police chief of Riviera Beach were both convicted of criminal offenses while in office. Such stories could be multiplied many times over. With all of the turbulence and setbacks, however, the progress in the racial distribution of services and public employment is undeniable. Blacks were participating in local public life in ways that would not have been possible before the Voting Rights Act.

The Voting Rights Act, it is clear, was just one step in a much longer struggle for political mobilization and representation. The Act was pivotal, however, because little of the subsequent history could have happened without it. As a direct test of this statement, political scientist Joel Thompson systematically compared the forty North Carolina counties covered by the Act with another forty-county sample from the same state, matched as closely as possible according to various demographic and economic criteria. Not only did the Voting Rights Act counties have greater increases in black voter registration and elected officials, but they also experienced more rapid growth in black incomes and occupational status and attracted more revenue from both county and outside governmental sources.[29] An earlier study compared Greene County, Alabama, where blacks gained control of county government between 1969 and 1972, with two other counties that were socioeconomically similar but remained in white control. Government employment, public and private investment, and black living standards all grew more rapidly in Greene than in the control counties.[30]

Economic gains from voting strength did not necessarily have to come through victorious black candidates. Lobbying and civic

participation could often secure concessions from white officeholders, especially when black voters constituted a swing vote
between competing candidates or factions. Economists Elizabeth
Cascio and Ebonya Washington show that the elimination of
literacy tests in 1965 was systematically associated with an increase in the share of state transfers to counties with higher black
population shares. The authors estimate that the mean county in
a literacy-test state saw an increase of 12.4 percent in per capita
transfers between 1957–1960 and 1977–1980, compared to
control-group counties. The shift in state resource allocation was
strongly associated with increased turnout in presidential elections but occurred well before any major black representation in
state government.[31]

Black Elected Officials and Public-Sector Employment

Successful black candidates were not the only channel for political impact, yet studies consistently find that the single most important factor in changing the relationship between black citizens and local government has been the emergence of black
public officials. Some observers emphasize the symbolic value of
visible black representation. One black political organizer in
Mississippi remarked, "The number of victories isn't as important as the fact that they symbolize a bit of black authority, a
gradual return to respect for those accustomed to having their
lives manipulated by white hands."[32] Tom McCain, the first African American since Reconstruction to run for office in Edgefield
County, South Carolina, argued, "There's an inherent value in
officeholding that goes far beyond picking up the garbage. A
race of people who are excluded from public office will always
be second class."[33]

As powerful as these subjective dimensions may be, they are
supplemented and reinforced by many very objective services
that black representatives provide for their constituents. Carol
Swain recounts the experience of sitting in the congressional of-

fice of John Lewis, observing a steady stream of ordinary people getting help with problems.[34] Lawrence Hanks provides the following list of services provided by black elected officials in Hancock County, Georgia, between 1966 and 1980: securing FHA loans, helping eligible constituents to apply for welfare, Social Security recertification, assistance with health care delivery, assistance with personal matters, and providing information on nongovernmental matters. Such routine services compose a surprisingly large share of the activity of many officials' work, and quite possibly white officeholders also try to assist black constituents in the post–Voting Rights Act era. But as Judge Edith Ingram of Hancock County explained, "A good 85 to 90 percent of the work that we do is non-office related work, but these people have no one else to depend on—they trust us, so we do it."[35] Similarly, a black official in Panola County, Mississippi, noted, "Blacks feel they can come to me and get answers to problems; they have a connection with the system."[36]

One of the most tangible and also most controversial ways in which political representation has benefited black citizens is in the racial composition of public-sector employment. There is little doubt that the impact has been positive. Table 6.4 shows black employment by department in the six Florida cities tracked by James Button, from 1960 to 2000. Both the number and share increased after 1960 in every department. The number of black supervisors grew more slowly, but these too began to rise after 1970, matching the educational and occupational upgrading of the private sector. National studies often report that the minority share of the population is the single most important factor accounting for minority public-sector employment, but for these six cities, Button and his colleagues find that black political power provides the stronger explanation.[37]

Because law enforcement officers were politically unaccountable to blacks in the South in the pre–Civil Rights era, the increased representation on police forces constitutes both a job

Table 6.4   Black Municipal Employment in Six Florida Cities,
1960–2000

Year	Police N(%)	Fire N(%)	Recreation N(%)	Public Works N(%)
	Black Employment by Department			
1960	14 (9.5)	0	9 (23.1)	84 (38.2)
1970	20 (9.0)	6 (3.5)	29 (29.0)	149 (48.9)
1980	62 (17.3)	22 (9.4)	63 (37.1)	215 (47.6)
1990	95 (19.9)	29 (10.8)	63 (35.6)	168 (36.8)
2000	108 (20.0)	42 (13.7)	77 (37.2)	194 (35.3)
	Black Supervisors by Department			
1960	0	0	2 (16.7)	0
1970	4 (7.6)	0	6 (28.6)	3 (8.8)
1980	9 (11.4)	2 (3.5)	15 (44.1)	12 (28.6)
1990	22 (19.6)	6 (7.2)	12 (34.3)	19 (27.5)
2000	35 (31.3)	11 (14.1)	13 (26.0)	26 (29.2)

Source: Button, Rienzo, and Croucher, *Blacks and the Quest for Economic Equality,* Table 4.1.

opportunity and a subjective improvement in a public service. Much the same can be said for school boards. Studies of school boards in Texas find that higher numbers of black and Latino school board members are associated with more minority teachers and administrators. The authors link these employment gains in turn with more equitable educational policies and improved minority performance.[38]

The biggest increases in black public-sector employment were in large cities with black city councils and mayors. When Atlanta first elected a black mayor in 1973, black employment rose from 38.1 to 55.6 percent of the total; black administrators jumped from 7.1 to 32.6 percent, and professionals from 15.2 to 42.2 percent.[39] In Richmond, Virginia, black city employment was restricted to service and maintenance jobs until 1963. Blacks attained a majority in the city council in 1977, after redistricting in response to a Supreme Court ruling rejecting a proposed annexation. As a direct result, the parity score for minority employment (the share of employment divided by the minority share of the population) increased from 0.756 to 1.10. As in Atlanta, employment shares rose most rapidly in administrative and professional categories. When a liberal black regime was replaced in 1982 by a more conservative black mayor backed by a multiracial coalition, the number of black professionals declined, but parity scores were stable or increased for most occupational categories. In other words, gains in black public-sector employment were consolidated and even extended, despite subsequent political fluctuations.[40]

Using a national panel of cities and metropolitan areas for 1971–2004, economists John V. C. Nye, Ilia Rainier, and Thomas Stratmann find that election of a black mayor in a city with a large black population had a large positive impact on black employment, labor force participation, and income.[41] The effects were greatest in the public sector, but private-sector black employment also increased. This result may have worked through the mayor's influence on the allocation of city contracts. One recent study found that contracting set-asides significantly raised the self-employment and employment rates of black men in these cities during the 1980s.[42]

WERE THESE GAINS AT THE EXPENSE OF WHITE SOUTHERNERS?

If we think of political offices and public-sector jobs as the "spoils" of electoral victory, then obviously white incumbents lost something when candidates backed by newly enfranchised black voters assumed office and assigned some positions to blacks that had previously been reserved for whites. Further, to the extent that the total supply of local public services was fixed or at least constrained by available revenues, a larger share for black citizens and neighborhoods meant that whites got less than they had before. Thus there was an unavoidable distributional aspect to local government, and some political scientists analyze local politics almost exclusively in these terms. Changing beneficiaries as the result of elections is a routine part of American political life, though the new racial order in the post–Voting Rights South may have been unique.

But from a longer-term perspective, what we want to know is whether black political representation and power were *primarily* concerned with redistribution of governmental "rents," in the parlance of economics. Perhaps fearing retaliation for past sins, white forecasts of impending doom were common. The mayor of Montezuma, Georgia, wrote, "Lord knows what would happen if we turned the rabble of their race loose at the polls. I have one very strong belief and that is that they would takeover Macon County and run it according to their own beliefs and consciences." A Democratic Party official from the same county predicted that black voting would "destroy Macon County and others that have a colored population exceeding the white." Less than ten years later, when the election of Maynard Jackson as Atlanta's first black mayor was imminent, his white opponent displayed billboards reading, "Atlanta's too young to die," and said, "One can almost see them singing and dancing in the streets in anticipation of a black takeover."[43]

By and large, these disaster scenarios did not occur. In many cases that have been recounted, black voting has encouraged participation in local politics and enhanced the quality of civic life.[44] In some localities, new black officeholders activated civic improvements and invigorated economic development projects. John McCown, a newly elected county commissioner, for example, founded a community-development corporation in Hancock County, Georgia, in 1970, which sponsored feasibility studies for local industry and assisted area farmers moving into catfish farming.[45] The town of Gretna, Florida, made significant progress after blacks assumed political power in 1970: new administrations were able to establish a town hall, a sewer system and treatment plant, a pilot solar energy system, and (by 1981) a large multipurpose municipal complex, with plans for an industrial park.[46] Returning to Panola County, Mississippi, after a twenty-year absence, Frederick Wirt found, "Among white leaders of Panola County there was generally a sense that voting changes had benefited not merely blacks, but whites as well. . . . Whites reported that black empowerment had helped them overturn the old power holders and the planters who had blocked racial and economic change."[47]

In some areas, local black power was long delayed because fearful whites resisted through various legal and political stratagems. But in Keysville, Georgia, when a protracted struggle over voting was finally settled in 1990, the town blossomed under the leadership of a black mayor and council. Within a few short years, Keysville had a new city hall, clinic, recreation center, fire station, street lights, and water tower, all of which benefited white residents as well as black. As Mayor Emma Gresham explained, "We had to prove to whites that we were not going to have power and leave them out. The burden was on us to include them."[48]

One of the main channels through which black officials were able to improve local economic conditions was vigorous pursuit of federal funds for health care facilities, housing, education, and other social services. In Lowndes County, Alabama, Charles Smith—the first black voter in 1965—became a county commissioner in 1972, "just in time to intervene on behalf of the group . . . organized to maintain the health center."[49] In Gretna black officials pushed through an annexation plan over white opposition, nearly doubling the town's population and qualifying it for a greater share of federal revenue-sharing funds. By the late 1970s Gretna's reliance on these funds was so extensive that critics called it the "federal government's town." Yet a county paper praised Gretna, saying it was "at the forefront of progress in Gadsden County."[50]

In Melissa Fay Greene's gripping narrative of McIntosh County, Georgia, where black political representation was delayed until 1978, the newly elected black county commissioner oversaw the creation of a hospital authority and a physician-staffed medical building deep in the county . . . brought plumbing and water to settlements where people used outhouses and wells . . . arranged for a renovation assistance program that aided homeowners in adding bathrooms to their cabins . . . saw that a multipurpose building was built for the antebellum black community on Sapelo Island [and] attracted a grant to build a mental health facility out in the county.[51]

Much of this was financed by the federal government, which of course required that the facilities be desegregated. But such projects infused outside funds into the community, and the new services were available to white as well as black residents.

These accounts from rural and small-town areas of the South, inspiring as some of them are, must be kept in perspective. Black political power has brought tangible economic benefits to black residents, and with the aid of federal funding some of the worst conditions of poverty have been alleviated. For the most part, these gains have not been realized at the expense of white residents. But with rare exceptions, ambitious plans for economic development in these areas have not been successful. They were poor prior to the Civil Rights era, and, allowing for some positive adjustment of standards over time, they remain poor today. For reasons far beyond the reach of local and county governments, economic growth in the South over the past half-century has been overwhelmingly concentrated in metropolitan areas. In order to assess the effects of voting rights on black and white well-being, we have to turn to the cities.

Biracial Coalitions for Economic Growth

White Atlantans were not alone in fearing that black political ascendancy in their city would kill economic progress by precipitating white flight and discouraging business investment. And some historians suggest that these scenarios actually came to pass. In his study of Atlanta, historian Kevin Kruse argues that whites responded to desegregation first by abandoning public spaces (buses, pools, parks) and ultimately by abandoning the city altogether (primarily to avoid integrated schools). Kruse concludes, "In an ironic touch, the Civil Rights Act succeeded in eliminating the last vestiges of segregation in the South but, in so doing, etched the worldview of segregationists ever more firmly onto the political landscape. . . . In the end, the new world of Atlanta looked much like the old."[52] As in other parts of the country, in the 1970s many southern central urban areas were all but given up as lost economic causes, at which point the achievement of black political representation seemed like a hollow prize. Over a longer time horizon, however, many of these cities have shown hopeful signs of resurgence, as they actively try to differentiate themselves in competing for diverse, mobile firms and individuals. New South cities are now well represented in lists of high-achieving urban areas.[53]

In many of these successful cities, black political representation did not threaten economic progress but instead fostered what Carl Abbott calls the "biracial coalition for economic growth." In as unlikely a setting as Jackson, Mississippi, according to voting-rights attorney Frank Parker,

> when the section 2 lawsuit appeared to make change to single-member districts inevitable, influential elements of the white political leadership and downtown business establishment supported the referendum to change Jackson's form of government. In part, they wanted to retain the ability to draw the district lines, but they also apparently believed that black representation in city government would end the controversy over exclusion of black representation and create a more stable environment for business growth and development.[54]

Were these expectations accurate? In 1997 Jackson elected Harvey Johnson Jr. as its first black mayor; he successfully backed a referendum for a convention center during his second term. In 2009 the self-styled "City with Soul" was ranked by *Forbes* magazine as the third-best "Bang for Your Buck" city in the nation, just behind Little Rock.[55]

A more famous example of urban growth in the post–Civil Rights era is Charlotte, North Carolina. A railroad center and cotton mill town in the nineteenth century, Charlotte emerged in the 1970s as the banking hub for the entire southeastern region. Although school desegregation was highly contentious, the city did not suffer white flight, in part because of the consolidation of city and county school districts in 1960. Consensus around the busing plan in the 1970s also solidified community support for the pro-growth agenda. The move to district representatives in 1977 increased black participation and contributed to passage of an airport bond issue in 1978, reversing an earlier defeat. The election of Civil Rights hero Harvey Gantt as mayor in 1981 seemed to symbolize the "biracial coalition around economic growth." True, the consensus on busing ultimately unraveled. But Charlotte was still rated as the best city for African Americans by *Essence* magazine in 1998, and fourth-best by *Black Enterprise* in 2001, at which point the city had become the third-largest banking center in the nation. Clearly neither desegregation nor black political voice was bad for economic progress.[56]

A greater economic challenge was Birmingham, Alabama, where steel output was already in decline during the 1950s, foreshadowing the massive job losses of the 1970s. Long before 1963, Birmingham's race relations were widely considered the worst in the nation, featuring more than fifty bombings between 1947 and 1963. When Richard Arrington was elected as Birmingham's first black mayor in 1979, the economic base was collapsing and whites were fleeing the city in droves. Hollow prize indeed.

But appearances can be deceiving. On closer inspection, one may observe that many local businessmen were well aware of the need for an alternative path for Birmingham, and efforts to restructure the economy had been under way for some time. As early as 1944, Birmingham was chosen by the University of Alabama as the site of its new medical college. In the 1950s commercial interests and their political allies saw the potential of using federal funds for hospitals and urban renewal as a way to revive the downtown area. In 1962 this group initiated a plan to reform the city government by shifting from the commission to a strong mayor-council form in an effort to streamline the development agenda associated with the medical center and thereby encourage merger with the suburbs. Desegregation was by no means a priority or even a goal of this reform agenda, but the need to deal with the federal government and concern for the city's reputation pushed the reformers into a moderate position on race issues. The reform referendum passed by a slim margin in November 1962; the civic breakdown of May 1963 occurred during an interregnum during which the outcome was under court appeal and no one was clearly in charge of city government. Thus a transition of some sort from the Bull Connor era would have happened even without the traumatic events for which Birmingham became world-famous.[57]

Seen in this light, the Civil Rights revolution was favorable to Birmingham's long-term development by opening decisions to black participation and reshaping these plans to gain black support. In the early 1950s the NAACP opposed the proposed hospital expansion, both because the facilities were segregated (as permitted under the Hill-Burton Act) and because of the absence of relocation plans for the displaced population. (This was before the NAACP was banned by the state in 1956.) The Birmingham Downtown Improvement Association proposed a master plan in August 1961, but a bond issue for implementation was defeated. During the 1960s federal approval and funding was held up until the hospital desegregated (in April 1965) and until planning committees added black members. By the end of the decade, the University of Alabama at Birmingham—an autonomous university as of 1969—was actively celebrating the diversity of its student body and workforce.[58]

Reform of Birmingham city government was affirmed by a ballot measure in December 1964, this time by a much wider margin and with the support of new black voters. As registration increased and the city moved into black-majority status in the

1970s, the influence of black voters was decisive in approval of bond issues to improve municipal services. The Chamber of Commerce opened its membership to blacks, and a new biracial Community Affairs Committee prompted cooperation between black and white moderates that would have been unthinkable in the Jim Crow era. Arrington's twenty years in office were marked by collaboration with the largely white business community and its program for central-city development.[59]

Since the 1980s Birmingham's growth has centered on the university and medical center, but with diversification into bio-technology, banking, insurance, and publishing, as well as construction. Although most of the area's population growth has been in the suburbs, new businesses have also moved into eighty square miles of largely vacant land annexed by the city.[60] The majority-black population has certainly shared in this turnaround; indeed Birmingham has generated more black professional and middle-class employment than Charlotte, relative to city size. Black-owned businesses have also recovered since 1982, assisted in part by the system of public-private partnerships initiated in 1989 (the Birmingham Plan), which markedly increased minority participation in both public and private sectors. These programs have been highly controversial, prompting federal investigations and charges of corruption against Arrington himself. But Birmingham has clearly recovered, and the gains from this recovery have been shared by whites as well as blacks in the metropolitan area.[61]

As for Atlanta, its success as the base of the southeastern regional economy is well-known, as is its status as a center for African American politics and culture. With the fourth-largest concentration of Fortune 500 companies, the world's busiest airport since 1998, prominent universities and related industries in information technology and telecommunications, Atlanta is now a world city—with black political leadership. It is hardly surprising that the metropolitan area has been by far the most popular destination for black in-migrants for decades. But what should be surprising, in light of earlier pessimistic assessments of its race relations and Civil Rights legacy, is that the city's white population has been growing even more rapidly since 1990, so that the white population share has increased faster than in any other U.S. city during this time.[62] If the city can attract young, educated, multiracial people in this way, its black political leaders must have been doing something right with the power they assumed in the 1970s under the aegis of the Voting Rights Act. There is much that might be said about the Atlanta phenomenon. What cannot be said is that black economic gains through political channels have come mainly at white expense.

THE VOTING RIGHTS ACT AND THE TWO-PARTY SOUTH

One of the most frequently quoted remarks of the Civil Rights era is what Lyndon Johnson is supposed to have said to his aide Bill Moyers after signing the historic 1964 bill: "I have just handed the South to the Republicans for a generation." It is quoted because it seems so prophetic. But as commonly used, the remark is deeply misleading. LBJ was not one for selfless political sacrifices. He well knew that the Civil Rights Act of 1964 badly damaged him and his party with the white South. But he also believed that the Voting Rights Act of 1965 would go far to repair this damage, by making liberal Democrats competitive in southern states. In a memo entitled "Negro Vote in the South," Presidential aide Lawrence O'Brien pointed out that black voters had provided LBJ's margin of victory in four southern states.[63] Martin Luther King expanded on this argument when the President called on his birthday in January 1965: "It's very interesting, Mr. President, to note that the only states you didn't carry in the South . . . have less than forty percent of the Negroes registered to vote. . . . It's so important to get Negroes registered in large numbers in the South. It would be this coalition of the Negro vote and the moderate white vote that will really make the new South."[64] This vision was sufficiently compelling to attract the votes of thirty-three southern Democrats in support of the Voting

Rights Act, including ten who had opposed the Civil Rights bill one year earlier.[65]

Far from turning the South over to the Republicans, the Voting Rights Act ushered in twenty-five years of vigorous new two-party competition. Figure 6.4 shows the division of senators and governors by party from 1960 to 2010. True, Republican strength increased almost immediately from its 1960 position of zero. But Democrats continued to be not only competitive but successful in statewide elections; the new competition had a moderating effect on both parties, as they tried to appeal for the first time to black voters. Thus moderate Democrats like John West of South Carolina, Reubin Askew of Florida, and Jimmy Carter of Georgia defeated segregationist opponents in the elections of 1970. In Arkansas, moderate Republican Winthrop Rockefeller won the governorship in 1966, only to lose four years later to moderate Democrat Dale Bumpers (who had defeated segregationist hero Orval Faubus in a Democratic primary runoff). Through the 1980s, Democratic senatorial candidates won by combining white with majority-black support, just as King had predicted in 1965.[66]

Appealing to black voters sounds promising, but did the advent of interparty competition have real consequences for ordinary people? One of the most direct effects was the rapid disappearance of racist rhetoric in campaigns, long a staple of regional politics. Veteran Southern Regional Council advocate Benjamin Muse noted that as early as 1966, the tone of political campaigns in the South "showed a revolutionary improvement over previous years."[67] In the once incorrigible state of South Carolina, observers reported that "the increase in African-American voter registration and turnout almost immediately eliminated the white supremacist rhetoric that had been a hallmark of the state's leaders."[68] Former Dixiecrat candidate Strom Thurmond, who became a Republican and endorsed Barry Goldwater in 1964, was one of the first prominent southern politicians to get the new message. After backing a segregationist Republican gubernatorial candidate in 1970 (who lost to progressive Democrat John West), Thurmond became the first southern senator to appoint a black staff aide and the first to sponsor an African American for a federal judgeship. For the rest of his career, Thurmond actively sought black votes, with considerable success.[69]

Within a few years of the Voting Rights Act, even the most unlikely parts of the South had changed their tune. Frank Parker describes the 1971 governor's race in Mississippi:

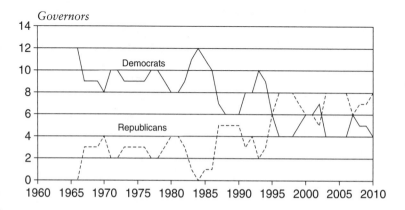

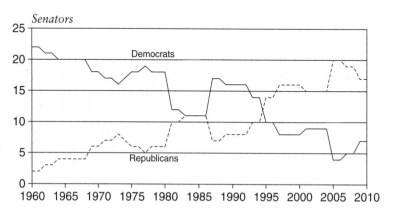

Figure 6.4 Comparison of U.S. governors with U.S. senators by party, 1960–2010.

Source: Statistical Abstract of the United States, various issues.

For the first time in the modern history of the state the two leading candidates . . . did not campaign as segregationists. [William] Waller's election in 1971 marked the beginning of the transition in Mississippi politics to ending the dominance of segregationist rhetoric in statewide campaigns. After 1971, none of the winning candidates for governor have employed open racial rhetoric in their campaigns, and in fact the candidates have appealed to black voters to get elected.[70]

A milestone for Alabama was reached in 1982, when archsegregationist George Wallace apologized for his racist past and openly solicited black votes in a new gubernatorial campaign. Stressing economic issues, Wallace easily defeated the Republican mayor of Montgomery, who deployed the law-and-order rhetoric of which Wallace was a past master.[71] Whatever one may say about hypocrisy and political opportunism, the new southern campaign rhetoric marked an epochal change in the relationship of African Americans to southern politics and government.

Voting Rights and Public Policy in Southern States

Civilizing public discourse was of inestimable value for black southerners. But did the massive number of new black voters have an impact on public policy in the states, particularly economic policies with effects on the lives of ordinary people? Isolating the "voting rights effect" is not easy because the 1960s saw many other important changes bearing on southern politics. The two most prominent were the reapportionment revolution initiated by *Baker v. Carr* (1962), which overthrew the historic overrepresentation of rural areas; and increased southern white voter turnout, which was partly a racial countermobilization but also reflected lower barriers to registration, the inflow of better-educated migrants into the South, and increased competition in southern general elections.[72] We cannot hope to disentangle the effects of each one of these developments. But V. O. Key's classic analysis held that white supremacy, single-party politics, and Black Belt dominance were components of a unified southern political formation, depriving the region of economically progressive state policies, to the ultimate detriment of both races.[73] We can at least examine broad trends in post–Voting Rights policies to see whether Key's implicit forecast was accurate.

One economic study found that expansion of the franchise after 1965 led to a sharp rise in welfare spending but had no other consistent impact on state and local spending.[74] The study was designed to test hypotheses about voting and the size of government rather than southern state policies, so the scope of the results is narrow. Voting rights did indeed lead to increased welfare coverage and payments in plantation Black Belt counties, where elites had long used managed relief programs in their own narrow interests.[75] But other studies report much broader effects on southern state budgets, including allocations for hospitals, roads, and libraries.[76] Kerry Haynie finds that greater black representation in state legislatures tended to raise spending on health, education, and social welfare.[77]

A policy area bearing directly on long-term economic well-being is public education. Many observers (including segregationists) predicted that desegregation of the schools would lead not only to resegregation through white flight but also to loss of political support for public schools. After the Voting Rights Act, however, southern gubernatorial campaigns increasingly featured nonracial themes of economic development and education.[78] Figure 6.5 graphs per pupil spending on K–12 education for six southern states from 1948 to 1965 as a fraction of the national average, showing that Georgia, North Carolina, South Carolina, and Virginia actually accelerated their progress during these years. Only in Mississippi and Alabama did spending decline during the turbulent period 1966–1970, after which growth resumed. Some of the increase reflected new federal support for public schools in low-income areas, but most of it was the result of new state policy priorities, led by a cohort of New South governors.

In South Carolina, after defeating a segregationist opponent with the help of black voters in 1970, Governor John West launched a major effort to reduce high school dropout rates, particularly among blacks. Increased state spending between 1965 and 1975 was largely driven by surging revenues rather than increased taxes (reflecting the booming Sun Belt economy), but the share of the budget allocated to education sharply increased.[79] In Alabama, Governor Albert Brewer (who assumed office after the death of Lurleen Wallace) steered a major education reform package through the state legislature in 1969, saying, "Our problem is not race [but education]." When funds ballooned in the Special Education Trust Fund, Brewer allocated them to teachers' salaries and capital improvements in schools. True, Brewer was defeated by George Wallace in 1970, but an atmosphere of expansionary optimism continued into the 1980s, culminating in the Education Reform Act of 1984.[80] Even Mississippi, long the most educationally backward state, belatedly got into the reform act. The state's compulsory education law,

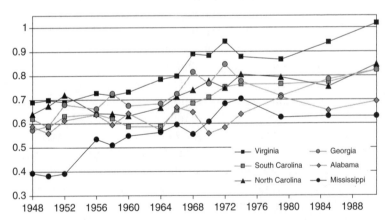

Figure 6.5 Per pupil spending in K–12 public schools as a percentage of U.S. average, 1948–1991.

Source: National Center for Education Statistics. *Digest of Education Statistics*, various years.

repealed in 1956 during the desegregation crisis, was reenacted in 1977. Gubernatorial candidate William Waller ran on an educational reform platform in 1979 and got most of his plan through the state legislature in 1982. With biracial support, state funding for kindergarten was introduced, teacher pay increased, and performance-based accreditation was instituted. Performance gains from a new assistant-teacher program were said to be "one of the most visible signs of educational progress in the state."[81] Mississippi was the last state to provide funding for kindergarten; every other state in the former Confederacy had enacted this reform between 1968 and 1978.[82]

It would be hopeless to attempt to delineate the precise political calculations that generated these reforms and funding allocations. Assertions that better-quality public schools were essential for economic development were advanced by both races in every state, though their persuasiveness is difficult to judge. No doubt some white politicians believed that increased funding for all schools would reduce the pressure for more thoroughgoing desegregation. Such thinking was evidently present in Florida, where voters overwhelmingly approved an antibusing referendum in 1972, but also approved an equal education opportunity program, embodied in Governor Reubin Askew's sweeping progressive educational reform act of 1973.[83] Trading racial integration for funding was a common form of interracial bargaining in the post–Voting Rights South. The fact that the bill would be shared with the federal government also doubtless influenced the willingness of white politicians to support improvements in public schools.

But American politics is always a complex package of mixed motives and compromises. At least black voters and their representatives were in on the negotiations during this phase of southern history. Once the massive-resistance logjam was broken, the new fluidity in southern politics meant that blacks did not necessarily require a majority in order to influence policy outcomes. It did, after all, take some political gumption for white politicians to support funding for a kindergarten program that opponents denounced as "day-care centers for blacks."[84] The least one can say is that this showed considerably more black political influence than in earlier times. The question looming over southern political history is whether the era of large black influence has now given way to a new regime of one-party state politics, in which black representatives are largely excluded from essential decision making because they are members of a permanent minority power with little chance of prevailing in statewide elections.

THE END OF THE SECOND RECONSTRUCTION?

The era of vigorous two-party competition came to an end in most southern states during the 1990s, as the Republican Party consolidated its dominant position as the home of white conservatives. This development culminated a longer-term trend, but the outcome marked a qualitative change in regional politics. Viewing southern party realignment in combination with complementary shifts in federal policy and judicial rulings, many observers saw the decade as the end of sympathetic accommodation to the Civil Rights revolution, a period often referred to as the Second Reconstruction.[85]

Was the rise of the southern Republican Right essentially a racial affair, a white reaction to black political and economic gains? There is much to be said for this perspective. At times the racial coding of campaign rhetoric is barely disguised, as in phrases like "He's one of us" or disdainful references to "special interest groups." The election of Civil Rights hero Harvey Gantt as mayor of Charlotte in 1983 seemed to symbolize the optimism of the new, more cooperative biracial era. But Gantt lost to a Republican in 1987, and the city's celebrated busing plan was soon dismantled. Gantt then lost senatorial elections in 1990 and 1996 to Jesse Helms, in campaigns that featured blatant racial appeals. Statewide campaigns in Georgia, South Carolina, and Mississippi were dominated by the racially charged issue of Confederate symbols on the state flag. In Duval County,

Florida, white election officials publicly rebuffed black political leaders.[86]

More comprehensive analyses, however, show that the new partisan alignment in the South was by no means a restoration of the pre–Civil Rights political order. The success of the Republican Right constituted a political innovation, a new ideological package of cultural and economic appeals that attracted relatively disparate groups into one coalition. Central to its success was the articulation of a nonracial ideology, in which low taxes and neighborhood schools echoed traditional American individualist values and a desire to escape intrusive government intrusions. In this formulation, the accomplishments of the Civil Rights Movement were embraced as objects of local and regional pride, often in the rhetoric of color blindness to oppose affirmative action and desegregation efforts. Decisive evidence in support of the *innovation* over the *redemption* interpretation lies in the fact that conservative Republican candidates found their strongest support not in the old Black Belt counties but in the growing suburbs of metropolitan areas, heavily populated by migrants from other parts of the country.[87]

Whatever the mixture of motivations and constituencies, the effect in many southern states has been to isolate African Americans politically and to stifle or reverse the policy programs they support. In Alabama, for example, the Plans for Excellence educational reform came to an abrupt halt with the election of Republican Guy Hunt in 1986, and the reform act itself was repealed in 1988. Subsequent efforts to revamp the state's school finance system were decisively turned back.[88] Convergence toward the national average in per pupil spending ceased or reversed in Florida, Georgia, Louisiana, North Carolina, South Carolina, Tennessee, and Texas. Most ominously, Republican control of the state legislature ended the advancement of black legislators to positions of leadership in such states as Georgia, South Carolina, and North Carolina.[89] More recent analysis of legislative influence finds that the positive effects of black representation on policy outcomes are vitiated when parties are highly racialized and the opposite party is in power—a way of describing most of the South since the 1990s.[90]

It is premature to declare that the era of the voting rights revolution and biracial coalitions in the South has come to an end. Black entry into the political process in southern counties and cities is not reversible, as may also be said of local gains in racial equity and cooperation. Prospects at the state level are less encouraging, for basic structural reasons. But Figure 6.4 suggests the one-party dominance is much more accentuated for senators, who are oriented toward national issues, than for governors, where fluid issues and diverse constituencies still foster reversals of party control. Nor is it the case that southern Republican governors are invariably committed to rigid policy agendas hostile to minority interests. Nonetheless, for the foreseeable future, the most urgent political task in the South will be cultivation of genuinely interracial coalitions.

CHAPTER 7

THE DOWNSIDE OF
THE CIVIL RIGHTS REVOLUTION

No revolution succeeds without costs and reactions, and the Civil Rights revolution is no exception. This chapter discusses three downsides that are often raised in discussions of the movement's long-term legacy: (1) the devastating effect of desegregation on black business districts, especially in southern cities and towns; (2) the persistence of poverty in the South, disproportionately among African Americans; and (3) the possibility that the political and ideological legacy of the Civil Rights era has served to impede further progress in recent decades. The purpose of this review is not to deplore, dismiss, or deny these developments and contentions but to try to understand how they relate historically to the Civil Rights revolution and how they have unfolded from a longer-term perspective.

THE RISE AND DECLINE OF BLACK
BUSINESS DISTRICTS

Many observers have noted that the opening of southern businesses to black customers and employees constituted a setback for black-owned businesses that catered to a semicaptive market protected by segregation. Peter Applebome concluded his extended stint as a southern correspondent for the *New York Times* by writing in 1996 that black nostalgia for the segregation era "has become a common theme throughout the South." The revolution, he wrote, was "a mixed blessing for southern blacks, who won a measure of integration into a white world at the expense of some of the enduring and nurturing institutions of the old black one."[1] Confirming Applebome's observation, many black writers use stronger language. According to business historian Robert E. Weems Jr., "White-owned businesses, rather than unfettered black consumers, were the primary beneficiaries of the Civil Rights Act of 1964."[2] Russ Rymer writes:

> Integration was by its nature incomplete. . . . Black customers eschewed the stores and banks—and insurance companies and beach resorts—to which they had long been relegated, propelled by the conviction, as the popular phrase went, that "the white man's ice is colder." Whites did not cross the same border to patronize black enterprises. Integration became the greatest opening of a domestic market in American history, but the windfall went in only one direction, with predictable, if unforeseen results: the whole economic skeleton of the black community, so painfully erected in the face of exclusion and injustice, collapsed as that exclusion was rescinded. In this way, integration wiped out or humbled an important echelon of the black community—the nonclergy leadership class that had fought so hard for civil rights and was needed to show the way to pragmatic prosperity.[3]

Weems and Rymer would have no problem accepting the evidence in Chapter 3 that desegregation was good for southern white business, but they emphasize the downside of the coin: adverse if unintended consequences for southern black business.

The rise of black businesses during the Jim Crow era was indeed remarkable, a development hailed by both W. E. B. Du Bois and Booker T. Washington. Southern cities typically did not have the northern form of residential segregation, a single neighborhood of concentrated black population, but instead featured "urban clusters" in areas considered undesirable by whites, often on the outskirts of the urban area. These patterns, combined with exclusion from downtown areas, created opportunities for black entrepreneurs, who opened corner grocery stores, saloons, billiard halls, beauty parlors, barbershops, and funeral homes for an almost exclusively black clientele. In Memphis, for example, the 1900 *City Directory* listed 248 black-owned businesses. By 1910 the number had more than doubled to 599, while Atlanta had 789, New Orleans 753, Nashville 534, and Savannah 212. The most rapid growth of black business during this era was in Richmond, Virginia, which fostered several interconnected "anchor business" complexes of banks, newspapers, and insurance, real estate investment, retail, and manufacturing enterprises. The much smaller city of Durham, North Carolina, nonetheless supported two centers of diverse and energetic black businesses. Durham's prize businesses were two major financial firms that were fully competitive in the open market: North Carolina Mutual Life Insurance Company and Mechanics and Farmers Bank. Because of its financial sophistication, Parrish Street in Durham was often called the "Wall Street of Negro America."[4]

Historical accounts stress that black business districts were not merely opportunities for profit but promoted a sense of community and self-reliance, along with churches, schools, and benevolent societies. Rymer provides compelling quotations from living memory about Ashley Street, the main artery of black Jacksonville, Florida, which from the 1920s into the 1950s supported theaters, ballrooms, taprooms, and a massive Masonic Hall. "I mean, Ashley Street was *it*," recalled jazz percussionist Billy Moore. "People used to dress up on Sunday and go strolling on Ashley, just like in New York you used to go strolling on 125th Street." Another Jacksonville native remembered, "We didn't have to ask the white man for nothing. *Nothing!* Back then, you could go from sunup to sundown and never bother with white people. That's how self-contained it was."[5]

An important business with strong links to black culture was the funeral home, often associated with burial insurance. Black mourning and funeral customs are said to trace back to roots in

West and Central Africa, placing a high value on a proper and dignified burial as an act of kinship. As a consequence, when the occupation of funeral director emerged as a profession in the late nineteenth century—associated with the distinctive skills involved in embalming—a black funeral industry grew in parallel with its white counterpart, offering one of the most viable business careers open to African Americans throughout the twentieth century. Perhaps the most famous black funeral director was A. J. Gaston of Birmingham, Alabama, who began his successful business career with a burial society, subsequently expanding into insurance, banking, construction, and motels. For Gaston and others, the economic independence of the funeral business allowed them to play an active role in the Civil Rights Movement, relatively free of threats of retaliation. Thus C. W. Lee, a prominent black funeral director in Montgomery, Alabama, led the National Negro Funeral Directors Association in its support for the bus boycott of 1955. Gaston and another funeral director, William E. Shortridge, were active in the Birmingham campaigns. Gaston offered his office building and motel as meeting places for movement leaders, one result being that his motel was bombed on May 12, 1963, at the height of the Birmingham protests.[6]

The decline and disappearance of black business districts and traditions are often lamented. Revisiting great Civil Rights sites in the 1980s, James Baldwin found "disappointment and let-down" nearly everywhere. "When downtown Atlanta was finally integrated," Hosea Williams told Baldwin, "blacks streamed out of their own neighborhoods to patronize previously off-limits white establishments. Black businesses failed."[7] But the fate of other black districts was far worse. As Rymer points out, Sweet Auburn in Atlanta "at least displays the fossil remains of its former vitality." The businesses on Ashley Street "are not only closed, all signs of them have vaporized." As Billy Moore put it, "When society integrated, it all crumbled." Another resident phrased it this way: "First we had segregation, and then integration. Then disintegration."[8] The black business district of Birmingham was also hard-hit. A 1975 study documented the decline of black-owned Birmingham businesses and concluded, "If current trends continue, the whole district may be transformed into a parking area."[9] One black legislator and businessman told a reporter in 1981, "Desegregation improved social conditions—it just didn't work out economically."[10]

The decline of black-owned insurance companies often receives special attention. Rymer laments the 1987 bankruptcy of Jacksonville's Afro-American Life Insurance Company, which was founded in 1901 by Abraham Lincoln Lewis and had once been Florida's largest employer of blacks. Weems calls this a "crumbling legacy," noting the fall from fifty black-owned insurance companies in 1962 to twenty-three in 1992, with a roughly commensurate fall in employment by these firms.[11] By the 1990s even the traditional black funeral business had come under competitive attack. The *Wall Street Journal* reported in 1997 that many family-owned black funeral homes that had long been mainstays of local communities had become targets of aggressive buyout bids from the mainstream white industry, "now quite willing to renounce its segregationist past in search of a new market share."[12]

The poignancy of these accounts is not diminished by pointing out that many other forces besides desegregation were also at work. The diffusion of the automobile and the proliferation of suburban malls undermined traditional central-city and small-town shopping areas all over the country, not just areas with concentrated black populations. Combined with scale economies in production and marketing, such forces generated a marked decline in self-employment rates for white males as well as blacks between 1940 and 1970.[13] In the case of Birmingham, the demise of the black business district was accelerated by the precipitous decline of the city's steel industry in the 1970s and 1980s, the result of international competition and tightened environmental regulations that had little to do with the Civil Rights Movement.[14]

One may also note that the decline in some types of black business were inevitable consequences of improvements in black income and life expectancy, not just desegregation. The clearest example is life insurance, which was overwhelmingly concentrated in "industrial" or home-collection policies, an extremely expensive form of coverage for which every week the " 'surance man" came to the door to collect the premium.[15] Priority for burial insurance may have been an expression of cultural values, but it was described by *Consumer Reports* in 1978 (in a passage cited by Weems) as "insurance that preys on the poor." The article concluded, "Anyone so poor as to need the weekly collection system would almost certainly be better off without the product."[16] To some extent, a similar pattern of reduced quality or value may have applied to other goods and services consumed in the semicaptive segregated market.[17] If so, then any sustained improvement in income, education, and living standards among African Americans was bound to have an adverse impact on businesses that catered to poor and constrained customers.

The Resurgence of Black-Owned Business in the South

When all due qualifications are made, however, there is no denying that desegregation disrupted existing black businesses and the communities of which they were a part. But it is appropriate to observe that the post–Civil Rights resurgence of southern African American communities has generated business opportunities as well as a sense of identity. We lack systematic data for earlier periods, but according to the *Survey of Minority-Owned Business Enterprises (SMOBE)*—added to the Economic Census in 1969 as part of the Civil Rights–era effort to broaden and encourage minority progress—as of 1977 there were more black-owned businesses in the South than in all other regions combined. The number of southern black-owned businesses grew from 92,838 in 1972 to 330,791 in 1992, and to 435,290 in 1997. By 2007 the number had increased to more than one million, a rate of growth considerably more rapid than that of the

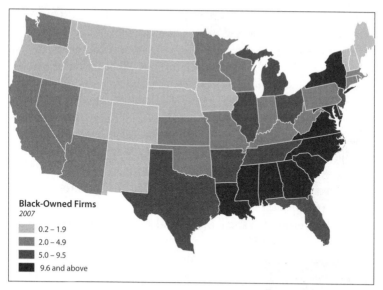

Map 7.1 Black-owned firms as a share of all firms in each state: 2007.
    Source: U.S. Census Bureau. *2007 Survey of Business Owners* (released February 8, 2011). Table 1.

southern black population.[18] To be sure, most of these businesses were small, not necessarily evidence of affluence. But the figures refute the myth that African Americans are less business-minded than other ethnic groups, under favorable conditions.

   These figures may overstate the true growth in the number of firms because the coverage of minority-owned businesses expanded over the years.[19] But the strongly regional character of black-owned business is undeniable (see Map 7.1). As measured by black-owned businesses as a share of all businesses, nine of the top eleven states in 2007 were in the South. Black-owned businesses constituted more than 10 percent of all businesses in ten southern Metropolitan Statistical Areas: Memphis (27.2 percent), Atlanta (23.1), Norfolk (15.8), Birmingham (15.8), Richmond (14.7), Miami (12.4), Charlotte (12.0), Houston (11.8), Raleigh (11.6), and Jacksonville (10.2).[20] Although the relationship between ethnicity and entrepreneurship has been extensively studied by economists and others, almost without exception this literature neglects the regional dimension of the topic, despite its glaring visibility on a national map. True, the location of black-owned business in the South largely reflects the geography of the black population. But southern racial demography was not seen as a business opportunity for most of southern history. The change is a post–Civil Rights phenomenon.[21]

Entrepreneurship studies can, however, help to identify some of the reasons for the southern black business resurgence. The chief determinants of small business participation are start-up capital (usually the owner's personal funds) and education. A family background in small business also helps in getting started, though it is less significant in determining success. In earlier eras, self-employment was often an alternative to the pursuit of education and a professional career (especially when these paths were blocked or discouraged), but the small-business opportunities emerging in recent decades—such as business services, finance, and real estate—are *positively* related to education and professional work experience. Black would-be entrepreneurs have clearly faced extra obstacles on each one of these counts in the past, probably more so in the South than elsewhere. But as the result of the Civil Rights revolution, the most favorable setting for black-owned business has been in the burgeoning metropolitan areas of the South. As economist Timothy Bates concludes, "In truth, the erosion of discrimination ushered in a new era of opportunity for black entrepreneurs."[22]

Political representation, economic and educational gains, and the rise of black-owned businesses have had mutually reinforcing effects in the South. Studies consistently show that the election of a black mayor has a positive impact on the number and sales of black-owned firms. The most immediate channel is through the allocation of municipal contracts. Although explicit minority set-aside programs were curtailed by the Supreme Court's 1989 *Croson* decision, the positive association between political and economic representation has continued. Because the benefits are found in black employment and incomes as well as contracts, it does not appear that the firms involved are typically "fronts" for white interests, as is often alleged.[23]

One unusual self-employment study that does consider geography explicitly finds a southern regional effect for black-owned business in 1990 that is both statistically significant and large. Seeking to interpret this finding—because evidently economists do not consider "region" per se to be a satisfactory explanation—the authors report that the black share of the metropolitan area population has no independent effect in itself, but the *income* of an area's black population is associated with both self-employment income and the self-employment rate. Thus this research confirms the presence of mutually reinforcing complementarities among black occupational gains, educational progress, and business opportunities.[24]

Atlanta is the best-known southern example. The city had never awarded a procurement contract to a black-owned company until 1973. But by the end of Maynard Jackson's first term in office in 1978, minority firms accounted for about one-third of Atlanta's construction contracts. The H. J. Russell construction company was founded in 1952, but its propulsion into national prominence dates from Jackson's 1974 Atlanta Plan for black business representation, predating federal set-aside programs by at least two years. In the post-*Croson* era, city departments have continued to encourage minority businesses through technical assistance programs to prepare them for bidding opportunities. Figure 7.1 shows the remarkable growth and diversity of Atlanta-area black-owned businesses since 1969. A 2011 survey by the Urban League rated the Atlanta metropolitan area first in the nation in the percentage of black-owned businesses relative to the black population.[25]

The most remarkable turnaround in black participation and economic performance was in Birmingham, site of the historic desegregation crisis of 1963, which left a legacy of racial bitterness. At the time of Richard Arrington's election as the city's first

black mayor in 1979, the area's economic base was in a state of
collapse, a poor prospect for investments of any kind. Studies in
the 1970s and 1980s ranked Birmingham last in the nation in its
support for black-owned business.[26]

Figure 7.2 shows that black-owned businesses in Birmingham
declined along with the area's economy in the 1970s; but they
recovered in both number and sales as of 1982. Some part of this
growth is attributable to the 10 percent minority participation
requirement in city contracts, first instituted by Mayor David
Vann (the last white mayor) in 1977. Early results were disap-
pointing, but a system of public-private partnerships initiated in
1989 (the Birmingham Plan) resulted in markedly increased minority participation in both public and private sectors.[27] The
sectoral diversity shown in Figure 7.3 suggests that the growth

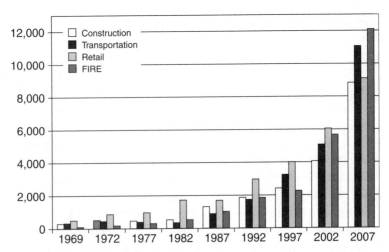

Figure 7.1 Black-owned businesses in Atlanta Metropolitan Statistical
Area, 1969–2007.
  Source: U.S. Bureau of the Census. *Survey of Minority-Owned
Business Enterprises,* various years. The surveys for 2002 and 2007 are
called *Survey of Business Owners.*
  Note: FIRE stands for finance, insurance, and real estate.

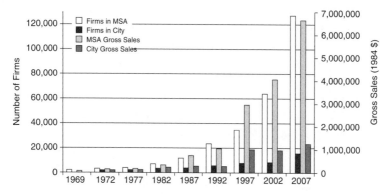

Figure 7.2 Black-owned businesses in Birmingham Metropolitan Statistical Area, 1969–2007.
    Source: U.S. Bureau of the Census. *Survey of Minority-Owned Business Enterprises.* Various years. The surveys for 2002 and 2007 are called *Survey of Business Owners.*

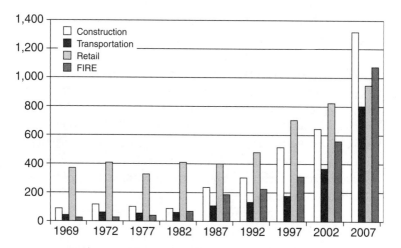

Figure 7.3 Black-owned businesses in Birmingham, 1969–2007.
    Source: U.S. Bureau of the Census. *Survey of Minority-Owned Business Enterprises.* Various years. The surveys for 2002 and 2007 are called *Survey of Business Owners.*
    Note: FIRE stands for finance, insurance, and real estate.

of Birmingham's black-owned business has not been merely the result of favoritism in city contracts.

It would be absurd to suggest that new generations of black-owned businesses in the South have replaced the old black business districts as symbols of community and identity. That would not be possible. Yet black-owned businesses clearly do draw upon the strengths of new black communities in southern cities, even though they no longer typically sell their goods and services to an exclusively racial clientele. Research clearly shows that black-owned businesses are more likely than their white counterparts to hire black employees, including those from low-income areas, so that the potential impact of these developments reaches well beyond the returns to the owners alone.[28] But business relationships can also foster social progress toward a more integrated society. When white Carolinian Joy Barnes walked into the Orangeburg, South Carolina, office of black entrepreneur and Civil Rights leader Earl Middleton in 1972 asking for a job, the ultimate result was a viable, biracial operation, even in the high-sensitivity field of real estate.[29]

POVERTY AND THE CIVIL RIGHTS REVOLUTION

Another frequently heard disparaging assessment of the Civil Rights legacy is that the movement essentially served the interests and aspirations of the black middle class but did little to help the poor. Thus Applebome quotes Selma resident Rose Sanders: "Now for the majority of the people in the Black Belt, who are black and poor, their lives have not significantly changed."[30]

Indeed despite the eye-catching regional progress and burgeoning metropolitan areas, southern poverty rates have remained persistently higher than the national average. Hopes that Civil Rights triumphs would usher in an era of expansive opportunities for all races and classes have been disappointed, so it is hardly surprising that the movement itself is often seen as a mirage in economic terms. The sense of disillusionment is perhaps felt even more keenly in southern cities with black political leadership than in bypassed rural areas. Of Birmingham, Glenn Eskew writes, "Clearly the civil rights movement failed to solve the problems of many black people.... The movement ... gained access for a few while never challenging the structure of the system."[31] The powerful images of destitute urban black hurricane victims in New Orleans seem to confirm this indictment. Kent B. Germany writes:

> The new skyscrapers of the Central Business District had become symbols of New Orleans's place in the new Dixie. However, these mirrored buildings, like some aspects of the Great Society, offered little direct benefit to most low-income New Orleanians.... [The 1960s and early 1970s] provided an interregnum of innovation that, regrettably, only narrowly tailored the arc of deprivation that has characterized the public history of poor southern blacks.[32]

But these negative appraisals understate the extent to which the Civil Rights era saw distinct improvements in well-being and opportunity for ordinary people. There is an element of tautology in statements that the movement served the interests only of the middle-class, since advancing educational and occupational attainment put people into middle-class status virtually by definition. Those still classified as poor in the twenty-first century—the rural poor or those living in racially concentrated inner cities—may understandably feel that a revolution fifty years earlier did not do much for them. But the absolute and relative size of the U.S. poverty population declined dramatically between 1959 and the 1970s, by far the largest component being poor black southerners. Most of these gains were direct or indirect consequences of the Civil Rights revolution. And for the most part this progress has persisted, despite the deterioration in the nation's political sympathy for the disadvantaged. The clearest case for these claims, and the best-developed historical literature, deals with access to modern medical care and facilities.

Hospital Desegregation and Racial Health Disparities in the South

It is hardly surprising that hospitals and other health services in the pre–Civil Rights South were highly segregated and that this segregation was associated with marked racial disparities in the quality of care and in health outcomes. More shocking is the fact that racial segregation was an explicit feature of the massive postwar federal program in support of hospital construction, known as the Hill-Burton Act of 1946. The author of the bill was veteran New Dealer Lister Hill of Alabama, who was responsible for the provision specifying that although federally sponsored hospitals could not discriminate on the basis of race, creed, or color, "an exception shall be made in cases where separate hospital facilities are provided for separate population groups, if the plan makes equitable provision on the basis of need for facilities and services of like quality for each such group." This "separate but equal" language survived the 1954 *Brown* decision, and in practice, federal authorities made no effort to enforce racial equality in access to hospital services. A 1963 survey reported that 85 percent of hospitals in the South practiced "some type of racial segregation or exclusion" (compared to less than 2 percent elsewhere). Of thirty-five single-race hospitals supported by Hill-Burton funds in North Carolina—the leading state by this measure—just four were for blacks. Black physicians were commonly denied admission and staff privileges at white institutions.[33]

The campaign to desegregate southern hospitals was a genuine part of the Civil Rights Movement. The decisive judicial decision was *Simkins v. Moses H. Cone Memorial Hospital* (1963), in which a U.S. circuit court held that the *Brown* principle applied to private hospitals that received public funds. George Simkins was a black dentist in Greensboro, North Carolina, who became a Civil Rights activist when ejected from a city-owned golf course in 1955. He persuaded the NAACP Legal

Defense Fund to take the city to court and won—the outcome being that the clubhouse was burned down and the course itself condemned and closed for the next seven years. One might well classify access to a golf course as a middle-class issue, but when one of Dr. Simkins's patients in serious condition was denied admission to nearby hospitals, the dentist contacted the NAACP attorneys and organized a group of plaintiffs to file a case with more far-reaching consequences. To the surprise of both parties, Attorney General Robert F. Kennedy intervened in the case on behalf of the plaintiffs in 1962, a rare example of the federal executive urging the courts to find an act of Congress unconstitutional. Although the ruling itself applied only to new Hill-Burton construction, and thus had little immediate impact on existing practices, it formed the basis of Section VI of the Civil Rights Act of 1964, which prohibited segregation or discrimination in any institution receiving federal funds.[34]

But court decisions and federal legislation might well have produced years of resistance, evasion, and litigation, as they did in many other areas of desegregation. What made the difference for health care was the advent of Medicare, signed into law by President Johnson on July 30, 1965. By offering generous cost-based funding, the program offered hospitals a positive incentive to take patients they would formerly have rejected, while at the same time giving the federal government a powerful financial threat to force compliance with Title VI. A hastily assembled team of more than five hundred people was dispatched from Washington in the fall of 1965 to monitor practices at southern hospitals. Although the first response in most cases was tokenism and denial, the mobilization of Civil Rights forces and professional communities—such as the Medical Committee for Human Rights, originally formed to provide care for injured demonstrators—proved remarkably effective. On June 30, 1966, the eve of Medicare implementation, President Johnson announced that more than 92 percent of the nation's hospital beds were in compliance with the Civil Rights law. This figure may have overstated the true rate of progress in the South, but between July and December 1966, the region's regime of hospital segregation was dismantled. Although political backlash weakened the enforcement effort and brought some relapses, by the early 1970s hospitals were the most integrated institutions in most southern communities.[35]

In the use of new federal funding to reward desegregation and penalize noncompliance, hospitals were not essentially different from public schools. As with public accommodations, hospitals feared the loss of white patients and physicians. But whereas whites had relatively easy access to still-segregated alternatives (private academies for their children, suburbs), most southern whites had no real choice but to utilize one of the small number of modern hospitals in the area. Those hospitals that held out, such as Baptist Hospital in Jackson, Mississippi, soon found that operation without Medicare funding was not financially viable. Medical historian David Barton Smith writes, "In essence, hospitals had to choose between affluence and compliance or bankruptcy." After acquiescence, as one black physician observed, everyone "acted like it was never any different, like segregation had never existed."[36]

The larger issue is whether hospital desegregation actually improved health outcomes. Figure 7.4 graphs post-neonatal infant mortality rates by race, in the South and in the North between 1955 and 1975, showing a downward break in 1965. Black rates fell relative to white rates in both regions, but the greatest gains were for blacks in the rural South. The 1965 discontinuity was particularly sharp in Mississippi, for which the mortality data have been analyzed by economists Douglas Almond, Kenneth Chay, and Michael Greenstone. The timing of the change strongly suggests an association with hospital desegregation, a conclusion confirmed by the authors' detailed econometric analysis of county-level data (showing that the timing of the fall in infant mortality corresponded closely to the timing of Medicare certification). This dramatic improvement was not the result of new breakthroughs in medical technology; treatments for infant diarrhea and pneumonia were well-known and standard in U.S. hospitals well before 1965, as indicated by the much more gradual and continuous decline in the white infant mortality rate from these diseases during this period. Mississippi was an extreme case, but similar improvements in black post-neonatal mortality occurred throughout the South after 1965.[37]

This evidence belies the claim that the Civil Rights revolution served only the middle class and did nothing for ordinary people. The gains were regional and racial, direct consequences

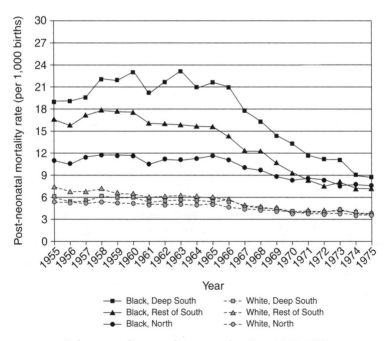

Figure 7.4 Infant mortality rates by race and region, 1955–1975.
Source: Kenneth Y. Chay and Michael Greenstone. "The Convergence in Black-White Infant Mortality Rates during the 1960's," *American Economic Review* 90 (2000): 328. Reprinted by permission of the American Economic Association.

of desegregation and the Civil Rights Movement. As with most of the economic advances for African Americans, they did not come at the expense of white southerners. To be sure, there were some costs. Because the greatest sensitivity and resistance was to racially mixed hospital rooms, desegregation was accompanied by a shift to single-patient occupancy, which undoubtedly increased hospital costs.[38] The larger context, however, was a massive expansion of access to advanced medical care for the elderly and poor of both races. Despite the shift in political climate and the persistence of racial health disparities in later years, most of the gains of the Civil Rights era were enduring. A study of racial segregation in hospital discharges during the 1990s concluded: *"In hospital care in the Medicare program, the South is the most racially integrated region of the country."*[39]

Southern Poverty and the War on Poverty

On August 20, 1964, less than two months after passage of the Civil Rights Act, Congress enacted the Economic Opportunity Act, launching the so-called War on Poverty. Neither President Johnson's poverty speech nor the Act itself mentioned race. Central to the political motivation for the initiative was a desire to move the national agenda away from race to issues of economic advancement that would benefit all low-income Americans. As southern journalist Nicholas Lemann reports, "The mantra of the people lobbying for the bill was that American poverty was mostly white and mostly nonurban." This approach followed the lead of southern moderates such as Governor Terry Sanford of North Carolina, who sought to sweeten the bitter pill of desegregation for white southerners by stressing the higher priority of education and economic progress. Sanford enjoyed great political success with these themes, and his 1963 North Carolina Fund (financed by the Ford Foundation) served in many respects as a model for the federal poverty program. In both cases, the underlying belief was that racial turmoil could not be contained unless desegregation were followed by economic gains, but that such a plan could gain general support if framed in nonracial terms with strong economic incentives and rewards. Poverty task force member Adam Yarmolinsky recalled, "We were busy telling people it *wasn't* just racial because we thought it'd be easier to sell that way, and we thought it was less racial than it turned out to be."[40]

As this rueful quote suggests, in its political goals the poverty program was a failure. The Office of Economic Opportunity (OEO) oversaw dozens of new programs in diverse areas related to poverty, including employment, health, education, and legal services. But the centerpiece was the Community Action Program, intended to foster grassroots initiatives on the theory that active participation by the poor would help to break the cycle of poverty. All activities were to be nondiscriminatory, but in the South especially groups in position to respond to the new funding opportunities were already organized along racial lines. In both rural and urban areas, Civil Rights activists saw Community Action Agencies as vehicles for extending their efforts toward economic objectives that had always been central to the movement. The OEO actively sought to ensure "maximum feasible" biracial representation of the poor. But when faced with a choice between financial resources and pushing for racial integration, Civil Rights groups had no doubt that the Office's first priority was economics.[41]

Even if the mobilization had not been racially structured, political opponents made sure that the public perceived poverty programs in just this way: as the deployment of federal funds to advance an integrationist agenda. Sometimes opposition had an identifiable basis in local economic relationships. OEO funding for the Southwest Alabama Farmers Cooperative Association, a marketing cooperative in the Alabama Black Belt, was attacked by the owner of the state's only pickle-processing plant as an assault on the free enterprise system.[42] By 1964 the historical southern politics of low-wage isolationism were no longer as powerful as they once had been; after mechanization, many black-majority

areas turned to active promotion of black out-migration. But
when OEO-sponsored groups offered encouragement and support to tenants, custodians, and welfare recipients, it is not hard
to see why many locals became hostile. More broadly, the programs offered a golden opportunity for political entrepreneurs
appealing to a white constituency still angry over desegregation.
Insurgent Republican Congressman James C. Gardner of North
Carolina made such attacks the hallmark of his political career,
denouncing the North Carolina Fund for "actively supporting
the civil rights groups in a so-called 'drive for change in [the] local power structure' which is in essence a shield for the so called
'black power' struggle."[43]

Thus the poverty program was embroiled in political turmoil
and litigation from the beginning. Whereas other components of
the Civil Rights agenda became accepted and even internalized in
regional rhetoric and behavior, this did not happen with poverty.
When Richard Nixon came into office in 1969, he appointed
Donald Rumsfeld (then a thirty-six-year-old congressman) to direct the OEO. Rumsfeld moved some of the more popular programs to other agencies—Job Corps to Labor, Head Start and
Comprehensive Health Centers to HEW. After the 1972 elections, Nixon appointed conservative activist Howard J. Phillips
as interim director, with instructions to close OEO's regional
offices and dismantle the organization altogether.[44] Looking
back, even sympathetic analysts concluded that "social policy
developments from 1965 to 1975" were characterized by "in-
consistency, inefficiency, and inequality. . . . When held up to generally accepted principles of efficiency and equity, the social policy legacy of the 1965–1975 decade does not score well."[45] One
can appreciate the political appeal of Ronald Reagan's quip:
"The federal government declared war on poverty, and poverty
won."[46]

Such is the impression, but what does the quantitative record
show? The official poverty rates have well-known shortcomings,
but for broad historical comparisons they are still informative.

Figure 7.5 shows that the South has remained the nation's high-poverty region. This regional poverty group has been disproportionately black throughout the period, though the majority of southern poor were white even in 1975—confirming the Great Society claim. Taking a longer view, however, the figure also shows that the most dramatic recorded reduction in poverty occurred between 1959 and the mid-1970s and that this was primarily a southern regional phenomenon. Because these dates correspond closely to those of the Civil Rights revolution in the South, one might have thought that the regional dimensions of poverty would be a major topic in poverty studies. To the contrary, the major national analyses of poverty pay almost no attention to the South.[47] A proximate reason for this neglect is that poverty data were not collected on a state or regional basis before 1969. The deeper reason is that the nation's attention turned

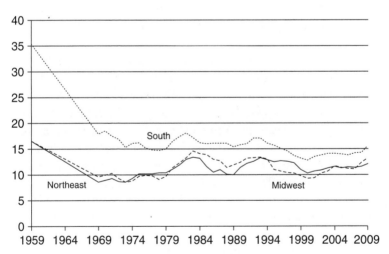

Figure 7.5 Poverty rates by region, 1959–2009.

Source: U.S. Bureau of the Census. Current Population Survey, Annual Social and Economic Supplements.

Note: Rates are the number of poor individuals as a percentage of the regional population.

in the late 1960s to the northern cities that became centers of racial violence.

Table 7.1 shows the fall in poverty between 1959 and 1978, the year when the national poverty rate reached its minimum of 11.4 percent. Poverty rates declined in all demographic categories at this time.[48] But nearly two-thirds of the decline in the number of poor during these years occurred in the South. The most dramatic change was in the rural South, where the black poverty rate fell from 77.7 to 37.2 percent. From the information available, we cannot tell how much of this decline was a direct consequence of out-migration. But the southern black rural population fell by 2.3 million, while the number of black poor in the North and West actually *increased* by nearly one million during the same period. Thus the primary locus of black poverty reduction was the South, and the chief vehicle was new access to jobs outside of agriculture, allowing significant numbers to share in the region's prosperity. This analysis is consistent with aggregate studies showing that the decline of the sharecropping-tenancy regime was a broad factor underlying the South's convergence to national per capita income levels.[49]

For the general U.S. population, cash transfers were the largest contributors to poverty reduction, primarily Social Security for the elderly, with secondary roles for public assistance, Unemployment Insurance, and Veterans' Benefits. But these programs were far less effective in reducing black poverty, because (owing to the disproportionate influence of southern representatives on the original legislation) blacks were disproportionately employed in occupations not covered by Social Security or Unemployment Insurance.[50] Thus most of the decline in numbers of black poor was in the working-age population. These gains had relatively little to do with the War on Poverty but everything to do with the Civil Rights revolution.

As previous chapters have shown, the Civil Rights Movement opened employment opportunities in southern cities and industries to black workers, including those with limited education.

Table 7.1 Poverty by Race and Region, 1959–1978 (numbers in thousands)

	USA		South		Black South		Black Rural	
	Number in Poverty	Poverty Rate	Number in Poverty	Poverty Rate	Number in Poverty	Poverty Rate	Number in Poverty	Poverty Rate
1959	38,766	22.0	19,166	35.4	7,505	68.5	4,925	77.7
1969	24,147	12.1	11,090	17.9	4,850	40.8	3,089	54.3
1978	24,497	11.4	10,255	14.7	4,429	34.1	2,202	37.2
Change 1959–1978	14,269		8,911		3,076		2,723	

Source: U.S. Bureau of the Census, Current Population Report, Consumer Income Series P-60, No. 130, Characteristics of the Population below the Poverty Level 1979, Table 4.

Over time these advances extended to jobs requiring greater skills and education. Racially selective out-migration from the southern countryside transpired over a much longer historical period, undoubtedly contributing to poverty reduction decades before that concept was defined and measured. But during the 1950s and 1960s, labor markets in northern cities were by no means welcoming to poor black southerners with limited education, so that interregional migration often simply transferred poverty from the rural South to the urban North.[51] The historical discontinuity came with the Civil Rights breakthroughs of the 1960s and 1970s, and the primary locus of change was the South. To be sure, black poverty rates in southern cities were also distressingly high in this era. But southern black poverty rates continued to fall, even after central-city poverty began to rise elsewhere in the country, in the 1970s and 1980s.[52] As limited and incomplete as they were, these advances were consequences of the Civil Rights revolution.

Nothing in this discussion is meant to deny or minimize the persistence of southern poverty nor its enduring racial character. Modern accounts of rural Black Belt counties describe a world still thoroughly segregated by race and permeated by racial mistrust.[53] The living standards of the poor have actually improved considerably since the 1960s, by such measures as electricity, running water, and access to health care. But health conditions in the region are still well below national standards, especially for children, and pathologies associated with poverty—alcohol and drug abuse, teenage pregnancy—persist as a source of national as well as regional shame.[54] My point is that these chronic conditions should not be understood as indications of a class-based character flaw in the Civil Rights generation, which oversaw the greatest reduction in poverty in American history. They do, however, reflect deep changes in state and national political priorities.

MISUSE AND ABUSE OF THE CIVIL
RIGHTS REVOLUTION

Throughout the post–Civil Rights era, political observers and participants have alleged and lamented that the core principles of the movement have been misused or abandoned, with adverse consequences for African Americans and perhaps for the country as a whole. The complaints come in many variants. One persistent version is that black political leaders have overemphasized race as a political and economic factor, thereby perpetuating rather than moderating racial tensions. In his preface to Abigail Thernstrom's book on the Voting Rights Act, Juan Williams writes, "Not surprisingly, black politicians wanted to protect their personal rise to power by arguing for safe seats under the act." Thernstrom herself adds that the Act "arguably serves as a brake on black political aspirations and a barrier to greater integration."[55] Some go so far as to argue that an "unholy alliance" has emerged between black representatives and conservative Republicans, at the expense of white southern Democrats.[56] A variation on this theme is the criticism advanced by political scientist William Julius Wilson, among others, that black leaders tend to support race-based programs such as affirmative action, as opposed to broad economic programs that would benefit and tend to unite the poor of all races and ethnicities.[57]

An alternative grievance, common among black commentators, is that black mayors have *not* given high priority to their black constituents but instead have catered to the interests of a largely white business elite. Many observers endorse political scientist Adolph Reed's contention that Atlanta's black political administrations are "by and large only black versions of the progrowth regimes that they have replaced."[58] Political scientist Elgie McFayden writes, "Today, African-American mayors, unlike the Civil Rights–era leaders of the 1960s, are often reluctant to pursue policies and programs viewed as extremely liberal, too expensive, or requiring a political fight."[59]

Perhaps the most disturbing critique holds that the political philosophy and rhetoric of the movement, emphasizing the injustice of racial distinctions, was quickly co-opted by "reformed" segregationists and utilized to thwart meaningful progress. Thus historian Joseph Crespino deplores the "triumphal narrative" that recounts how "a color-blind, religiously-oriented civil rights movement shamed the rest of white America into living up to its own stated principles. . . . Whatever noble uses to which the closèd-society metaphor may have been put in the past, today it is often the tool of this fundamentally conservative narrative."[60] Key to this successful reversal was what historian Matthew Lassiter calls the "suburban ideology of racial innocence," summarized by legal historian Anders Walker as "the ability to reframe resistance to Civil Rights in racially neutral, constitutional terms."[61] In 1985 even the Ku Klux Klan adopted this theme, holding a rally at the Martin Luther King historic site in Atlanta to protest the "corruption" of King's message of equality by the "anti-white" policy of affirmative action.[62]

This lament is most bitter with respect to school integration. As early as 1966, Mississippi officials deployed the rhetoric of color blindness to resist moves toward "racial balance" in public schools.[63] By dropping explicit racial criteria, argues education historian Scott Baker, South Carolina officials utilized test scores to "institutionalize a more rational, legally defensible and durable system of white supremacy in education."[64] Many critics on both Left and Right would subscribe to Raymond Wolters's flat declaration: "Integration has been a failure."[65] Legal scholar Robert Justin Lipkin argues that the *Brown* decision's emphasis on racial integration reflects an "invidious paternalism" that is morally undesirable if not indeed offensive, one that has delegitimized affirmative action programs that might have been more effective than desegregation.[66] In taking this position, Lipkin echoes the doubts that many black parents had all along about the priority of racial integration in their struggle for better schools.[67]

It is not my purpose to refute or dismiss these diverse contentions. They should all be taken seriously, and each one contains some truth. But the economic successes of the southern Civil Rights Movement offer a strong counterargument. Two million African American in-migrants from other parts of the country since 1970 testify to the reality of these changes. However much Civil Rights leaders might have played their rhetorical and political cards differently, they must have been doing something right.

Yet critiques of the Civil Rights legacy highlight a deep and persistent tension between the rhetoric and the reality on the ground. The movement presented itself to the world in universalist terms, calling for an end to invidious racial distinctions, laws, and practices. But race-conscious political mobilization and race-based remedies were essential to its success. It was not that the rhetoric was insincere. In a racially stratified society, there was no practical alternative to building on preexisting identities and networks. Local boycotts of downtown areas were calls for the black community to exercise its economic power collectively. Antipoverty groups in pursuit of federal funding soon found that interracial organizing was difficult, contentious, and disruptive. When calls for "black power" emerged in 1966, the new militancy was shocking to many sympathizers and threatening to white southerners. But as Stokely Carmichael repeatedly explained, the slogan meant only that black people "have the right to organize themselves politically and . . . via the vote seize the power."[68] As Peniel E. Joseph puts it, southern Civil Rights–era organizing traditions were not abandoned in the late 1960s and early 1970s but "updated with a new face and political edge."[69]

Similarly, courts and federal administrators who were serious about enforcing Civil Rights laws after years of evasion and delay had little choice but to establish more or less explicit racial criteria for compliance in employment and in school desegregation cases. The same held true in the protracted struggle against vote dilution and for political representation. One may deplore

the need to take race into account at all in legislative redistricting, and one may plausibly hold that the choices actually made
have had adverse consequences for political incentives and outcomes. The central historical point is that the racial consequences
of redistricting decisions could not be ignored. In a race-conscious
society, anyone who claims to have ignored race has in effect
made a racial decision. The proper extent of race-consciousness
in redistricting is certainly subject to debate, and black representatives are no less subject to self-interested incumbency bias than
others. But the rise of racial representation in the South cannot
be blamed for the polarization of national politics nor for the
conservative trend in national policies, as detailed empirical
studies have shown.[70]

Despite the tensions, the record shows that the uneasy partnership between universality and racial identity has been historically productive. The War on Poverty did not succeed in its
goals, and it did not survive as a program, but it contributed to
the ongoing political mobilization of black southerners, which
ultimately generated more black elected officials and a higher
level of political representation than elsewhere in the country. An
example of an enduring benefit is the proliferation of community
health centers, which provide basic care to poor populations
throughout the South (though not reflected in official poverty
statistics). The program has survived multiple political attacks
over many presidential administrations. By 2011 more than
1,100 community health centers provided primary care at more
than 8,500 delivery sites in medically underserved areas.[71] According to health administrator Daniel Hawkins, "Civil Rights
and the War on Poverty were key to the program's birth, and the
need to care for the underserved is the key to growth. But the real
key to success is the community's feeling of ownership over their
centers—that's what has sustained and nurtured us through it
all."[72] Health care historian Bonnie Lefkowitz writes, "In South
Carolina, Mississippi, and Texas, the centers not only drew
strength from the civil rights movement, they irrevocably altered

the white power structure that controlled the economic and environmental determinants of disease."[73]

Some slippage between political actors and their constituents is inevitable in any process of representation. And there is bound to be some divergence between the interests of the middle class and those of the poor. But throughout the period in question, most black southerners have believed (in the phrase of political scientist Michael Dawson) that "their own self-interests are linked to the interests of the race."[74] This belief has had sufficient validity that gains have been realized at all parts of the socioeconomic scale. And according to one detailed study of voting patterns in southern legislatures, there is virtually no evidence of an "unholy alliance" between black legislators and conservative Republicans—except perhaps on the issue of redistricting itself.[75] Thus the hybrid post–Civil Rights system, in which race has been informally and unofficially acknowledged as a basis for representation and community definition, has worked tolerably well in the South. Under it, African Americans have experienced real and complementary gains in both political and economic spheres. A candid assessment of progress in the post–Civil Rights South must acknowledge that race-conscious political and economic mobilization has played a large role.

The Postracial South?

One way of rationalizing the gap between color-blind ideals and race-conscious reality is to argue that race-based criteria were necessary as a transitional matter to overcome the historical legacies of slavery, segregation, and discrimination. This logic was compelling when segregated employment structures and school systems were being dismantled during the 1970s and 1980s. But since then many have argued that the day for race-conscious policies has passed or soon will. In the 2003 *Grutter v. Bollinger* case, Justice Sandra Day O'Connor wrote, "We expect that 25 years from now, the use of racial preferences will no longer be necessary to further the interest [in racial diversity] approved today."

Well before that date, in 2007, Chief Justice John Roberts concluded his opinion in *Parents Involved in Community Schools v. Seattle School District No. 1,* "The way to stop discrimination on the basis of race is to stop discriminating on the basis of race."

Yet the evidence is clear that strong racial consciousness persists in important spheres of life such as politics, residence, and schooling, notwithstanding undeniable progress in racial attitudes and economic status. This persistence is at least as strong in the South as elsewhere, though the qualitative dynamics often differ by region. Black congressional candidates typically receive about one-third of the southern white vote, a marked change from earlier times. But this vote share is distinctly less (by ten percentage points, according to one estimate) than an otherwise comparable white candidate would receive.[76] Black mayors who perform well in office are often reelected with the support of white voters, another sign of progress. But perceptions of performance are strongly conditioned by race, especially in sensitive areas such as evaluating the police.[77] Abigail Thernstrom suggests that "racial animus is a marginal element in American politics" today. But while "racial animus" as such has surely lessened, scholars and journalists find it virtually impossible to record the political histories of southern elections without putting racially polarized perceptions and issues on center stage.[78] Studies of racial representation in Congress show that although the racial composition of delegations has little effect on roll-call votes, black representatives make a decisive difference for constituency services, hiring black staff members, locating district offices, and establishing a sense of trust with black constituents.[79]

Opinion surveys consistently show marked black-white differences in attitudes and perceptions on issues pertaining to race or where race is even tangentially involved. A 1993 survey in North Carolina found that 70 percent of blacks believed that "most whites in North Carolina have prejudiced views," while only 38 percent of whites agreed; 64 percent of blacks believed that "law enforcement in [North Carolina] is tougher on blacks," compared to just 19 percent of whites.[80] National opinion polls continue to report similar gaps on such questions as the pervasiveness of racial discrimination, the fairness of the criminal justice system, and the appropriate role of government in promoting racial justice.[81] Racial cleavages were on stark display in the aftermath of Hurricane Katrina, when more than six in ten African Americans attributed the slow government response to the fact that the majority of victims were poor and black; nine of ten non-Hispanic whites believed that neither race nor class was a significant factor. When Trayvon Martin was fatally shot in Sanford, Florida, more than 70 percent of blacks believed that race was a major factor in the events leading up to the shooting and in the police response; only 35 percent of nonblacks shared this view.[82]

The Civil Rights Movement accomplished many things, including an evident improvement in racial tolerance in the South. But it did not create a color-blind or postracial world. In a society for which racial consciousness is still strong, delegitimizing race as a basis for policy can be a political tactic, with real consequences. Adopting and deploying the Civil Rights rhetoric of color blindness has often proved useful in this strategy. Thus when political scientists find that "racial issues matter more for blacks than whites," is this because whites simply take their dominant group identity for granted and hence believe it is best left unmentioned?[83]

As vexing as it can be to hear Civil Rights rhetoric used in the service of white affluence, it is difficult to sustain an argument that the entire movement would have done better with a more explicitly racial appeal from the start. As of 1950 blacks were a minority group in every southern state. During the ten years between the Montgomery bus boycott and the Voting Rights Act, they had no conventional political representation even as a minority; that status changed only moderately during the next decade. Thus isolating the white South politically was essential for gaining the outside support the movement needed, and for this purpose a transcendent, universalized depiction of the struggle was ideal. The ability to hold out a vision of a future in which the white South would also be liberated was an enormous asset—even if the invitation was initially rejected almost everywhere.[84] Longer-term success derived from the indigenous political and economic mobilization that federal protection fostered and permitted. This is not to argue that the best of all possible decisions was taken in every instance; clearly many were debatable and may still be debated. But even the most cynical interpretation of white acquiescence as "strategic accommodation" must acknowledge how far the outcomes were from the white South's original objectives.[85]

The more urgent question is whether the southern conservative counterrevolution has or will have adverse *economic* consequences that threaten the progress documented in this book. There is reason for concern. Although numerous surveys and studies show that white southern racial hostility has moderated over the past fifty years, unobtrusive measures of racial attitudes—designed to remove the effects of social desirability on responses—find distinctly higher levels of racial prejudice in the South than in the non-South.[86] Political scientists Nicholas Valentino and David Sears find a strong association between southern ideological conservatism and what they call "modern" or "symbolic" racial attitudes, reflected in beliefs that black economic disadvantages are caused by poor work ethic, or that blacks make excessive demands and get too many concessions from government.[87] These studies reveal racial cleavages persisting in a pronounced regional pattern, despite radical change in the norms of socially acceptable language regarding race. They raise the possibility that behavior might also change in response to new political and economic incentives.

One recent study suggests that such changes are already under way in state policies on public finance and welfare expenditures. Sociologists Katherine Newman and Rourke O'Brien show that southern states depend on regressive sales taxes as a revenue source (as opposed to property and income taxes) to a far greater extent than states in other parts of the country. The regressivity of the sales taxes is accentuated by including food for home consumption as a taxable item—in Alabama and Mississippi at the full rate, and at lower rates in other southern states. The result is a marked difference in tax liability at the poverty line, as shown in Figures 7.6 and 7.7, between southern and northeastern states. Although these taxes cannot be identified as the *cause* of southern poverty, Newman and O'Brien show that their impact is sufficient to aggravate material hardships and behaviors associated with poverty, such as failure to see a doctor or dentist when needed, teenage pregnancies, and crime. The authors conclude, "The poor in the southern region are at a greater disadvantage than their counterparts in other parts of the country *because* the state and local tax burdens they face make them even poorer. A

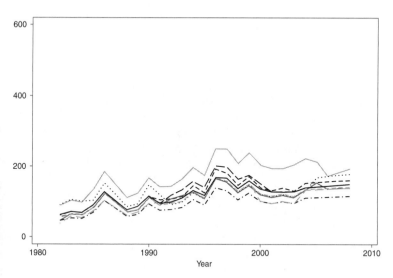

Figure 7.6 State/local sales tax liability for family of three at the poverty line: Northeast, 1982–2008. Each line represents a different state.

Source: Katherine S. Newman and Rourke O'Brien. *Taxing the Poor.* Berkeley, CA: University of California Press, 2011, p. 128. Reprinted by permission of the University of California Press.

particularly pernicious driver of these differences lies in the sales taxes the poor must pay (alongside the nonpoor), especially the food taxes that many southern states and localities assess."[88]

Newman and O'Brien trace distinctive southern tax policies back to the 1930s, and in several states to constitutional tax limitation rules adopted in the 1960s and 1970s in the wake of the Voting Rights Act. But regional differences in tax structure have actually widened in recent decades, roughly coincident with the consolidation of conservative Republican majorities in southern states. The same is true for public assistance programs. Analysis of responses to the welfare reform of 1996, which gave states greater choice in setting eligibility rules, shows that the adoption of "get tough" policies was strongly associated with the percentage of African Americans on the state's welfare rolls.[89]

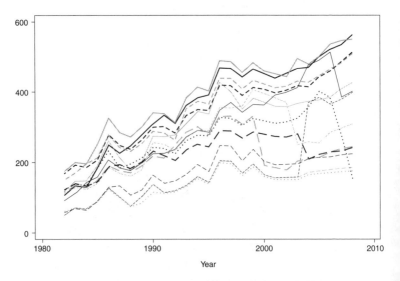

Figure 7.7 State/local sales tax liability for family of three at the poverty line: South, 1982–2008. Each line represents a different state.

Source: Katherine S. Newman and Rourke O'Brien. *Taxing the Poor.* Berkeley, CA: University of California Press, 2011, p. 129. Reprinted by permission of the University of California Press.

This variable is highly correlated with southern location, though this geographical mapping is seldom mentioned in quantitative studies. The policies, of course, affect poor whites and Hispanics as well as blacks. But racialized perceptions of the poor play a powerful role in framing issues and directing political priorities.

Racial associations are perhaps even stronger with respect to crime and incarceration. The vast expansion of the U.S. prison population since 1980 is obviously more than a southern phenomenon. But of the fifteen states with the highest rates of incarceration per capita in 2008, ten were in the South.[90] Because the prison population is racially skewed, felon disfranchisement laws—not confined to the South but pervasive within the region—cut heavily into the size of the southern black electorate.[91]

The problem is not that the ideals of the Civil Rights era were inadequate, nor that southern black leaders have abandoned them. Whether southern Republicans are really driven by racial hostility hardly matters. The essence of the situation is that ascendant conservative coalitions in southern states have little incentive to accommodate the preferences of black voters, much less to promote active programs on their behalf. Ultimately the only realistic response is to build sustainable multiracial coalitions that can compete politically in these states. My conclusion is that the inclusive values of the Civil Rights Movement will be needed even more in the future than they were in the past.

CHAPTER 8

CIVIL RIGHTS ECONOMICS

Historical Context and Lessons

The book is a work of economic history, not a prescriptive policy analysis nor a test of theoretical hypotheses about relationships between race and economics. Unlike many histories, this one has no precise ending date. But the objective has been historical nonetheless, an attempt to assess the economic effects of the mid-1960s Civil Rights revolution across subsequent decades in four important areas: public accommodations, labor markets, schools, and voting rights. Tracking these effects is not a simple task of measurement but inevitably extends to matters of interpretation and economic analysis: What were the historical origins of segregation and other forms of race discrimination, and how did these persist over time? How did Civil Rights legislation and enforcement alter these practices, and did resistance to change intensify or diminish over time? How did gains for African Americans affect the economic well-being of white southerners? Although historical studies with no clear end date cannot identify outcomes with precision, we can ask in each case whether the dynamic of change was completed, continued through time, or interrupted or reversed by later historical developments.

In the early 1960s the public accommodations debate was contentious and emotional in character, impinging as it did on socially sensitive areas of racial interaction and the rights of business establishments. The specter of social equality translated into fears of losing white patronage, prompting a negative initial response from business almost everywhere in the South, yet public accommodations became the movement's clearest success story. Exertion of economic pressure over months and years brought reluctant acquiescence by local business groups. The surprisingly positive results of these local negotiations in turn unleashed a political dynamic within the business community that produced strong federal legislation far earlier than anticipated. Within a decade this hot-button issue was all but forgotten, leaving in its wake a prosperous region that could now open its doors unapologetically to travelers, performers, and entrepreneurs from all over the world.

Labor market desegregation was more protracted and litigious. For white southern workers, racial hostilities were aggravated by understandable economic fears. More perplexing from an economic perspective is that southern employers were almost equally fearful. Not only did they anticipate adverse reactions from white employees, but they bought into prevailing prejudices about the competence and vitality of black workers. The learning process began only after federal authorities and the courts made it clear that firms had no choice but to institute meaningful changes in their racial policies. In textiles, the transition from resistance to promotion took place very rapidly, within a year or two of "the change." Elsewhere adjustments were slower and more reluctant. Ultimately, however, many and perhaps most southern employers developed internal systems to accommodate racial integration, and these systems were retained even after major swings in the national political climate. Changes of this type occurred throughout the country, but by far the largest and most persistent gains were in the South. A key variable, it appears, is black representation—in communities, in schools, in political office, and in the personnel departments of business firms.

Desegregation succeeded in public accommodations and employment largely because, although business did not play a leading role in either case, incentives were reconfigured so that profit-seeking firms came to support new policies as a matter of self-interest. For public schools, the main decision-making bodies were more clearly political, so that internalizing the benefits of integration was often not possible. As a result, acquiescence in school desegregation came only in response to threats of financial losses from the federal government and of legal consequences from the courts. In this setting, thoroughgoing racial integration has proven elusive. Nonetheless, despite all manner of delays, evasions, and circumventions, the historical record shows that school desegregation was far more extensive and sustained in the South than elsewhere in the country and that this policy generated significant gains for southern black students by measures ranging from educational attainment to test scores to adult occupational status. Despite widespread fears, there is no evidence that any of this progress came at the expense of southern white students. This is a remarkable record of achievement for a set of policies whose political and ideological supports have receded over time.

The final Civil Rights reform examined here is the Voting Rights Act, often celebrated for its historic success and renewed multiple times by large bipartisan votes in Congress. Southern black voter registration jumped dramatically in the 1960s, but translating votes into meaningful political representation proved to be even more contentious and long delayed than desegregation. Persistent effort paid off, however, and by the 1980s there were far more black elected officials in the South than elsewhere, and representation relative to the black share of the population was also far higher. What Chapter 6 adds to this political narrative is evidence that representation has made a difference for economic life as well. With voting rights, black citizens have shared more fairly in public services, public-sector jobs, and municipal contracts. Beyond racial equity, voting rights ushered in an era of competitive two-party politics in southern states, channeling public energies toward growth-enhancing investments in schools, transportation, and recreational facilities. Although politics by its very nature is concerned with distributional issues, the benefits of regional growth have been shared by white as well as black southerners, and in this larger sense expanding the electorate was a win-win proposition like other components of the Civil Rights revolution.

No one should understand this summary as the celebration of a mission completed, a narrative with a happy ending after which we can now turn our attention to new problems and concerns. Nothing in this book argues that racial prejudice and discrimination have been eradicated in the South, much less that the region has entered a new postracial age. The Civil Rights revolution did not overthrow the economic system, and progress toward racial equality has been far from complete. Visionaries who foresaw the prospect of more fundamental change in the 1960s have reason to be disappointed. In contrast to celebration and triumphal finality, the book has posed a series of narrowly framed questions and answered them by documenting meaningful economic gains in historical context. In essence, *historical context* means relative to conditions and trends prior to the protests of the 1960s and the legislation of 1964 and 1965. By this standard, the economic advances of black southerners were remarkable and have largely been sustained. By contrast, reduction in the regional poverty rate largely came to an end after 1980. Thus the South has been the locus of both the movement's greatest economic success and its greatest disappointment.

For voting rights, the positive dynamic launched in 1965 came to an end in the 1990s. The Voting Rights Act itself survives for the present, and black political power in the cities seems secure. But two-party competition at the state level dwindled with the consolidation of conservative Republican majorities, which make no serious effort to compete for the black vote. Not only has black political influence been diminished, but in the wake of the high black turnout for Barack Obama in 2008 (carrying North Carolina, Virginia, and Florida), southern states have taken the lead in enacting measures designed to discourage registration and make voting itself more difficult. Although similar legislation has been proposed in all parts of the country, in the South the barely disguised racial dimension evokes uncomfortable echoes of the Jim Crow era. Equally targeted in modern times, however, has been the rapidly growing Hispanic population.[1]

LESSONS OF THE PAST?

A better way to understand this historical record is to say that it illustrates what can be accomplished under favorable conditions through concerted, purposeful government policy in a mutually supportive partnership with grassroots political mobilization. The achievements of the southern Civil Rights revolution provide an example of a strong interventionist central government policy that worked. The movement itself is rightly known as a largely nonviolent insurgency that succeeded through the exercise of economic and moral pressure. But the movement could not have accomplished its goals without outside help—though, to be sure, the movement itself was instrumental in evoking that help. On the spectrum of policy instruments, Civil Rights enforcement by federal agencies and the courts could at times be fairly characterized as coercive and heavy-handed; it was indubitably imposed by an outside force, with little sympathy or understanding for local and regional cultural traditions. Yet through these policies, the federal government managed not only to compel immediate compliance through the force of law, but also, in time, to bring about a longer-term reconfiguration of the profit-seeking strategies of private businesses. Further, these interventions achieved an outcome that was evidently market-enhancing rather than stifling and restrictive in its economic impact.

Civil Rights history also offers a hopeful counterexample to the hypothesis widely accepted among development economists that ethnic and racial diversity has adverse consequences for economic growth.[2] Or perhaps it is the exception that proves that rule. Racial polarization certainly did inhibit southern regional progress, first through the repressive institutions and practices of segregation, and then through political conflict that discouraged outside investments and deterred coalitions in support of common objectives. But Civil Rights history shows that such polarization is not eternally fixed by exogenous demographic structures. Once the landmark federal legislation was in place, a combination of pressures and incentives fostered new biracial coalitions in states and metropolitan areas that restarted the engines of the southern growth machine. As behavior changed under pressure, racial tolerance within the region clearly improved over time, though race-consciousness has by no means disappeared.

Even as the Civil Rights revolution extends our sense of what is possible in economic life, a full assessment of the record must also acknowledge that specific aspects of the historical context facilitated these outcomes. Most immediately, the South was an emerging regional economy with strong underlying growth prospects. Enthusiasm for attracting outside investment gave the movement economic leverage, while ongoing growth made it possible for the regional economy to absorb African Americans without reducing the well-being of white southerners. Because one of the bases for growth was the South's supply of relatively cheap unskilled labor, the movement was able to quickly provide economic gains to workers with limited education merely by dismantling racial barriers to these jobs. But even in the presence of such incentives, the white South, left to its own devices, would not have initiated major changes in the racial order. Another crucial background condition was the expanding role of the federal government in the 1960s into areas such as education and health care. Federal financial subsidies offered both a carrot for compliance and the threat of a stick for continued defiance. Massive new funding, however, merely provided potential leverage in the struggle against segregation. The potential became decisive only when federal authorities and the courts used it to demand meaningful desegregation on the part of school districts, employers, local governments, and hospitals. Federal responsiveness was never as strong or as consistent as Civil Rights forces wanted, but it was critical for sustaining the revolution. The persistence of federal and judicial pressure reflected in turn the unique political isolation of the South during this era, another key feature of the historical context.

Thus the Civil Rights revolution does not provide us with a well-defined package of lessons to be transported across historical time and space, neither for the specifics of economic policy nor for the political supports that made the economic gains possible. The economic challenges of the twenty-first century differ from those of the 1960s in fundamental ways. Although both blacks and whites often blame the race issue for their economic disappointments, the larger common source of their struggles has been the diminished performance of the national economy since the 1970s. Except for the Internet boom of the 1990s, real wage growth has been slow to negative for the past generation, especially for low-skilled workers. Labor-intensive manufacturing industries that were central to midcentury southern growth were decimated by foreign competition in the 1990s. Salary premiums for the college-educated have increased, but access to higher education has been limited by rising tuition costs as well as poor educational preparation in the precollege years. These problems are aggravated for African Americans and other minorities, but when so many others are also struggling, the case for special attention on grounds of historical injustice is more difficult to make. In general, conditions of slow economic growth are uncongenial to a political agenda grounded on fairness and social justice.[3]

Recent economic trends within the South are, if anything, even less hopeful. After decades of convergence toward national standards, per capita incomes for the region have peaked at around 90 percent of the U.S. average, with many states stalled well below this level. Progress in relative school funding has similarly slowed to a crawl, even while the low-cost source of historical educational gains—school desegregation—has lost political and legal favor. A recent University of North Carolina report on the status of southern development finds that much of the region receives low marks for its investment in infrastructure, schools, the environment, and technology. Southern state governments still pursue industrial recruitment plans, but they typically do so on the basis of low taxes and cheap labor, an approach that seems to have reached the limits of its effectiveness. These same state governments often seem to show little interest in the well-being of their poorest citizens. One contributor to the UNC report remarked, "The states [primarily southern] with the highest levels of poverty tend to be the most powerfully committed to the notion that government should not do anything about it."[4]

It is far from clear that these state policy regimes really serve the interests of the majority of their citizens. For example, southern states have resisted the gay rights revolution, despite evidence that such intolerance is a deterrent for high-technology business.[5] Alabama's restrictive immigration law (2011) inflicted heavy costs on state businesses as well as on Latinos.[6] If this is so, then the Civil Rights era may indeed offer some lessons for the present. The basic strategy of the southern movement was to combine a morally compelling appeal with a credible case that accommodating demands for inclusion would actually serve the economic interests of a larger community. Because Jim Crow segregation barriers were racial, advancing the interests of the black middle class often served the interests of the black poor as well, giving them a common basis for political mobilization. Appropriately adjusted for the times, these broad features will have to be present for successful political insurgencies in the future. The case is there to be made, but doing so will call for defining issues so as to build coalitions across racial, ethnic, and class lines. That is a tall order indeed, but the basic lesson is well understood among southern black political leaders and their allies. As they undertake this daunting project, they cannot do better than to draw upon the heritage of the Civil Rights revolution.

NOTES

1 CIVIL RIGHTS, ECONOMICS, AND THE AMERICAN SOUTH

1. Eskew, "Memorializing the Movement," pp. 357, 373–374.

2. Filmmaker Stanley Nelson presented his documentary *Freedom Riders* in Tunisia in December 2010, two weeks before the Jasmine Revolution in that country. Although no one claimed a direct causal connection, it was reported that the Q and A session was "quite intense." Mark Jenkins, "Film Forward Program Reaches Out to Underserved Areas, Challenges Stereotypes," *Washington Post,* May 6, 2011.

3. Chappell, *Inside Agitators,* pp. xxv, 61. The second quotation paraphrases a comment from Lyndon Johnson's speech at the signing ceremony for the Voting Rights Act.

4. Quoted in Chafe, Gavins, Korstad, and Ortiz, *Remembering Jim Crow,* p. 182.

5. Sokol, *There Goes My Everything,* p. 328.

6. Quoted in Eskew, "Memorializing the Movement," p. 364.

7. Quoted in Litwack, *How Free Is Free?,* p. 100.

8. Litwack, *How Free is Free,* pp. 109–110.

9. Applebome, *Dixie Rising,* pp. 17, 215.

10. Wolters, *Race and Education,* p. 11.

11. The gradual process through which blacks acquired political influence in northern cities is recounted in Gregory, *Southern Diaspora,* pp. 241–273. On progress against segregation, see Cohen, *Consumers' Republic,* pp. 175–183; Sugrue, *Sweet Land of Liberty,* chapter 5. By

the time of the Civil Rights Act of 1964, most nonsouthern states and virtually all nonsouthern cities had public accommodations laws. See Konvitz and Leskes, *A Century of Civil Rights*, p. 157; Gregory, *Southern Diaspora*, p. 267.

12. Licht, *Getting Work*, pp. 45, 141; Whatley and Wright, "Race, Human Capital, and Labour Markets," pp. 281–283; Vedder and Gallaway, "Racial Differences in Unemployment"; Sundstrom, "Last Hired, First Fired?"

13. Whatley, "Getting a Foot in the Door." In contrast, firms in Atlanta reverted to prewar lines of segregation. On municipal jobs, see Sugrue, *Sweet Land of Liberty*, pp. 112–113. On fair employment laws, see Collins, "Race, Roosevelt, and Wartime Production"; Konvitz and Leskes, *A Century of Civil Rights*, pp. 197–201; Collins, "The Labor Market Impact of State-Level Antidiscrimination Laws."

14. Myrdal, *American Dilemma*, pp. 662–666.

15. Margo, *Race and Schooling in the South*, chapter 6.

16. Myrdal, *American Dilemma*, p. 1013.

17. Rodriguez and Weingast, "The Positive Political Theory of Legislative History," argue that the Civil Rights Act of 1964 was carefully tailored to minimize its impact outside of the South.

18. Analyzing the events of 1967, the Kerner Commission found that just one of eight "major disorders," and only 16 percent of all disorders, occurred in the southern and border states (National Advisory Commission, *Report*, p. 66). Later studies using larger data sets similarly find that the incidence of disorders and their adverse effects on property values were far more severe in the Northeast and Midwest than in the South and West (Collins and Margo, "The Economic Aftermath of the 1960s Riots," pp. 853, 857, 860). The apparent deviation in 1968 is attributable to major riots in April 1968 in Baltimore and Washington, D.C., which are counted in the census South.

19. Muse, *The American Negro Revolution*, p. 287.

20. This argument was advanced in 1964 by Victor Schiro, mayor of New Orleans. Quoted in Germany, *New Orleans after the Promises*, p. 36.

21. From Dunbar's introduction to Watters and Cleghorn, *Climbing Jacob's Ladder*, p. xiii.

22. Carson, *In Struggle*; Morris, *The Origins of the Civil Rights Movement*; Payne, *I've Got the Light of Freedom*.

23. See particularly Hill, *The Deacons for Defense*.

24. Joseph, *The Black Power Movement*, pp. 21, 146. The comparison between southern self-defense groups and the Black Panther Party is from the essay by Simon Wendt in the Joseph volume.

25. I expressed this view myself in 1986, declaring that "the entity formerly known as the Southern economy no longer exists" (*Old South, New South,* p. vii). For a corrective, see my "Persisting Dixie," pp. 77–90.

26. Lassiter, *The Silent Majority,* pp. 18–19.

27. Cobb, *The South and America,* pp. 162–163; U.S. Bureau of the Census, *The Black Population: 2010* (September 2011). The census South includes Delaware and Maryland, both of which have large African American population shares.

28. Burns and Burns, *A People's Charter,* p. 326. A similar "before and after" dividing line is implied by the title of Timothy Minchin's book *From Rights to Economics.*

29. Jackson, *From Civil Rights to Human Rights,* p. 58; Eskew, *But for Birmingham,* pp. 199, 326.

30. Quoted in J. Freedom Du Lac, "Road through Segregation," *Washington Post,* Sept. 12, 2010.

31. Interview quoted in Morris, *Origins,* p. 177.

32. Quoted in Cohen, *A Consumers' Republic,* p. 190.

33. Korstad, *Civil Rights Unionism;* Honey, *Southern Labor and Black Civil Rights.*

34. Krochmal, "An Unmistakably Working-Class Vision," esp. pp. 941–951. On the importance of jobs in Atlanta's public accommodations struggle, see Brown-Nagin, *Courage to Dissent,* p. 168.

35. Graham, *The Civil Rights Era,* pp. 70, 95; Jackson, *From Civil Rights to Human Rights,* pp. 182–183.

36. Smith, *Race, Labor and Civil Rights,* pp. 81–85.

37. Sugrue, *Sweet Land of Liberty,* p. 273.

38. Thernstrom and Thernstrom, *America in Black and White,* p. 96.

39. This line of argument dates from Becker, *The Economics of Discrimination,* but perhaps the strongest statement in a Civil Rights context is by Richard Epstein, *Forbidden Grounds,* pp. 126–140, 244–259.

40. Wright, "Public Accommodations," pp. 87–88; Brown-Nagin, *Courage to Dissent,* p. 220.

41. Mangum, *The Legal Status of the Negro,* p. 174. The only significant exceptions were a North Carolina statute requiring separate toilets in manufacturing plants and a South Carolina law mandating segregation in cotton textiles. These laws were passed in 1913 and 1915, respectively, long after segregation in textiles was well entrenched; they were not imitated in other equally segregationist states. See Murray, *States' Laws on Race and Color,* pp. 341–342, 414–415.

42. Delgado and Stefancic, *The Derrick Bell Reader,* p. 37.

43. Bloom, *Class, Race, and the Civil Rights Movement*, pp. 2, 5.

44. Moreno, *Black Americans and Organized Labor*, p. 222.

45. On the origins of urban segregation, see Cell, *The Highest Stage of White Supremacy*, pp. 176–191; Hale, *Making Whiteness*, p. 130. On Atlanta, see Newman, *Southern Hospitality*, pp. 47, 95, 103; Bayor, *Race and the Shaping of Twentieth-Century Atlanta*, pp. 93, 108–113; Brown-Nagin, *Courage to Dissent*, pp. 152–156.

46. National Planning Association, *Selected Studies of Negro Employment in the South*, p. 175.

47. Chappell, "Disunity and Religious Institutions," p. 137.

48. Sokol, *There Goes My Everything*, p. 116.

49. This case is persuasively argued by Tony Badger in "Segregation and the Southern Business Elite," pp. 105–109, and "Brown and Backlash," pp. 40–45. For a survey of southern white community leaders showing that their first preference was segregation even in the 1960s, see Cramer, "School Desegregation and New Industry."

50. This phrase is from Seymour Drescher's account of equally rapid change in attitudes regarding the slave trade (*Capitalism and Antislavery*, p. 86).

51. Thornton, *Dividing Lines*, pp. 96–113.

52. Stern, *Calculating Visions*, p. xi; Kotz, *Judgment Days*, pp. 8, 14.

53. Valelly, *The Two Reconstructions*, pp. 193–197.

54. This is the central theme in Minchin, *From Rights to Economics*. A good survey of post–Civil Rights southern labor history is Minchin and Salmond, *After the Dream*.

55. Thornton, *Dividing Lines*, p. 500. In his study of Mississippi counties, *Freedom Is a Constant Struggle*, Kenneth Andrews finds that strong movement organization was a good predictor of black civic engagement after the passage of the Civil Rights Act.

56. See Kotlowski, *Nixon's Civil Rights*.

57. Nicholls, *Southern Tradition and Regional Progress*. Geographer Robert Lewis argues that most southern industrial growth through the 1950s was "dominated by a narrowly based economy rooted in earlier industrial forms" ("World War II Manufacturing and the Postwar Southern Economy," p. 840).

58. Lemann, *The Promised Land*, pp. 47–49. James Cobb notes that some local officials made no secret of this desire when they began to publicize the comparatively generous welfare payments available in northern states (*The South and America Since World War II*, p. 98).

59. The literature on the political and legislative histories of the Civil Rights and Voting Rights Acts is too large to summarize. Good general treatments include Graham, *The Civil Rights Era*; Kotz, *Judgment Days*;

Stern, *Calculating Visions;* Whalen, *The Longest Debate.* A particularly useful account of the role of southern black migrants to northern cities in pushing a Civil Rights agenda is Gregory, *The Southern Diaspora.*

60. Florida has been dropped from the South Atlantic region in Figure 1.3 because the timing of its growth was quite different from the rest of the region, for reasons largely unrelated to Civil Rights issues.

61. "60,000 in Atlanta Welcome Braves," *New York Times,* Apr. 9, 1965; "Charleston, Home of Catfish Row, Stages First 'Porgy,'" *New York Times,* June 27, 1965; Roy Reed, "Birmingham Leads Arts in the South," *New York Times,* Nov. 16, 1974. The Houston Colt 45s joined the National League as an expansion team in 1962, after the city had quietly desegregated its public accommodations in 1960. In 1965 the American Football League's All-Star game was moved from New Orleans to Houston after players protested the exclusion of blacks from New Orleans hotels and businesses.

2   THE POLITICAL ECONOMY OF THE JIM CROW SOUTH

1. Pope, "Southern Homesteads for Negroes," pp. 201–212. In an ingenious study, "Land and Racial Wealth Inequality," Melinda Miller compares the wealth accumulation of freedmen in southern states to that of the Cherokee Nation in Oklahoma, who were guaranteed the right to claim unused land on the public domain. The relative economic status of the Oklahoma freedmen was distinctly better.

2. Jaynes, *Branches without Roots,* pp. 156–157. Other useful accounts of the transition include Davis, *Good and Faithful Labor;* Harris, "Plantations and Power"; Ransom and Sutch, *One Kind of Freedom;* Shlomowitz, "The Squad System"; Wayne, *The Reshaping of Plantation Society.*

3. Woodman, *New South, New Law.*

4. Brooks, "The Agrarian Revolution in Georgia," p. 67. On the Anglo-American legal tradition, see Karsten, "'Bottomed on Justice,'" pp. 213–261.

5. Hill, "Interstate Migration," p. 305; Scroggs, "Interstate Migration of the Negro Population," pp. 1034–1043.

6. Lemann, *The Promised Land,* p. 20.

7. Rapid black upward mobility on the postbellum Yazoo-Mississippi Delta is documented by Willis, *Forgotten Time,* pp. 3, 44–54, 58–75.

8. Higgs, "Firm-Specific Evidence," p. 241.

9. U.S. Bureau of the Census, 1933, Table 11 for each state.

10. Worthman, "Black Workers and Labor Unions," p. 392.

11. Becker, *The Economics of Discrimination;* Arrow, "The Theory of Discrimination."

12. Cited in Higgs, "Racial Wage Differentials in Agriculture," p. 310.

13. U.S. Industrial Commission, *Final Report,* 10:446, 471.

14. Whatley and Wright, "Race, Human Capital, and Labour Markets," pp. 276–278.

15. Sundstrom, "Half a Career," pp. 423–440.

16. Kousser, *The Shaping of Southern Politics,* pp. 41–62, 240–242. For an account of black agrarian activism, see Willis, *Forgotten Time,* pp. 115–143. C. Vann Woodward celebrated interracial Populist collaboration in *Tom Watson, Agrarian Rebel* (1938).

17. Key, *Southern Politics in State and Nation* (1949); Woodward, *Origins of the New South* (1951).

18. Kousser, *The Shaping of Southern Politics.* The quote is by Congressman Eaton J. Powers of Mississippi (p. 144). See also Perman, *Struggle for Mastery.*

19. Feldman, *The Disfranchisement Myth,* pp. 1–10, 21–47, 166–168.

20. Feldman, *The Disfranchisement Myth,* p. 13; Kousser, *The Shaping of Southern Politics,* pp. 183–195; "Governor Hoke Smith Beaten in Georgia," *New York Times,* June 5, 1908.

21. U.S. Industrial Commission, *Final Report,* p. 119.

22. Quoted in Anderson, *The Education of Blacks,* p. 96.

23. Harlan, *Separate and Unequal,* p. 235, 248–269; Kousser, *The Shaping of Southern Politics,* p. 229.

24. Jones, *Negro Education,* p. 28.

25. Gerber, "Public School Expenditures," pp. 309–322; Halcoussis, Ng, and Virts, "Property Ownership," pp. 128–139; Walters, Barnhouse, James, and McCammon, "Citizenship and Public Schools," pp. 34–52.

26. Kousser, "Progressivism for Middle-Class Whites Only," p. 191.

27. Feldman, *The Disfranchisement Myth,* pp. 15, 207–208; Williamson, *The Crucible of Race,* pp. 183–189; Willis, *Forgotten Time,* pp. 154–156.

28. Smith, "Race and Human Capital," pp. 685–698.

29. Wright, "Cheap Labor and Southern Textiles," pp. 619–628; Wright, *Old South, New South,* pp. 147–155.

30. Margo, *Race and Schooling in the South,* chapter 2.

31. A formalization of this equilibrium is Schwab, "Is Statistical Discrimination Efficient?"

32. Quoted in Anderson, *The Education of Blacks,* p. 84, emphasis added.

33. Anderson, *Education of Blacks in the South,* pp. 209–228.

34. Bond, *Negro Education in Alabama,* pp. 232, 240–243; Harris, "Stability and Change," pp. 378–380.

35. Fishback, "Can Competition among Employers Reduce Governmental Discrimination?," pp. 311–328.

36. Johnson, *Patterns of Negro Segregation,* p. 90.

37. Woodward, *Strange Career of Jim Crow,* pp. 32–33.

38. Rabinowitz, *Race Relations in the Urban South;* Rabinowitz, *Race, Ethnicity and Urbanization.*

39. Cell, *The Highest Stage of White Supremacy.*

40. Perman, *Struggle for Mastery,* pp. 61, 168, 248–260. In Arkansas the Democratic Convention of 1890 approved a separate-coach law "with a whoop and a hurrah," (p. 62) along with an election reform platform.

41. Ayers, *Promise of the New South,* p. 17; Perman, *Struggle for Mastery,* pp. 250–252.

42. Ayers, *Promise of the New South,* p. 142; Rabinowitz, *Race, Ethnicity, and Urbanization,* pp. 155–156; Perman, *Struggle for Mastery,* pp. 250–252; Welke, *Recasting American Liberty,* pp. 345–352.

43. This account is drawn from Palmore, "The Not-So-Strange Career," pp. 1777–1780.

44. Palmore, "The Not-So Strange Career," pp. 1804–1816.

45. Roback, "The Political Economy of Segregation," pp. 893–917; Meier and Rudwick, "The Boycott Movement against Jim Crow Streetcars," pp. 756–775.

46. Rabinowitz, *Race, Ethnicity and Urbanization,* pp. 144–146, 160–162.

47. Isenberg, *Downtown America,* pp. 188–192, 207.

48. Doyle, *New Men, New Cities, New South,* pp. 290–291, 303–304; Hale, *Making Whiteness,* p. 145; Newman, *Southern Hospitality,* pp. 47–50, 57, 95–99.

49. "President Resents Negro's Criticism," *New York Times,* Nov. 13, 1914.

50. Gilmore, *Defying Dixie,* p. 17. On the modernity of segregation, see Hale, *Making Whiteness,* p. 130; Cell, *Highest Stage of White Supremacy,* pp. 176–191.

51. This section and the one following draw upon Wright, "The New Deal and the Modernization of the South."

52. Oakes, "The Present Becomes the Past," pp. 149–163. Harold Woodman shows that although their labor practices fostered

backwardness, the plantations themselves were modern, well-organized, well-financed "emerging agribusinesses, using low-cost black labor" ("Political Economy," p. 257).

53. Bleakley, "Disease and Development," pp. 73–117; Troesken, *Water, Race and Disease,* pp. 1–12, 65–92. On manufacturing growth, see Wright, *Old South, New South,* pp. 61–62.

54. Hayes, *South Carolina and the New Deal,* p. 71.

55. Tindall, *Emergence of the New South,* pp. 477, 493. Figures on total WPA highway miles are from Federal Works Agency, *Final Report on the WPA Program,* p. 135.

56. Schulman, *From Cotton Belt to Sunbelt,* p. 91. "Living out of bags" and other phrases are from Kirby, *Rural Worlds Lost,* pp. 115–116.

57. Phillips, *This Land, This Nation,* pp. 83–107; Brown, *Electricity for Rural America,* pp. 67–75.

58. FDR's fireside chats were recalled in oral interviews reported in Bindas, *Remembering the Great Depression,* p. 40.

59. The forester is quoted in Boyd, "The Forest Is the Future," p. 174. The soil erosion estimates are from Odum, *Southern Regions of the United States,* p. 38.

60. Kirby, *The Countercultural South,* p. 49; Boyd, "The Forest Is the Future," pp. 179–180.

61. Hayes, *South Carolina,* p. 129; Phillips, *This Land, This Nation,* pp. 96–97, 126, 170–175; Whayne, *A New Plantation South,* pp. 168–170.

62. Fishback, Haines, and Kantor, "The Impact of the New Deal," pp. 93–122.

63. Hayes, *South Carolina,* pp. 64, 84; Biles, "The Persistence of the Past," p. 155; Lowitt, "The TVA, 1933–1945," p. 49; Brown, "Farm Children in the South," pp. 178–180.

64. Smith, *The New Deal in the Urban South,* pp. 122, 133–134.

65. Fleming, "The New Deal in Atlanta," pp. 15–16, 27–28.

66. Goldfield, *Cotton Fields and Skyscrapers,* pp. 181–182. The figures on water treatment are from Tarr, "Sewerage and the Development of the Networked City," p. 171.

67. Badger, *New Deal/New South,* p. 33.

68. Sitkoff, *A New Deal for Blacks;* Sullivan, *Days of Hope;* Gilmore, *Defying Dixie.* John Brueggemann concludes that the balance of forces "pulled the administration toward social policy that was moderately favorable and thus historically dramatic in terms of the interests of blacks" ("Racial Considerations and Social Policy in the 1930s," p. 168).

69. On the influence of southern planters on federal legislation, see Alston and Ferrie, *Southern Paternalism and the American Welfare State*; Lieberman, *Shifting the Color Line*; Quadagno, *The Color of Welfare*; Katznelson, *When Affirmative Action Was White*. Nonracial motivations for the southern position are stressed by Davies and Derthick, "Race and Social Welfare Policy," pp. 217–235. On planter control of local administration, among many possible citations, see Whayne, *A New Plantation South*, pp. 167, 175, 216. On Louisiana, see De Jong, *A Different Day*, p. 96. On mechanization, see Whatley, "Labor for the Picking."

70. Jones, *The Tribe of Black Ulysses*, p. 90. For other examples of black displacement prior to the New Deal, see Wolters, *Negroes and the Great Depression*, pp. 113–117.

71. Carlton and Coclanis, *Confronting Southern Poverty in the Great Depression*, pp. 25, 54, 139–143. On black job displacement, see Smith, *New Deal in the Urban South*, pp. 20–21; Heinemann, "Blue Eagle or Black Buzzard?," p. 97; Holmes, "The Blue Eagle as 'Jim Crow Bird,'" pp. 276–283.

72. Brown, *Race, Money and the American Welfare State*, pp. 78–80.

73. Biles, "The Persistence of the Past," p. 153; Sundstrom, "Last Hired, First Fired?," p. 417.

74. Grant, *The TVA and Black Americans*, pp. xvi, 23, 30, 48, 71, 86, 134–135.

75. This discussion draws upon Katznelson, *When Affirmative Action Was White*, pp. 113–140; Turner and Bound, "Closing the Gap or Widening the Divide." Katznelson draws in turn upon Onkst, "First a Negro" Frydl, *The GI Bill*.

76. Schulman, *From Cotton Belt to Sunbelt*, pp. 92–93.

77. On technological developments by International Harvester and other firms, see Whatley, "Southern Agrarian Labor Contracts," pp. 64–68; Fite, "Mechanization of Cotton Production," pp. 194–195, 198–204.

78. Kirby, "Black and White in the Rural South," p. 442.

79. Northrup, *The Negro in the Paper Industry*, p. 45.

80. Margo, *Race and Schooling in the South*, chapter 6.

81. National Planning Association, *Selected Studies of Negro Employment in the South*, p. 175. On Dewey's singularity, see Nicholls, *Southern Tradition and Regional Progress*, p. 185.

82. Greenberg, *Race and State in Capitalist Development*, pp. 228–229.

83. "Anti-Negro Acts Are Laid to G.M.," *New York Times*, Nov. 30, 1961.

84. Sandoval-Strausz, *Hotel,* p. 302; Gregory, *The Southern Diaspora,* p. 267.

85. Collins, "Race, Roosevelt, and Wartime Production," pp. 272–286.

86. Thornton, *Dividing Lines,* pp. 91–102.

87. Franklin, "History of Racial Segregation," p. 9.

88. C. Vann Woodward, "New South Fraud Is Papered by Old South Myth," *Washington Post,* July 9, 1961.

3   SOUTHERN BUSINESS AND PUBLIC ACCOMMODATIONS

1. Applebome, *Dixie Rising,* p. 17.

2. Muse, *American Negro Revolution,* p. 80.

3. Johnson, *Patterns of Negro Segregation,* p. 56.

4. Lewis, *Walking with the Wind,* p. 50.

5. *Negro Travelers' Green Book,* p. 3.

6. See Pollitt, "Dime Store Demonstrations," p. 316: "In some few instances, this discrimination is required by statute or city ordinance. In most instances, it is a matter of custom and tradition, and fear of losing white business if Negroes are served."

7. Wright, "Public Accommodations," pp. 87–88; Brown-Nagin, *Courage to Dissent,* p. 220. For example, Durham repealed its segregation ordinance in 1961, after the Supreme Court remanded a sit-in case to determine the ordinance's role in the arrest and conviction of the demonstrators. DeJarmon, "Public Accommodations," pp. 85–86.

8. Schmidt, "The Sit-ins and the State Action Doctrine."

9. Epstein, *Forbidden Grounds,* p. 128.

10. Oppenheimer, *The Sit-in Movement of 1960,* p. 126.

11. Quoted in Wolff, *Lunch at the Five and Ten,* p. 122.

12. *Women's Wear Daily,* May 10, 1960, emphasis added.

13. Quoted in Chafe, *Civilities and Civil Rights,* p. 136. See Isenberg, *Downtown America,* pp. 188–192.

14. *Women's Wear Daily,* April 14, 1960.

15. For additional reiterations of corporate hands-off policies, see *Women's Wear Daily,* March 21, 1960; April 27, 1960; May 10, 1960; May 18, 1960; *New York Times,* February 11, 1960; March 15, 1960; April 27, 1960; May 18, 1960.

16. Morris, *Origins of the Civil Rights Movement,* pp. 188–205.

17. Schmidt, "The Sit-ins and the State Action Doctrine," p. 776; Andrews and Biggs, "The Dynamics of Protest Diffusion," pp. 752–777; Biggs, "Who Joined the Sit-ins and Why," pp. 321–336. John Lewis describes his feelings of resentment when Thurgood Marshall arrived in Nashville at the height of the sit-ins, telling the activists they had made

their point and urging them to turn the issue over to the courts (*Walking with the Wind,* p. 113).

18. Mitchell and Peace, *Angry Black South,* pp. 101–103.

19. Kirk, *Redefining the Color Line,* pp. 63, 101.

20. Kirk, *Redefining the Color Line,* pp. 140, 143–144, 154.

21. Quoted in Thornton, *Dividing Lines,* p. 302.

22. Oppenheimer, *Sit-in Movement,* pp. 146–152; Luders, "Economics of Movement Success," pp. 986–990.

23. Chong, *Collective Action,* p. 174.

24. Quoted in Daniel, *Lost Revolutions,* p. 300.

25. This account is drawn from Ehle, *The Free Men.* The figures on segregation in Chapel Hill businesses are from a survey by the *Daily Tar Heel* in January 1964 (pp. 152–153).

26. Chafe, *Civilities and Civil Rights,* p. 136; Wolff, *Lunch at the Five and Ten,* pp. 173–174.

27. Halberstam, *The Children,* p. 178. Halberstam cites the estimates of Vivian Henderson, a Fisk economist who had studied black purchasing power in Nashville.

28. *Women's Wear Daily,* March 21, 1960; March 26, 1960; April 11, 1960; April 15, 1960.

29. Quoted in Isenberg, *Downtown America,* p. 210. Woolworth sales rose nationally by 11.8 percent in the first five months of 1960. Kress sales in the South fell by 15–18 percent, but the company claimed that a decline in 1960 had been expected anyway (Oppenheimer, *The Sit-in Movement,* p. 180).

30. *Women's Wear Daily,* May 10, 1960.

31. *New York Times,* May 15, 1960. For additional reports of retail losses in the South, see *Wall Street Journal,* May 16, 1960; November 18, 1960; December 20, 1960; January 16, 1962; September 6, 1962; March 11, 1963; May 16, 1963.

32. Fairbanks, *For the City as a Whole,* p. 238.

33. Randolph and Tate, *Rights for a Season,* pp. 180–185; *New York Times,* January 22, 1961.

34. Muse, *Ten Years of Prelude,* p. 206.

35. *Women's Wear Daily,* September 9, 1960.

36. *Women's Wear Daily,* May 16, 1963.

37. *Wall Street Journal,* July 15, 1963.

38. *New York Times,* May 6, 1961.

39. *Wall Street Journal,* July 15, 1963.

40. Most of the Federal Reserve department store figures were published by the Census Bureau in its *Monthly Retail Trade Report.* But there were unaccountable omissions. I thank Janet Swan of the Minneapolis

Federal Reserve Library for locating a complete microfilm copy. The survey was transferred to the Census Bureau in 1966. Because seasonality is severe in these types of data, no attempt has been made to interpret monthly fluctuations. All the figures in the graphs represent annual totals for calendar years. Nashville data are unfortunately not available.

41. Nor do the figures differentiate between sales in the downtown areas and in the suburbs of the metropolitan area. Much of the growth in the 1970s undoubtedly reflects suburbanization. The turning points in the 1960s, however, seem closely associated with Civil Rights issues.

42. Fairbanks, *For the City as a Whole,* p. 238; Jones and Long, *Negotiation of Desegregation,* pp. 19–20.

43. Jacoway, "Taken by Surprise," p. 37; Kirk, *Redefining the Color Line,* pp. 157–158.

44. Spitzberg, *Racial Politics in Little Rock,* p. 146. The black negotiators rejected the proposed restriction.

45. *Jet,* April 4, 1963, p. 17.

46. This summary draws on Hornsby, "A City That Was Too Busy to Hate," pp. 120–150; Pomerantz, *Where Peachtree Meets Sweet Auburn,* pp. 257–278; Brown-Nagin, *Courage to Dissent,* pp. 149–164. The first quotation appears in Kruse, *White Flight,* p. 182. The statement by Rich is from Brown-Nagin, *Courage to Dissent,* p. 155.

47. This summary draws on Morris, "Birmingham Confrontation Reconsidered," pp. 621–626; Eskew, *But for Birmingham,* pp. 194–199; Thornton, *Dividing Lines,* pp. 265–319.

48. Chappell, *Inside Agitators,* pp. 166, 197–200.

49. Box 30, "Oberdorfer Files on Southern Business," Burke Marshall Papers, John F. Kennedy Library, Boston.

50. On June 5, 1963, the *New York Times* reported, "All three Savannah movie houses, which racially integrated their theaters yesterday, resumed segregation today." In Jacksonville, Florida, local Civil Rights leaders reported in March 1964 that some restaurants "promised to serve Negroes and then backed out," while theaters returned to segregation after a trial period (*New York Times,* March 26, 1964).

51. Paschall, *It Must Have Rained,* pp. 55, 63–64; Hornsby, "A City That Was Too Busy to Hate," p. 135. Allen's memoir is quoted in Cortner, *Civil Rights and Public Accommodations,* p. 31.

52. *New York Times,* March 1, 1963.

53. *New York Times,* June 4, 1963.

54. *New York Times,* June 5, 1963.

55. Radio and Television Report to the American People on Civil Rights, June 11, 1963, John F. Kennedy Presidential Library website.

56. See, for example, the Justice Department file memo from Frank I. Michelman dated June 17, 1963, reporting a telephone conversation with Mr. Merritt of the National Association of Chain Drug Stores. Merritt noted the forthcoming editorial in *Chain Store Age* and similar commentary in *American Druggist,* a magazine for independents. Merritt also reported that chainwide desegregation instructions had been issued by Liggett's, Walgreen, and Eckard (Box 29, Marshall Papers).

57. *Kiplinger,* July 26, 1963.

58. *New York Times,* June 29, 1963.

59. *New York Times,* January 12, 1964.

60. *Wall Street Journal,* February 3, 1964.

61. *Wall Street Journal,* July 2, 1964.

62. Cortner, *Civil Rights and Public Accommodations,* pp. 6, 29, 64.

63. Muse, *Revolution,* pp. 75, 156–157.

64. These examples are drawn from the Department of Justice litigation case files, now at the National Archives in College Park, MD (Record Group 60, Class 168).

65. U.S. Commission on Civil Rights, *Twenty Years after Brown,* p. 73.

66. U.S. Department of Justice, *Annual Report of the Attorney General,* 1965–1977; Lerman and Sanderson, "Discrimination in Access to Public Places," pp. 216–226.

67. Cortner, *Civil Rights,* p. 92.

68. "The Supreme Court: Without a Doubt," *Time,* December 25, 1964; Don Milazzo, "Ollie's Barbecue Closes, but the Sauce Will Live On," *Birmingham Business Journal,* September 21, 2001. Cortner refutes the common belief that the Ollie's Barbecue case turned on interstate meat shipments (*Civil Rights,* p. 193). The restaurant was reopened by two of the McClung sons at a new location in 2005.

69. Bell, *And We Are Not Saved,* pp. 62–63. See also Bell, "Economic Determinism and Interest Convergence," pp. 27–54.

70. Folder: Compliance Meetings Undated, Box 22, Marshall Papers. Manger notes that a similar report at a meeting on June 27 "brought about some rather critical discussion" from two black participants. Fellow panel member James Forman took particular exception to Manger's comment that southern businessmen expressed no objection to "Negroes who were clean and well-dressed using public accommodation facilities." Manger responded that he had heard this concern expressed many times and that hotel and motel operators were in fact allowed by law to set standards of dress, and so on. The meeting reportedly ended "on a very friendly note," but it is not hard to see the contrast

between the black perception of the issues and the mode of persuasion used between one white businessman and another.

71. Hyman and Sheatsley, "Attitudes toward Desegregation"; Greeley and Sheatsley, "Attitudes toward Racial Integration."

72. Black and Black, *Politics and Society,* pp. 111–112, 200.

73. Abbott, "The Norfolk Business Community," pp. 101, 113.

74. Quoted in Salmond, *Southern Struggles,* p. 161.

75. Ehle, *Free Men,* p. 327.

76. Quoted in Chafe, *Civilities,* p. 287. By 1970 the Chamber was firmly in favor of "the liberation of white and black together from this heritage of bondage" (Sokol, *There Goes My Everything,* p. 323).

77. Interview in Raines, *My Soul Is Rested,* p. 82.

4 DESEGREGATING SOUTHERN LABOR MARKETS

1. Butler, Heckman, and Payner, "The Impact of the Economy and of the State," p. 240.

2. This paragraph draws upon Arrow, "Models of Job Discrimination"; Wright, *Old South, New South,* pp. 187–192; Whatley and Wright, "Race, Human Capital, and Labour Markets," pp. 273–281.

3. Fredrickson, "Four Decades of Change," pp. 71, 75.

4. Rowan, "The Negro in the Textile Industry," p. 135; Fredrickson, "Four Decades of Change," p. 73.

5. Kidder, "Federal Compliance Efforts," pp. 354–356; Butler, Heckman, Payner, "The Impact of the Economy," pp. 243, 309–314; Minchin, *Hiring the Black Worker,* pp. 52–53.

6. Quoted in Minchin, *Hiring the Black Worker,* p. 51; Minchin, "Federal Policy and the Racial Integration of Southern Industry," pp. 157–158.

7. Minchin, *Hiring the Black Worker,* pp. 53–55. On the legislative history, see Burstein, *Discrimination, Jobs and Politics,* pp. 9, 53. For adverse industry reaction to the Charlotte forum, see "Negro Gains Found in Textile Industry," *New York Times,* Jan. 12, 1967.

8. Quoted in Fredrickson, "Four Decades of Change," p. 73. Statistical results on federal contracts are in Kidder, "Federal Compliance Efforts," pp. 356–360, and Butler, Heckman, Payner, "The Impact of the Economy and the State," pp. 321–325.

9. Minchin, *Hiring the Black Worker,* pp. 265–266. See also the table of turnover rates on p. 183. Roy Reed, "Industry in South Woos Negro Labor," *New York Times,* May 19, 1969; Reese Cleghorn, "The Mill: A Giant Step for the Southern Negro," *New York Times,* Nov. 9, 1969.

10. Greenberg, *Crusaders in the Courts,* p. 446. Similarly, Minchin writes, "The desegregation of textiles and paper occurred at a time of declining employment opportunities" (*From Rights to Economics,* p. 43).

11. Minchin, *Hiring the Black Worker,* p. 32; Reed, "Industry in South," p. 42. For additional references to black mill workers sending their children to college, see Cleghorn, "The Mill"; Byerly, *Hard Times Cotton Mill Girls,* pp. 138, 154.

12. Donohue and Heckman, "Continuous versus Episodic Change," pp. 1608–1610. The contrast between southern textiles and northern construction is emphasized in MacLean, *Freedom Is Not Enough,* pp. 78–103.

13. Ferman, *The Negro and Equal Employment Opportunities,* p. 65; Marshall, *Negro Employment in the South,* vol. 2; Marshall and Christian, *Employment of Blacks in the South,* p. 182.

14. Chen, *The Fifth Freedom,* pp. 182–196.

15. Minchin, *Color of Work,* p. 65, citing a 1967 interview by Herbert Northrup and his own interview of the manager of industrial relations at the Union Camp Company in Savannah, Georgia.

16. Minchin, *Color of Work,* pp. 49, 62–64, 149–162, 213–214; Minchin, *From Rights to Economics,* pp. 38–39.

17. This account draws upon Smith, *Race, Labor and Civil Rights,* especially chapters 2–6.

18. Boyd and another janitor did take the test, which consisted of fifty relatively complex questions to be answered in twelve minutes, though the job they were applying for was hauling coal. Neither man passed.

19. This promotion was not altogether smooth. After first trying to persuade Boyd not to apply for the supervisory job, plant managers then promoted a white man along with Boyd to the same position, making it a two-man job (Smith, *Race, Labor and Civil Rights,* pp. 178–179)!

20. Blumrosen, "The Legacy of *Griggs,*" pp. 1, 3, 10.

21. Ashenfelter and Heckman, "Measuring the Effect of an Antidiscrimination Program"; Freeman, "The Changing Labor Market for Black Americans"; Chay, "The Impact of Federal Civil Rights Policy"; Chay and Honore, "Estimation of Semiparametric Censored Regression Models"; Leonard, "The Impact of Affirmative Action on Employment"; Leonard, "The Impact of Affirmative Action Regulation and Equal Employment Law on Black Employment"; Carrington, McCue, and Pierce, "Using Establishment Size to Measure the Impact of Title VII."

22. Minchin, *Hiring the Black Worker,* p. 59.

23. Leonard, "The Impact of Affirmative Action Regulation," pp. 60–61; Blumrosen, "The Legacy of *Griggs,*" p. 10.

24. Stainback, Robinson, and Tomaskovic-Devey, "Race and Workplace Integration," pp. 1205–1207. The effectiveness of fair-employment laws outside the South is demonstrated in Collins, "The Labor-Market Impact of State-Level Anti-Discrimination Laws, 1940–1960."

25. Minchin, *From Rights to Economics,* pp. 34–36.

26. Butler, Heckman, and Payner, "The Impact of the Economy and the State," pp. 233–234.

27. Fossett, Galle, and Kelly, "Racial Occupational Inequality, 1940–1980."

28. Hyde, "A Righteous Collusion." On trends in retail sales employment, see Perry, "The Negro in the Department Store Industry," pp. 41, 47, 86, 105–108; Fletcher, "The Negro in the Drugstore Industry," pp. 46, 49, 82–87.

29. This account is drawn from Watkins, *The Black O,* pp. 69–70, 111, 125–132, 231.

30. A recent restatement is Moreno, *Black Americans and Organized Labor.*

31. Norrell, "Caste in Steel," p. 685; Nelson, "CIO Meant One Thing for the Whites," pp. 116–117. Among many accounts of race and unionism in the South, see Honey, *Southern Labor and Black Civil Rights.* An economic analysis of segregation in southern railroads is Sundstrom, "Half a Career."

32. Botson, *Labor, Civil Rights, and the Hughes Tool Company,* pp. 163–186. The quotation is on p. 166.

33. Greenberg, *Race and State in Capitalist Development,* pp. 231–233.

34. Habbe, *Company Experience with Negro Employment,* p. 145.

35. Quoted in Minchin, *From Rights to Economics,* p. 32.

36. In addition to Duke Power, another example is provided by Nelson for the Atlantic Steel Company. After making concessions on the issue of transfer rights, the company unilaterally imposed a test-taking criterion as a condition for such transfers ("CIO Meant One Thing for the Whites," p. 135).

37. Draper, *Conflict of Interests,* pp. 29, 121.

38. Draper, *Conflicts of Interest,* pp. 37, 104–105, 158.

39. Donohue, Heckman, and Todd, "The Schooling of Southern Blacks."

40. Card and Krueger, "School Quality and Relative Black/White Earnings," pp. 167–168. See Figure 5.1.

41. Smith, "Race and Human Capital"; Smith and Welch, "Black Economic Progress Since Myrdal."

42. U.S. Industrial Commission, *Final Report*, p. 497.

43. William H. Baldwin Jr., quoted in Anderson, *The Education of Blacks in the South*, pp. 84, 91. Baldwin was a railroad entrepreneur from Boston who came to the South in 1894 to reorganize the region's railroads. He employed thousands of black workers.

44. Anderson, *Education of Blacks in the South*, pp. 222–228.

45. Minchin, *Color of Work*, pp. 37–38.

46. Southern Regional Council, *The Negro and Employment Opportunities in the South*, reports on Houston, Chattanooga, Atlanta.

47. Southern Regional Council, report on Houston, pp. 791–793.

48. Card and Krueger, "School Quality and Black-White Relative Earnings," pp. 153, 164–165. For the black cohort born between 1940 and 1949 and residing in the South in 1980, Card and Krueger estimate the rate of return to schooling as 7.69 percent for the southern-born and 9.49 percent for the northern-born (p. 164). Card and Krueger are unable to identify a statistically significant effect of black school quality on returns prior to the Civil Rights Act (p. 183).

49. Mingle, *Black Enrollment in Higher Education*.

50. Freeman, *Black Elite*, pp. 34–36.

51. Peter Braestrup, "U.S. Panel Split over Negro Jobs," *New York Times*, June 18, 1962.

52. Braestrup, "U.S. Panel Split over Negro Jobs"; Peter Braestrup, "White House Urged to Use Compulsion in Negro Job Drive," *New York Times*, Aug. 19, 1962.

53. Southern Research Council, "Plans for Progress: Atlanta Survey," Jan. 1963, Box 33, BM to RFK (Mar. 2, 1963), Burke Marshall Papers, John F. Kennedy Library, Boston; John D. Pomfret, "Negro-Job Pledge Is Found Flouted," *New York Times*, Apr. 16, 1963.

54. Gourlay, *The Negro Salaried Worker*, pp. 14, 77–78; Habbe, *Company Experience with Negro Employment*, pp. 6–8, 110–118, 124–127, 128–131.

55. Henry C. Baker, "A Voluntary Approach," in Northrup and Rowan, *The Negro and Employment Opportunities*, pp. 111–121.

56. Dobbin, *Inventing Equal Opportunity*, chapters 1–5. A similar thesis is presented in Delton, *Racial Integration in Corporate America*.

57. Dobbin, *Inventing Equal Opportunity*, p. 158. For evidence on the spread of personnel offices and affirmative action policies, see the graphs on pp. 54, 87, 115, 117, 123. See also Bureau of National Affairs, *Equal Employment Opportunity*.

58. Anne B. Fisher, "Businessmen Like to Hire by the Numbers," *Fortune*, Sept. 16, 1985; "Rethinking Weber."

59. Dobbin, *Inventing Equal Opportunity*, pp. 14–15, 45–49, 56–61; Kennesaw State University Oral History Project, interview with Hugh L. Gordon, July 18, 2000.

60. Leonard, "The Impact of Affirmative Action," p. 58.

61. Dobbin, *Inventing Equal Opportunity*, p. 135.

62. Beginning in 1966, private sector firms with more than fifty employees (twenty-five if federal contractors) were required to submit yearly reports on the racial/ethnic and sex composition of their workforce. The thresholds were changed in 1983 to 150 employees, fifty for federal contractors.

63. On industrial decline and midwestern black workers, see Bound and Freeman, "What Went Wrong?"

64. The shares reported in Table 4.4 are virtually the same as those found in the corporations surveyed by the Bureau of National Affairs in 1975. See *Equal Employment Opportunity: Programs and Results*, Figure 4 on p. 13.

65. Button and Rienzo, "The Impact of Affirmative Action," p. 5; Stoll, Raphael, and Holzer, "Black Job Applicants and the Hiring Officer's Race"; Giuliano, Levine, and Leonard, "Manager Race and the Race of New Hires," esp. pp. 608–611.

66. Fredrickson, "Four Decades of Change," p. 75. For evidence on black migration into textile states during 1965–1970, see McHugh, "Black Migration Reversal," p. 179.

67. Margo, *Race and Schooling in the South*; Tolnay, "Educational Selection in the Migration of Southern Blacks"; Vigdor, "The Pursuit of Opportunity." Tolnay and Vigdor report that the degree of educational selectivity in black out-migration declined over time. But comparisons over time are complicated by the general extension of black schooling in the South and by the mechanization of agriculture, which added a "push" factor at the low end of the educational distribution. Vigdor's data show that the median black interstate migrant age eighteen to twenty-seven in 1970 was a high school graduate ("Pursuit of Opportunity," p. 416).

68. Southern Regional Council, *The Negro and Employment Opportunities*, report on Chattanooga.

69. Vigdor, "The New Promised Land," Tables 3, 5, 6. Vigdor notes, "The fact that the time series cross, rather than converge, indicates that economic processes more complex than mere regional convergence are at play" (p. 27).

70. Frey, "The New Great Migration," pp. 95–100; Hunt, Hunt, and Falk, "Who Is Headed South?," pp. 103–110. The apparent statistical anomaly (that more whites move into the South though the black southern migration rate is higher) is explained by the much larger white population base in the national totals.

71. Suzi Parker, "Defying Past, Blacks Head South," *Christian Science Monitor,* June 8, 1998.

72. Sam Roberts, "New York City Losing Blacks, Census Shows," *New York Times,* Apr. 3, 2006.

73. David Firestone, "As a Region's Economy Booms, So Does Interest in Its Politics," *New York Times,* Mar. 7, 2000.

74. Ben Bain, "New 'Migration' Sends Black Americans Back to Their Roots in the South," *Financial Times,* Dec. 6, 2005.

75. Black median income in the West (not shown in the figure) was reported as somewhat higher than in the South in 2000, though it fluctuated erratically year-to-year, presumably because of small sample sizes. Whether or not black incomes were higher, the West also experienced net black out-migration between 1995 and 2000, in favor of the South. See Frey, "The New Great Migration," p. 105.

76. This argument is advanced in Donohue, "Is Title VII Efficient?" A rebuttal is presented by Epstein, *Forbidden Grounds,* pp. 77–78, 257–259. The quote from Hatch is from "Loading the Economy," p. 264, arguing that racial affirmative action imposed massive costs on the private sector.

5   THE ECONOMICS OF SOUTHERN SCHOOL DESEGREGATION

1. Donohue, Heckman, and Todd, "The Schooling of Southern Blacks," pp. 236–240. Even the concept that black teachers were acceptable in black schools required an extended campaign, largely successful by 1919 despite the absence of black political representation. See Fairclough, *Teaching Equality,* p. 8.

2. Donohue, Heckman, and Todd, "The Schooling of Southern Blacks," pp. 244–251; Card and Krueger, "School Quality," pp. 165–173; Cecelski, *Along Freedom Road,* p. 29.

3. Kluger, *Simple Justice,* pp. 291, 367, 542, emphasis added.

4. Professor Kenneth Clark presented evidence that black children preferred white dolls to brown dolls, but he did not show that black children in segregated schools favored white dolls more than did those in integrated schools. As Professor Ernest van den Haag pointed out, if anything, Clark's evidence seemed to support the opposite conclusion (Kluger, *Simple Justice,* pp. 355–356). On the variability of

psychological findings, see St. John, *School Desegregation,* esp. pp. 42–86, 107.

5. Kluger, *Simple Justice,* pp. 577, 707–708.

6. Wolters, *Burden of Brown,* p. 80; Patterson, *Brown v. Board of Education,* p. 100; Irons, *Jim Crow's Children,* p. 190; Cascio, Gordon, Lewis, and Reber, "From Brown to Busing," Table 1; Jacoway and Williams, *Understanding the Little Rock Crisis.* Ernest Green, the only senior of the Little Rock Nine, graduated in June 1958, with Martin Luther King Jr. in attendance.

7. Jeffrey, *Education for the Children of the Poor,* pp. 107–109.

8. *Alexander v. Holmes County Board of Education* 396 U.S. 1218 (1969).

9. Cascio, Gordon, Lewis, and Reber, "Paying for Progress," Tables III–VI; Giles, "HEW versus the Federal Courts," pp. 84–88.

10. Jacoway, "Taken by Surprise"; Jacoway, *Turn Away Thy Son,* pp. 137, 300–308, 349–352.

11. Kruse, *White Flight,* pp. 148, 200; Cramer, "School Desegregation and New Industry"; Hornsby, "A City That Was Too Busy to Hate"; and Chafe, "Greensboro NC."

12. Reber, "Court-Ordered Desegregation." Reber's study uses a national sample of large school districts with at least one court-ordered desegregation plan between 1961 and 1986.

13. Clotfelter, "Tipping," pp. 30, 41–47 and Table 4; Clotfelter, *After Brown,* pp. 110–114. The level of the "tipping point" came in for discussion across the South; Fairclough notes that a threshold of 30 percent black was frequently claimed in Louisiana (*Race and Democracy,* p. 453).

14. Pride and Woodard, *The Burden of Busing,* pp. 134–136.

15. See, for example, Rossell and Hawley, *Consequences of Desegregation,* pp. 32–33.

16. On the historical origins of southern school districts, see Fischel, *Making the Grade,* pp. 170–183.

17. This paragraph is drawn primarily from Orfield, *Public School Desegregation.* On the effects of school district size, see Reber, "Court-Ordered Desegregation."

18. Orfield and Eaton, *Dismantling Desegregation;* Boger and Orfield, *School Resegregation.* A 2007 report of the U.S. Commission on Civil Rights supported withdrawal of the courts from such matters with the following argument: "By its nature, judicial supervision supplanted the decisions of locally elected officials and professional educators with those of an unelected judge without special training or expertise in educational policy" (*Becoming More Separate?,* p. xi).

19. Guryan, "Desegregation and Black Dropout Rates," pp. 932–934.

20. Reber, "School Desegregation and Educational Attainment for Blacks." See also Reber, "From Separate and Unequal to Integrated and Equal?"

21. Boozer, Krueger, and Wolkon, "Race and School Quality since *Brown v. Board of Education*," Table 8. The authors also found that the post-desegregation cohorts were more likely to attend integrated colleges and to work with a larger share of nonblack coworkers.

22. Ashenfelter, Collins, and Yoon, "Evaluating the Role of *Brown*," Tables 2–4.

23. Chay, Guryan, and Mazumder, "Birth Cohort and the Black-White Test-Score Gap." The fall in black postnatal mortality rates is elaborated more fully in Almond, Chay, and Greenstone, "The Civil Rights Act of 1964, Hospital Desegregation and Black Infant Mortality in Mississippi."

24. Johnson, "Long-Run Impact of School Desegregation." Johnson's research will appear in *Desegregation and (Un)equal Opportunity*, to be published by the Russell Sage Foundation.

25. This list follows Ashenfelter, Collins, and Yoon, "Evaluating the Role of *Brown*." The last possibility is supported by Grawe and Wahl, "Blacks, Whites, and *Brown*," who find a positive effect of the *Brown* decision on black earnings, even before significant school desegregation had occurred.

26. Quoted in Wolters, *Burden of Brown*, p. 285.

27. Quoted in Wolters, *Burden of Brown*, p. 127.

28. Wolters, *Burden of Brown*, p. 173.

29. Fairclough, *Race and Democracy*, pp. 449–453.

30. Clotfelter, *After Brown*, p. 93.

31. Rossell and Hawley, *Consequences of School Desegregation*, pp. 23–29.

32. James T. Wooten, "Private Schools Thrive in South, but Finances Restrict Quality," *New York Times*, Feb. 1, 1970; Jack Rosenthal, "White Academies Termed Inferior," *New York Times*, July 2, 1970; Nevin and Bills, *The Schools That Fear Built*, pp. 68, 177.

33. Regan Loyola Connolly, "Private Schools Diversify," *Montgomery Advertiser*, Jan. 12, 2004.

34. Schofield, "Review of Research," pp. 599–602.

35. Frankenberg and Orfield, *Lessons in Integration*, p. 14.

36. Baker, *Paradoxes of Desegregation*, pp. xxii, 135.

37. Bryson and Bentley, *Ability Grouping of Public School Students*, pp. 25–26, 54–67, 117–119.

38. Clotfelter, *After Brown*, pp. 130, 145–146; Clotfelter, Ladd, and Vigdor, "Classroom-Level Segregation."

39. Clotfelter, *After Brown,* pp. 139–145.

40. Clotfelter, *After Brown,* p. 139; Sara Corbett, "A Prom Divided," *New York Times Magazine,* May 24, 2009, pp. 24–29.

41. McElreath, "The Cost of Opportunity," p. 22.

42. This paragraph draws upon Douglas, *Reading, Writing and Race,* pp. 44–45, 52–55, 80–83; Lassiter, *The Silent Majority,* pp. 131–160; Hanchett, *Sorting Out the New South City,* pp. 224, 227–248.

43. Gaillard, *Dream Long* Deferred, p. xi; Douglas, *Reading, Writing and Race,* pp. 250–251; Lassiter, *The Silent Majority,* pp. 210–211; Applebome, *Dixie Rising,* p. 168.

44. See, for example, Lee A. Daniels, "In Defense of Busing," *New York Times,* Apr. 17, 1983.

45. Douglas, *Reading, Writing, and Race,* pp. 196, 249–250. School administer quoted in Gaillard, *The Dream Long Deferred,* p. 135.

46. Douglas, *Reading, Writing, and Race,* pp. 76–77, 139; Smith, *Boom for Whom?,* pp. 57–59.

47. Douglas, *Reading, Writing, and Race,* pp. 233–234.

48. Smith, *Boom for Whom?,* pp. 217–220. The phrase "biracial coalition around economic growth" is from Abbott, *New Urban America,* p. 257.

49. This summary draws upon Smith, *Boom for Whom?,* pp. 121–201; Mickelson, Smith, and Southworth, "Resegregation, Achievement, and the Chimera of Choice," pp. 129–138.

50. Mickelson, Smith, and Southworth, "Resegregation," esp. pp. 142, 145, 149–151.

51. See the articles listing Charlotte-Mecklenburg district awards in Mickelson, Smith, and Southworth, "Resegregation," note 6, and Smith, "Development and the Politics of School Desegregation and Resegregation," note 43.

52. Compare Armor, *Forced Justice,* and Orfield and Lee, *Historic Reversals.*

53. Minow, *In Brown's Wake,* p. 26.

54. U.S. Commission on Civil Rights, *Becoming Less Separate?*

55. Clotfelter, Ladd, and Vigdor, "Federal Oversight, Local Control and the Specter of 'Resegregation' in Southern Schools." This finding does not imply that reduced judicial scrutiny had no effect. The authors suggest that school segregation might have declined in the absence of these decisions because the level of residential segregation fell during this period.

56. Lutz, "The End of Court-Ordered Desegregation," pp. 150–164. An analysis of all districts with at least two thousand students that were under court supervision in 1990 reports that the timing of release was

not tightly linked to success in achieving integration and that the greatest consequent increases in black-white segregation occurred in the South. See Reardon, Grewal, Kalogrides, and Greenberg, "*Brown* Fades." Reardon et al. find no evidence of "reverse white flight" after release from court oversight.

57. The NAEP is administered by federal officials who visit participating schools. Since, in addition, it is not a high-stakes test with financial consequences for schools and students, the NAEP has not been the object of cheating allegations that have received much attention in recent years. It is, however, subject to potential bias because of variations in participation rates. See Amrein and Berliner, "High-Stakes Testing."

58. Because a breakdown of regional scores by race is available only beginning in 1975, the black score for 1971 was estimated under the assumption that the white-black ratio did not change between 1971 and 1975. Thus Figure 5.6 probably understates the rise in black scores between these years.

59. The West region is excluded from the figures because relatively few blacks are in that region; hence the estimated standard errors are large. Average black scores in the West are slightly lower than the Southeast.

60. Sam Dillon, "Racial Gap in Testing Sees Shift by Region," *New York Times,* July 15, 2009. The article discusses the 2009 report by the U.S. Department of Education, Institute of Educational Sciences, National Center for Education Statistics, *Achievement Gaps.*

61. The pattern for mathematics is essentially similar, but these scores are available only beginning in 1978.

62. Evidence for North Carolina is presented in Vigdor and Nechyba, "Peer Effects in North Carolina Public Schools," though they question the causal role of peer effects. The broader hypothesis relating test scores to peer effects of socioeconomic status is discussed in Vigdor and Ludwig, "Segregation and the Test Score Gap."

63. Wiese, "African-American Suburbanization," p. 228. This paragraph is drawn from Wiese's essay.

64. This account draws upon Smith, "Still Swimming against the Tide?," pp. 1145–1208.

65. Emily Bazelon, "The Next Kind of Integration," *New York Times Magazine,* July 20, 2008, pp. 38–43; Robert Barnes, "New Look at School Integration," *Washington Post,* Sept. 20, 2010; Alan Finder, "As Test Scores Jump, Raleigh Credits Integration by Income," *New York Times,* Sept. 25, 2005

66. Kahlenberg, *Rescuing Brown vs. Board of Education,* pp. 3–4. Additional southern examples of voluntary integration strategies are

provided in Holley-Walker, "After Unitary Status," pp. 891–907. Holley-Walker highlights Seminole County, Florida, whose policy considers racial integration, socioeconomic status, and other forms of diversity in a way that may prove to be a model for other districts (pp. 899–901).

6   THE ECONOMIC CONSEQUENCES OF VOTING RIGHTS

1. Allan M. Winkler, "Voting Rights Act Has Stormy History," *Eugene (Oregon) Register-Guard,* June 22, 1982; Blum, *Unintended Consequences,* p. 1.

2. The quote is from Johnson's speech at the signing ceremony, quoted in Blum, *Unintended Consequences,* p. 3.

3. The 1940 and 1947 figures are from various NAACP surveys, and the 1952 estimate is from the Southern Regional Council. See Price, *The Negro Voter in the South* and *The Negro and the Ballot in the South.* On the white primary and the poll tax campaigns, see Lawson, *Black Ballots,* pp. 23–85.

4. Keech, *Impact of Negro Voting,* p. 39.

5. Thornton, *Dividing Lines,* pp. 29, 48.

6. Price, *The Negro Voter in the South,* p. 59.

7. Lawson, *Black Ballots,* pp. 167–220.

8. Watters and Cleghorn, *Climbing Jacob's Ladder,* p. 376; Garrow, *Protest at Selma,* pp. 11, 19.

9. Lawson, *Black Ballots,* pp. 261–287. Marshall's views on the limits of federal powers under the Constitution were summarized in his 1964 book, *Federalism and Civil Rights* (quote on p. 24). The 1962 turning point in registration is documented in Timpone, "Mass Mobilization or Government Intervention?"

10. This summary draws upon Lawson, *Black Ballots,* pp. 307–330; Bullock and Gaddie, *The Triumph of Voting Rights,* pp. 11–13; Timpone, "Mass Mobilization," p. 435; U.S. Commission on Civil Rights, *Political Participation.*

11. For comprehensive data by state for 1980–2006, see Tables B.1 and B.2 in Bullock and Gaddie, *Triumph of Voting Rights.* The increase in southern white registration rates is discussed in Stanley, *Voter Mobilization and the Politics of Race,* pp. 4–16, 23–102.

12. Lawson, *In Pursuit of Power,* pp. 35, 99, 107.

13. Campbell and Feagin, "Black Politics in the South," pp. 138, 140–41; Valelly, *Two Reconstructions,* p. 211. Campbell and Feagin report figures for the entire South. The numbers for the covered states are from U.S. Commission on Civil Rights, *The Voting Rights Act,* p. 328.

14. U.S. Commission on Civil Rights, *The Voting Rights Act,* p. 336.

15. Lawson, *In Pursuit of Power;* Bullock and Gaddie, *Triumph of Voting Rights,* p. 32.

16. Parker, *Black Votes Count,* p. 54.

17. Davidson and Grofman, *Quiet Revolution,* pp. 32–36, 335–350.

18. Quoted in Bullock and Gaddie, *Triumph of Voting Rights,* p. 16.

19. See the state tables in Bullock and Gaddie, *Triumph of Voting Rights,* pp. 42, 68, 92, 124, 148, 176, 204.

20. *Voting Rights—and Wrongs,* p. 15. The earlier book was *Whose Votes Count?* Thernstrom continues to be critical of applications of the Voting Rights Act outside of this historical context.

21. This paragraph is drawn from Bullock and Gaddie, *Triumph of Voting Rights,* pp. 43, 70–72, 125–126, 150, 177, 296, 316, 330–334. African Americans have served on the supreme court in several states. On the sources of Wilder's electoral support, see Davidson and Grofman, *Quiet Revolution,* p. 278.

22. John Herbers, "Dr. King and 770 Others Seized in Alabama Protest," *New York Times,* Feb. 2, 1965.

23. Raines, *My Soul Is Rested,* p. 228.

24. Quoted in Button, *Blacks and Social Change,* p. 4. Many other skeptics are cited in Campbell and Feagin, "Black Politics in the South," pp. 130–131.

25. Keech, *The Impact of Negro Voting,* pp. 53–65, 75–78.

26. Wirt, *Politics of Southern Equality,* pp. 166–175; Lawson, *Black Ballots,* p. 339.

27. Hanks, *The Struggle for Black Political Empowerment,* pp. 65–66.

28. Button, *Blacks and Social Change,* p. 71.

29. Thompson, "The Voting Rights Act in North Carolina," pp. 144, 149, 151.

30. Coombs, Alsikafi, Bryan, and Webber, "Black Political Control," 398–406; Perry, "The Socioeconomic Impact," 214–218.

31. Cascio and Washington, "Valuing the Vote." State transfers were primarily for education but also included funds for highways and general spending.

32. Quoted in Lawson, *In Pursuit of Power,* p. 301.

33. Quoted in Thernstrom, *Voting Rights—and Wrongs,* p. 14.

34. Swain, *Black Faces,* pp. 89–97. My wife and I had the same experience in the office of Congresswoman Eva Clayton in 1998.

35. Hanks, *Struggle for Black Empowerment,* pp. 69–70. Lists of services provided are on pp. 178–179.

36. Wirt, *"We Ain't What We Was,"* p. 69.

37. Button, Rienzo, and Croucher, *Blacks and the Quest,* pp. 75–102; Gainous, Button, and Rienzo, "African Americans and Municipal Employment." See also Wirt, *"We Ain't What We Was,"* pp. 72–74.

38. Meier and England, "Black Representation and Educational Policy"; Meier, Juenke, Wrinkle, and Polinard, "Structural Choices and Representational Biases."

39. Eisinger, "Black Employment in Municipal Jobs," p. 385.

40. This account draws on Byng, "Responding to Black Political Interests," pp. 209–223. Stein and Condrey, "Integrating Municipal Workforces," find that local black political strength (either a black mayor or a white mayor dependent on black electoral support) was the primary factor accounting for the pace of municipal workforce integration.

41. Nye, Rainier, and Stratmann, "Do Black Mayors Improve Black Employment Outcomes?"

42. Chatterji, Chay, and Fairlie, "The Impact of City Contracting Set-asides." Explicit set-asides were barred by the Supreme Court in 1989, but black mayors might still be sensitive to racial equity in contract policy.

43. McDonald, *Voting Rights Odyssey,* pp. 95–96, 151.

44. Valelly, "Net Gains," pp. 316–319.

45. Hanks, *The Struggle for Black Political Empowerment,* pp. 74–76.

46. Button, *Blacks and Social Change,* pp. 52–62.

47. Wirt, *"We Ain't the Way We Was,"* p. 67.

48. McDonald, *Voting Rights Odyssey,* pp. 238–245. Steven Light tells a similar story for Tallulah, Louisiana, a poor town in a black-majority parish in the northeastern part of the state. After a redistricting suit was settled in 1992, black political leadership launched a concerted economic development campaign, with mixed results. See *"The Law Is Good,"* pp. 101–137.

49. Couto, *Ain't Gonna Let Nobody Turn Me Round,* p. 251.

50. Button, *Blacks and Social Change,* p. 60.

51. Green, *Praying for Sheetrock,* p. 250.

52. Kruse, *White Flight,* pp. 105–130, 233, 242.

53. Florida, *Rise of the Creative Class;* Hackler, *Cities in the Technology Economy;* Markusen and Schrock, "The Distinctive City." The phrase "hollow prize" was first applied to black mayors in 1969 by Paul Friese.

54. Parker, *Black Votes Count,* p. 209.

55. Francesca Levy, "America's Best Bang-for-the-Buck Cities," Forbes.com, Nov. 30, 2009.

56. This account draws on Smith, *Boom for Whom?*, pp. 217–220. See also Hackler, *Cities in the Technology Economy*, pp. 127–129; Leinberger, "New Kind of Growth."

57. Scribner, *Renewing Birmingham*, pp. 34, 57, 79; Connerly, *"The Most Segregated City,"* pp. 102–128.

58. Conner, "Building Moderate Progress," chapter 5.

59. Scribner, *Renewing Birmingham*, pp. 59–61, 127–130; Connerly, *"The Most Segregated City,"* pp. 125, 208; Perry, "The Evolution and Impact of Biracial Coalitions," p. 232; Thornton, *Dividing Lines*, pp. 370–379.

60. David Firestone, "Mayor Improves Image of Birmingham but Not Racial Split," *New York Times*, July 18, 1999.

61. Michael E. Kanell, "Birmingham: Steel Town Reforges Itself with Mix of Automaking, Banking and Biotech," *Atlanta Journal-Constitution*, June 23, 2002.

62. Rob Gurwitt, "Atlanta and the Urban Future," *Governing Magazine*, July 1, 2008.

63. Stern, *Calculating Visions*, p. 211.

64. Quoted in Valelly, *The Two Reconstructions*, p. 198.

65. Brady and Sinclair, "Building Majorities," p. 1054.

66. Black and Black, *Rise of Southern Republicans*, p. 135. The division of offices across the southern states is of course not necessarily a good index of the competitiveness of elections for these offices within states. But more sophisticated indices show two-party competitiveness in virtually all southern states as of the 1970s. See Lamis, *The Two-Party South*, pp. 42, 46, 66, 85, 94, 110, 121, 137, 159, 170, 184, 195.

67. Muse, *American Negro Revolution*, p. 265.

68. Davidson and Grofman, *Quiet Revolution in the South*, p. 215.

69. Cohodas, *Strom Thurmond*, pp. 412–413, 451; Stanley, *Voter Mobilization*, pp. 142–143; Thernstrom, *Whose Votes Count?*, p. 3. West's 1970 campaign is recounted in Black, *Southern Governors*, pp. 84–85.

70. Parker, *Black Votes Count*, p. 300.

71. Lawson, *In Pursuit of Power*, p. x.

72. Stanley, *Voter Mobilization*, pp. 14, 50–52, 57–70.

73. Key, *Southern Politics*, esp. pp. 1–18.

74. Husted and Kenny, "The Effects of the Expansion of the Voting Franchise," pp. 54–82. The authors use literacy tests and poll taxes as their measures of suffrage restriction, which would primarily target the South. But they also control for many state-level variables that are highly correlated with the South, such as the black share of the population and

the percentage living in metropolitan areas. They also include state-year dummies, making it virtually impossible to identify regional patterns in their results.

75. Bensel and Sanders, "The Impact of the Voting Rights Act," pp. 56–63.

76. Valelly, *Two Reconstructions,* p. 199.

77. Haynie, *African-American Legislators,* chapter 4. The states covered were Arkansas, Illinois, Maryland, New Jersey, and North Carolina for the legislative years 1969, 1979, and 1989.

78. Black, *Southern Governors,* pp. 161, 299, 305.

79. Harvey, *A Question of Justice,* pp. 117, 132, 141–144.

80. Harvey, *A Question of Justice,* pp. 41–63; Rudder, "Educational Reform in Alabama."

81. Jenkins and Person, "Educational Reform in Mississippi," pp. 82–107; Bolton, *The Hardest Deal of All,* p. 217.

82. Cascio, "Maternal Labor Supply," Table 1.

83. Harvey, *A Question of Justice,* pp. 84–73.

84. Quoted in Jenkins and Person, "Educational Reform in Mississippi," p. 104.

85. See, for example, the subtitle of J. Morgan Kousser's 1999 book: *Minority Voting Rights and the Undoing of the Second Reconstruction.* Accounts of political transition include Lamis, *Southern Politics in the 1990s;* Black and Black, *The Rise of Southern Republicans.*

86. Parker, *Black Votes Count,* p. 201; Edsall and Edsall, *Chain Reaction,* chapters 7 and 10; Cobb, *The South and America,* pp. 183, 267; Corrigan, *Race, Religion, and Economic Change,* p. 25.

87. Lublin, *Republican* South, pp. 149–169. The most complete syntheses are Lassiter, *The Silent Majority;* Shafer and Johnston, *The End of Southern Exceptionalism.* For a critique, see Kousser, "The Immutability of Categories and the Reshaping of Southern Politics."

88. Rudder, "Educational Reform in Alabama," pp. 118–122; Bullock and Rozelle, *The New Politics of the Old South,* pp. 82–83.

89. Bullock and Gaddie, *The Triumph of Voting Rights,* pp. 93, 176, 207.

90. Preuhs, "The Conditional Effects of Minority Descriptive Representation," pp. 585–599.

7   THE DOWNSIDE OF THE CIVIL RIGHTS REVOLUTION

1. Applebome, *Dixie Rising,* pp. 17, 215.

2. Weems, *Desegregating the Dollar,* p. 69.

3. Russ Rymer, "Integration's Casualties," *New York Times Magazine,* Nov. 1, 1998, p. 48. Rymer's account of the black business com-

munity in Jacksonville, Florida, and its demise, is elaborated in *American Beach,* pp. 93–270.

4. This summary draws upon Ingham, "Building Businesses, Creating Communities," pp. 639–665; Woodard, *Black Entrepreneurs in America,* pp. 19–22; Butler, *Entrepreneurship and Self-Help among Black Americans,* pp. 103–199; Rogers, *The African American Entrepreneur,* pp. 59–86.

5. Rymer, *American Beach,* pp. 134–135; Rymer, "Integration's Casualties," p. 50.

6. Smith, *To Serve the Living,* pp. 18–25, 27–31, 142–155; Jenkins and Hines, *Black Titan,* pp. 78–81, 163, 213.

7. Vincent Canby, "Film: Revisiting the Civil Rights South," *New York Times,* Mar. 3, 1982.

8. Rymer *American Beach,* pp. 214, 220.

9. Wilson, "The Ecology of a Black Business District," p. 365.

10. Reginald Stuart, "Businesses Owned by Blacks Still Fighting an Uphill Battle," *New York Times,* July 26, 1982.

11. Weems, "A Crumbling Legacy," pp. 29–32.

12. Angelo B. Henderson, "Death Watch? Black Funeral Homes Fear a Gloomy Future as Big Chains Move In." *Wall Street Journal,* July 18, 1997.

13. Fairlie and Robb, *Race and Entrepreneurial Success,* p. 20.

14. Thomas Lippman, "Twilight of the God of the Forge." *Wall Street Journal,* July 25, 1982.

15. Rymer, *American Beach,* p. 226. In 1962, according to Andrew Brimmer, industrial life insurance represented more than 60 percent of the life insurance of black-owned companies, compared to only 6 percent for all insurance companies nationwide ("The Negro in the National Economy," pp. 308–319).

16. Weems, "A Crumbling Legacy," p. 35.

17. Writing in 1936, Abram Harris referred to high prices and poor quality at small, black-owned shops as the equivalent of a "tariff" on black consumers. Harris went on to note that the advent of chain stores had led to the "collapse of racial protectionism" (*The Negro as Capitalist,* pp. 177–178).

18. U.S. Census Bureau, *Survey of Minority-Owned Business Enterprises,* issued every five years beginning in 1972. As of 2002, the publication is called *Survey of Business Owners* (www.census.gov/econ/sbo).

19. Shortcomings of using *SMOBE* across time periods are described in Boston, "Trends in Minority-Owned Businesses," pp. 200–203.

20. 2007 *Survey of Business Owners,* Black-Owned Firms, Table 4. This list does not include Washington, DC–Arlington, VA–Alexandria, VA (18.0 percent) or Baltimore (16.5 percent).

21. See Bates, *Race, Self-Employment, and Upward Mobility;* Fairlie and Robb, *Race and Entrepreneurial Success;* Bogan and Darity, "Culture and Entrepreneurship."

22. Bates, *Race,* p. 144. This summary draws on Bates, pp. 142–162, 189–206; Fairlie and Robb, *Race and Entrepreneurial Success,* pp. 49–143.

23. Bates and Williams, "Racial Politics"; Chatterji, Chay, and Fairlire, "The Impact of City Contracting Set-asides"; Mangum, "Public Contracting"; Nye, Rainier, and Stratmann, "Do Black Mayors Improve Black Employment Outcomes?"

24. Black, Holtz-Eakin, and Rosenthal, "Racial Minorities, Economic Scale, and the Geography of Self-Employment," Tables 7, 10, 11, 12.

25. National Urban League, *State of Urban Business 2011.*

26. Peter Applebome, "Bitter Memories of Bias Accompany City's Gains," *New York Times,* Aug. 10, 1990; Stuart, "Businesses Owned by Blacks Still Fighting."

27. LaMonte, *Politics and Welfare,* pp. 240–242; Perry, "Evolution and Impact," pp. 242–244.

28. Boston, *Affirmative Action,* pp. 25–32; Boston, "The Role of Black-Owned Business," pp. 165–166; Bates, *Banking on Black Business,* pp. 90–91, 146.

29. Dorothy Gaites, "A Black Entrepreneur Vaults Racial Barriers in a Southern Town," *Wall Street Journal,* Apr. 29, 1992. Barnes assisted with Middleton's memoir, *Knowing Who I Am,* published in 2008, shortly before his death.

30. Applebome, *Dixie Rising,* pp. 66, 69.

31. Eskew, *But for Birmingham,* p. 331.

32. Germany, *New Orleans after the Promises,* pp. 298–299.

33. U.S. Commission on Civil Rights, *Civil Rights '63,* pp. 132, 141; Smith, *Health Care Divided,* pp. 46–47; Quadagno, "Promoting Civil Rights through the Welfare State," pp. 73–75.

34. This account is drawn from Smith, *Health Care Divided,* pp. 89–110. The Supreme Court declined to review the *Simkins* decision in March 1964.

35. Dittmer, *The Good Doctors,* pp. 112, 124, 135–140; Smith, *Health Care Divided,* p. 141; Quadagno, "Promoting Civil Rights," pp. 69, 81.

36. Smith, "The Politics of Racial Disparities," pp. 249, 258, 263. On white patient protest as a "nonevent escaping the notice of local news media," see Smith, *Health Care Divided,* pp. 232, 320.

37. Chay and Greenstone, "The Convergence in Black-White Infant Mortality Rates"; Almond, Chay, and Greenstone, "The Civil Rights Act of 1964."

38. Smith, *Health Care Divided,* p. 232; Smith, "The Politics of Racial Disparities," p. 264; Dittmer, *The Good Doctors,* p. 139.

39. Smith, *Health Care Divided,* p. 221, emphasis in original.

40. Lemann, *The Promised Land,* p. 156; Korstad and Leloudis, *To Right These Wrongs,* pp. 42–43, 82–83.

41. Ashmore, *Carry It On,* pp. 57–71; Germany, *New Orleans,* pp. 81, 95; Korstad and Leloudis, *To Right These Wrongs,* pp. 175–215.

42. Ashmore, *Carry It On,* pp. 12–13, 216–229.

43. Korstad and Leloudis, *To Right These Wrongs,* pp. 291–297.

44. Ashmore, *Carry It On,* pp. 278–279; Korstad and Leloudis, *To Right These Wrongs,* pp. 347–349.

45. Haveman, *A Decade of Federal Antipoverty Programs,* p. 14.

46. Reagan said this many times. The precise quote is from his 1988 State of the Union address.

47. See Haveman, *A Decade of Federal Antipoverty Studies,* and Plotnick and Skidmore, *Progress against Poverty,* which barely mention the South. The tradition continues in more recent research, such as Lin and Harris, *The Colors of Poverty.*

48. Stoll, "Race, Place, and Poverty Revisited," p. 207.

49. Wheat and Crown, *State Per-Capita Income,* esp. pp. 170–171.

50. Haveman, *A Decade of Antipoverty Programs,* pp. 92, 97; Plotnick and Skidmore, *Progress against Poverty,* p. 160. These estimates do not include food stamps, a form of in-kind assistance extensively used in the South but not counted toward the poverty income target.

51. See Wright, *Old South, New South,* pp. 246–247, 251–252; Cogan, "The Decline in Black Teenage Employment," Table 1. The regional transfer of poverty is a central theme in Lemann, *The Promised Land.*

52. U.S. Bureau of the Census, Current Population Reports, Series P-60, *Characteristics of the Population below the Poverty Level,* annual from 1974.

53. Duncan, *Worlds Apart,* pp. 73–151; Wirt, *"We Ain't What We Was,"* pp. 118–141; Mason, "The Poverty Hurdle," pp. 279–296; Fleming, *In the Shadow of Selma,* pp. 283–313.

54. Goldhagen et al, "Health Status of Southern Children"; Newman and O'Brien, *Taxing the Poor,* pp. 57–86.

55. Thernstrom, *Voting Rights,* pp. xviii, 3.

56. Jeffrey Toobin, "The Great Election Grab," *New Yorker,* Dec. 8, 2003.

57. Wilson, *Declining Significance of Race.*

58. Reed, "A Critique of Neo-progressivism," p. 168.

59. McFayden, "African-American Mayors," p. 129.

60. Crespino, "Mississippi as Metaphor," p. 116.

61. Lassiter, *The Silent Majority*, p. 142; Walker, *The Ghost of Jim Crow*, p. 151.

62. Dwyer and Alderman, *Civil Rights Memorials*, p. 43.

63. Bolton, *The Hardest Deal of All*, p. 125.

64. Baker, *Paradoxes of Desegregation*, p. xvii.

65. Wolters, *Race and Education*, p. 11. See also Irons, *Jim Crow's Children*, esp. p. 289.

66. Lipkin, "Haunted by Brown," pp. 210, 214–215. For rebuttals to Lipkin, see the essays by Hayman and Ware, and by Finkelman, in the same volume.

67. Bolton, *The Hardest Deal*, pp. xvii, 78; Cecelski, *Along Freedom Road*; Brown-Nagin, *Courage to Dissent*, pp. 307–408.

68. Quoted in Ashmore, *Carry It On*, pp. 185–186. On the tendency for antipoverty organizing to follow racial lines, see Germany, *New Orleans*, pp. 81–95; Korstad and Leloudis, *To Right These Wrongs*, pp. 175–197.

69. Joseph, *The Black Power Movement*, p. 21. In the same volume, Simon Wendt contrasts black self-defense efforts in the South, which repelled white attackers and complemented nonviolent political action, with the aggressive, militant Black Power militancy in northern cities ("The Roots of Black Power," pp. 145–165).

70. Abramowitz, Alexander, and Gunning, "Incumbency, Redistricting, and the Decline of Competition"; Grose, *Congress in Black and White*, pp. 12, 58–62, 78–81.

71. U.S. Department of Health and Human Services, Health Resources and Services Administration, "Primary Care: The Health Center Program" (www.hhs.gov, accessed August 31, 2012).

72. Quoted in Lefkowitz, *Community Health Centers*, p. 26.

73. Lefkowitz, *Community Health Centers*, p. 137.

74. Quoted in Ford, *African Americans in Georgia*, p. 57.

75. Menifeld and Shaffer, *Politics in the New South*, pp. 96–105, 188–191.

76. Grose, *Congress in Black and White*, pp. 30–31.

77. Howell, *Race, Performance, and Approval of Mayors*, pp. 14, 55, 104–105, 138–142.

78. Thernstrom, *Voting Rights*, p. 3; Liu and Vanderleeuw, *Race Rules*, pp. 97, 123; Ford, *African Americans in Georgia*, pp. 72–97.

79. Grose, *Congress in Black and White*, pp. 7–9, 87–109, 110–133.

80. Kousser, *Colorblind Injustice*, p. 272.

81. Frank Newport, "Blacks, Whites Differ on Government's Role in Civil Rights," *USA Today*/Gallup Poll 149087, August 19, 2011.

82. Potter, *Racing the Storm,* p. 69; Frank Newport, "Blacks, Non-blacks, Hold Sharply Different Views of Martin Case," *USA Today/* Gallup Poll 153776, June 5, 2012.

83. Lublin, *The Republican South,* p. 27. On the resonance between Civil Rights rhetoric and the new conservatism, see Irons, *Reconstituting Whiteness,* pp. 193–201; Lawrence, "Forbidden Conversations."

84. Chappell, *A Stone of Hope,* chapters 3–8.

85. Crespino, *In Search of Another Country,* pp. 267–268.

86. Kuklinski, Cobb, and Gilens, "Racial Attitudes and the 'New South.'"

87. Valentino and Sears, "Old Times There Are not Forgotten."

88. Newman and O'Brien, *Taxing the Poor,* pp. 25–29, 90–114, 122–132.

89. Soss, Schram, Vartanian, and O'Brien, "Setting the Terms of Relief"; Soss, Fording, and Schram, "The Color of Devolution."

90. Newman and O'Brien, *Taxing the Poor,* pp. 83–84.

91. Behrens, Uggen, and Manza, "Ballot Manipulation and the 'Menace of Negro Domination'"; King and Mauer, *The Vanishing Black Electorate.*

8 CIVIL RIGHTS ECONOMICS

1. On voting laws, see Weiser and Norden, *Voting Law Changes in 2012.* For a discussion of Latino political influence in the South (suggested limited impact through 2008 outside of Florida and Texas), see Stanley, "The Latino Vote in 2008."

2. For a survey, see Ranis, "Diversity of Communities and Economic Development."

3. For a general treatment of this relationship, see Friedman, *The Moral Consequences of Economic Growth.*

4. Gene Nichol, "Southern Poverty, Southern Politics," p. 186. See Gitterman and Coclanis, *A Way Forward,* particularly the essays by Lacy Ford, Lance D. Fusarelli, and Jerry Weitz.

5. James B. Stewart, "Intolerance May Carry a Price for States," *New York Times,* May 12, 2012.

6. Miriam Jordan, "Alabama Immigrant Law Irks Business," *Wall Street Journal,* Aug. 24, 2011.

BIBLIOGRAPHY

Abbott, Carl. *The New Urban America: Growth and Politics in Sunbelt Cities.* Chapel Hill: University of North Carolina Press, 1987.
———. "The Norfolk Business Community." In *Southern Businessmen and Desegregation*, ed. Elizabeth Jacoway and David R. Colburn. Baton Rouge: Louisiana State University Press, 1982.

Abramowitz, Alan I., Brad Alexander, and Matthew Gunning. "Incumbency, Redistricting, and the Decline of Competition in U.S. House Elections." *Journal of Politics* 68 (2006): 75–88.

Almond, Douglas V., Kenneth Y. Chay, and Michael Greenstone. "The Civil Rights Act of 1964, Hospital Desegregation, and Black Infant Mortality in Mississippi." NBER Working Paper, 2008.

Alston, Lee. J., and Joseph P. Ferrie. *Southern Paternalism and the American Welfare State.* New York: Cambridge University Press, 1999.

Amrein, Audrey L., and David C. Berliner. "High-Stakes Testing, Uncertainty and Student Learning." *Education Analysis Policy Archives* 10 (2002): 1–74.

Anderson, James D. *The Education of Blacks in the South, 1860–1935.* Chapel Hill: University of North Carolina Press, 1988.

Andrews, Kenneth T. *Freedom Is a Constant Struggle: The Mississippi Civil Rights Movement and Its Legacy.* Chicago: University of Chicago Press, 2004.

Andrews, Kenneth T., and Michael Biggs. "The Dynamics of Protest Diffusion: Movement Organizations, Social Networks, and News

Media in the 1960 Sit-ins." *American Sociological Review* 71 (2006): 752–777.

Applebome, Peter. *Dixie Rising: How the South Is Shaping American Values, Politics and Culture.* New York: Random House Torch-books, 1996.

Armor, David J. *Forced Justice: Desegregation and the Law.* New York: Oxford University Press, 1995.

Arrow, Kenneth. "Models of Job Discrimination." In *Racial Discrimination in Economic Life,* ed. A. H. Pascal. Lexington, MA: Heath-Lexington, 1972.

———. "The Theory of Discrimination." In *Discrimination in Labor Markets,* ed. O. Ashenfelter and A. Rees. Princeton, NJ: Princeton University Press, 1973.

Ashenfelter, Orley, William J. Collins, and Albert Yoon. "Evaluating the Role of *Brown vs. Board of Education* in School Equalization, Desegregation, and the Income of African Americans." *American Law and Economics Review* 8 (2006): 213–248.

Ashenfelter, Orley, and James J. Heckman. "Measuring the Effect of an Antidiscrimination Program." In *Evaluating the Labor Market Effects of Social Programs,* ed. Orley Ashenfelter and James Blum. Princeton, NJ: Industrial Relations Section, Princeton University, 1976.

Ashmore, Susan Youngblood. *Carry It On: The War on Poverty and the Civil Rights Movement in Alabama, 1964–1972.* Athens: University of Georgia Press, 2008.

Ayers, *The Promise of the New South: Life After Reconstruction.* New York: Oxford University Press, 1992.

Badger, Anthony. "Brown and Backlash." In *Massive Resistance: Southern Opposition to the Second Reconstruction,* ed. Clive Webb. New York: Oxford University Press, 2005.

———. *New Deal/New South.* Fayetteville: University of Arkansas Press, 2007.

———. "Segregation and the Southern Business Elite." *Journal of American Studies* 18 (1984): 105–109.

Bailey, Conner, Peter Sinclair, John Bliss, and Karnai Perez. "Segmented Labor Markets in Alabama's Pulp and Paper Industry." *Rural Sociology* 61 (Fall 1996): 475–497.

Baker, Peter. *Paradoxes of Desegregation: African-American Struggles for Educational Equity in Charleston, South Carolina, 1926–1972.* Columbia: University of South Carolina Press, 2006.

Barnett, Paul. *An Analysis of State Industrial Development Programs in the Thirteen Southern States.* Knoxville: University of Tennessee Press, 1944.

Bartley, Numan. "In Search of the New South: Southern Politics after Reconstruction." In *The Promise of American History,* ed. Stanley T. Kutler and Stanley N. Katz. Baltimore: Johns Hopkins University Press, 1982.

Bates, Timothy. *Banking on Black Business.* Washington, DC: Joint Center for Political and Economic Studies, 1993.

———. *Race, Self-Employment, and Upward Mobility: An Illusive American Dream.* Washington, DC: Woodrow Wilson Center Press, 1997.

Bates, Timothy, and Darrell L. Williams. "Racial Politics: Does It Pay?" *Social Science Quarterly* 74 (1993): 507–522.

Bayor, Ronald H. *Race and the Shaping of Twentieth-Century Atlanta.* Chapel Hill: University of North Carolina Press, 1996.

Becker, Gary. *The Economics of Discrimination.* 1957. Chicago: University of Chicago Press, 1971.

Behrens, Angela, Christopher Uggen, and Jeff Manza. "Ballot Manipulation and the Threat of 'Negro Domination': Felon Disfranchisement in the United States, 1850–2002." *American Journal of Sociology* 109 (2003): 559–605.

Bell, Derrick. *And We Are Not Saved: The Elusive Quest for Racial Justice.* New York: Basic Books, 1987.

———. "Economic Determinism and Interest Convergence." In *The Derrick Bell Reader,* ed. Richard Delgado and Jean Stefancic. New York: New York University Press, 2005.

Bensel, Richard F., and M. Elizabeth Sanders. "The Impact of the Voting Rights Act on Southern Welfare Systems." In *Do Elections Matter?,* ed. Benjamin Ginsberg and Alan Stone. Armonk, NY: M. E. Sharpe, 1986.

Biggs, Michael. "Who Joined the Sit-ins and Why? Southern Black Students in the Early 1960s." *Mobilization: An International Journal* 11 (2006): 321–336.

Biles, Roger. "The Persistence of the Past: Memphis in the Great Depression." In *Hope Restored,* ed. Bernard Sternsher. Chicago: Ivan R. Dee, 1999.

Bindas, Kenneth J. *Remembering the Great Depression in the Rural South.* Gainesville: University Press of Florida, 2007.

Black, Dan, Douglas Holtz-Eakin, and Stuart Rosenthal. "Racial Minorities, Economic Scale, and the Geography of Self-Employment." *Brookings-Wharton Papers on Urban Affairs,* 2001, 245–286.

Black, Earl. *Southern Governors and Civil Rights: Racial Segregation as a Campaign Issue in the Second Reconstruction.* Cambridge, MA: Harvard University Press, 1976.

Black, Earl, and Merle Black. *Politics and Society in the South.* Cambridge, MA: Harvard University Press, 1987.

———. *The Rise of Southern Republicans.* Cambridge: Cambridge University Press, 2002.

Bleakley, Hoyt. "Disease and Development: Evidence from Hookworm Eradication in the American South." *Quarterly Journal of Economics* 122 (2007): 73–117.

Bloom, Jack M. *Class, Race, and the Civil Rights Movement.* Bloomington: Indiana University Press, 1987.

Blum, Edward. *The Unintended Consequences of Section 5 of the Voting Rights Act.* Washington, DC: AEI Press, 2007.

Blumrosen, Alfred. "The Legacy of *Griggs:* Social Progress and Subjective Judgments." *Chicago-Kent Law Review* 63 (1987): 1–41.

Bogan, Vicki, and William Darity Jr. "Culture and Entrepreneurship: African American and Immigrant Self-Employment in the United States." *Journal of Socio-Economics* 37 (2008): 1999–2019.

Boger, John Charles, and Gary Orfield, eds. *School Resegregation: Must the South Turn Back?* Chapel Hill: University of North Carolina Press, 2005.

Bolton, Charles C. *The Hardest Deal of All: The Battle over School Desegregation in Mississippi, 1870–1980.* Jackson: University Press of Mississippi, 2005.

Bond, Horace Mann. *Negro Education in Alabama: A Study in Cotton and Steel.* 1939. Tuscaloosa: University of Alabama Press, 1994.

Boozer, Michael A., Alan B. Krueger, and Shari Wolkon. "Race and School Quality Since *Brown v. Board of Education.*" *Brookings Papers on Economic Activity: Microeconomics,* 1992, 269–338.

Boston, Thomas D. *Affirmative Action and Black Entrepreneurship.* London: Routledge, 1999.

———. "The Role of Black-Owned Businesses in Black Community Development." In *Jobs and Economic Development in Minority Communities,* ed. Paul Ong and Anastasia Loukaitou-Sideris. Philadelphia: Temple University Press, 2006.

———. "Trends in Minority-Owned Businesses." In *America Becoming: Racial Trends and Their Consequences,* vol. 2. Washington, DC: National Academy Press, 2001.

Botson, Michael R., Jr. *Labor, Civil Rights, and the Hughes Tool Company.* College Station: Texas A&M Press, 2005.

Bound, John, and Richard Freeman. "What Went Wrong? The 1980s Erosion of the Economic Well Being of Black Men." *Quarterly Journal of Economics* 107 (1992): 201–232.

Boyd, William. "The Forest Is the Future." In *The Second Wave: Southern Industrialization from the 1940s to the 1970s,* ed. Philip Scranton. Athens: University of Georgia Press, 2001.

Brady, David, and Barbara Sinclair. "Building Majorities for Policy Changes in the House of Representatives." *Journal of Politics* 46 (1984): 1033–1060.

Brimmer, Andrew. "The Negro in the National Economy." In *The American Negro Reference Book,* ed. John P. Davis. Englewood Cliffs, NJ: Prentice-Hall, 1966.

Brooks, R. P. "The Agrarian Revolution in Georgia, 1865–1912." *Bulletin of the University of Wisconsin* 639, 1914.

Brown, D. Clayton. *Electricity for Rural America: The Fight for the REA.* Westport, CT: Greenwood Press, 1980.

———. "Farm Children in the South." *Agricultural History* 53 (1979): 172–180.

Brown, Michael K. *Race, Money and the American Welfare State.* Ithaca, NY: Cornell University Press, 1999.

Brown-Nagin, Tomiko. *Courage to Dissent: Atlanta and the Long History of the Civil Rights Movement.* New York: Oxford University Press, 2011.

Brueggemann, John. "Racial Considerations and Social Policy in the 1930s." *Social Science History* 26 (2002): 139–177.

Bryson, Joseph E., and Charles P. Bentley. *Ability Grouping of Public School Students.* Charlottesville, VA: Michie, 1980.

Bullock, Charles S., III, and Ronald Keith Gaddie. *The Triumph of Voting Rights in the South.* Norman: University of Oklahoma Press, 2009.

Bullock, Charles S., III, and Mark J. Rozell, eds. *The New Politics of the Old South.* 4th ed. Lanham, MD: Rowman & Littlefield, 2010.

Bureau of National Affairs. *Equal Employment Opportunity: Programs and Results.* Personnel Policies Forum Survey No. 112. Washington, DC, March 1976.

Burns, James MacGregor, and Stewart Burns. *A People's Charter:* New York: Knopf, 1991.

Burstein, Paul. *Discrimination, Jobs and Politics: The Struggle for Equal Employment Opportunity.* Chicago: University of Chicago Press, 1985.

Butler, John Sibley. *Entrepreneurship and Self-Help among Black Americans.* 1991. Albany: State University of New York Press, 2005.

Butler, Richard J., James J. Heckman, and Brook Payner. "The Impact of the Economy and the State on the Economic Status of Blacks: A Study of South Carolina." In *Markets in History,* ed. D. Galenson. Cambridge: Cambridge University Press, 1989.

Button, James W. *Blacks and Social Change: Impact of the Civil Rights Movement in Southern Communities.* Princeton, NJ: Princeton University Press, 1989.

Button, James W., and Barbara Rienzo. "The Impact of Affirmative Action: Black Employment in Six Southern Cities." *Social Science Quarterly* 84 (2003): 1–14.

Button, James W., Barbara A. Rienzo, and Sheila L. Croucher. *Blacks and the Quest for Economic Equality: The Political Economy of Employment in Southern Communities in the United States.* University Park: Pennsylvania State University Press, 2009.

Byerly, Victoria. *Hard Times Cotton Mill Girls.* Ithaca, NY: ILR Press, 1986.

Byng, Michelle D. "Responding to Black Political Interests in the Post-Civil Rights Era." *Sociological Inquiry* 68 (1998): 203–227.

Campbell, David, and Joe R. Feagin. "Black Politics in the South: A Descriptive Analysis." *Journal of Politics* 37 (1975): 129–162.

Card, David, and Alan Krueger. "School Quality and Relative Black/White Earnings." *Quarterly Journal of Economics* 107 (1992): 151–200.

Carlton, David L., and Peter A. Coclanis, eds. *Confronting Southern Poverty in the Great Depression.* Boston: Bedford Books, 1996.

Carrington, William J., Kristin McCue, and Brooks Pierce. "Using Establishment Size to Measure the Impact of Title VII and Affirmative Action." *Journal of Human Resources* 35 (2000): 503–523.

Carson, Clayborne. *In Struggle: SNCC and the Black Awakening of the 1960s.* Cambridge, MA: Harvard University Press, 1981.

Carter, Susan B., Scott Sigmund Gartner, Michael R. Haines, Alan L. Olmstead, Richard Sutch, and Gavin Wright. *Historical Statistics of the United States, Earliest Times to the Present: Millennial Edition.* New York: Cambridge University Press, 2006.

Cascio, Elizabeth U. "Maternal Labor Supply and the Introduction of Kindergartens into American Public Schools." *Journal of Human Resources* 41 (2009): 140–170.

Cascio, Elizabeth, Nora Gordon, Ethan Lewis, and Sarah Reber. "From Brown to Busing." *Journal of Urban Economics* 64 (2008): 296–325.

———. "Paying for Progress: Conditional Grants and the Desegregation of Southern Schools." *Quarterly Journal of Economics* 125 (2010): 445–482.

Cascio, Elizabeth U., and Ebonya Washington. "Valuing the Vote: The Redistribution of Voting Rights and State Funds Following the Voting Rights Act of 1965." NBER Working Paper 17776, 2012.

Cecelski, David S. *Along Freedom Road: Hyde County, North Carolina, and the Fate of Black Schools in the South.* Chapel Hill: University of North Carolina Press, 1994.

Cell, John W. *The Highest Stage of White Supremacy: The Origins of Segregation in South Africa and the American South.* Cambridge: Cambridge University Press, 1982.

Chafe, William H. *Civilities and Civil Rights.* New York: Oxford University Press, 1980.

———. "Greensboro, NC." In *Southern Businessmen and Desegregation,* ed. Elizabeth Jacoway and David R. Colburn. Baton Rouge: Louisiana State University Press, 1982.

Chafe, William H., Raymond Gavins, Robert Korstad, and Paul Ortiz, eds. *Remembering Jim Crow: African Americans Tell about Life in the Segregated South.* New York: New Press, 2001.

Chappell, David L. "Disunity and Religious Institutions in the White South." In *Massive Resistance,* ed. Clive Webb. New York: Oxford University Press, 2005.

———. *Inside Agitators: White Southerners in the Civil Rights Movement.* Baltimore: Johns Hopkins University Press, 1994.

———. *A Stone of Hope: Prophetic Religion and the Death of Jim Crow.* Chapel Hill: University of North Carolina Press, 2004.

Chatterji, Aaron K., Kenneth Y. Chay, and Robert W. Fairlie. "The Impact of City Contracting Set-asides on Black Self-Employment and Employment." Working Paper, August 2010.

Chay, Kenneth Y. "The Impact of Federal Civil Rights Policy on Black Economic Progress." *Industrial and Labor Relations Review* 51 (1998): 608–632.

Chay, Kenneth Y., and Michael Greenstone. "The Convergence in Black-White Mortality Rates during the 1960s." *American Economic Review* 90 (2000): 326–332.

Chay, Kenneth Y., Jonathan Guryan, and Bhashkar Mazumder. "Birth Cohort and the Black-White Test-Score Gap." NBER Working Paper 15078, 2009.

Chay, Kenneth Y., and Bo E. Honore. "Estimation of Semiparametric Censored Regression Models: An Application to Black-White Earnings Inequality during the 1960s." *Journal of Human Resources* 33 (1998): 4–38.

Chen, Anthony S. *The Fifth Freedom: Jobs, Politics, and Civil Rights in the United States, 1941–1941.* Princeton, NJ: Princeton University Press, 2009.

Chong, Dennis. *Collective Action and the Civil Rights Movement.* Chicago: University of Chicago Press, 1991.

Clotfelter, Charles. *After Brown: The Rise and Retreat of School Segregation.* Princeton, NJ: Princeton University Press, 2004.

———. "'Tipping' and Private School Enrollment." *Journal of Human Resources* 11 (1976): 28–50.

Clotfelter, Charles, Helen F. Ladd, and Jacob L. Vigdor. "Classroom-Level Segregation and Resegregation in North Carolina." In *School Resegregation: Must the South Turn Back?,* ed. John Charles Boger and Gary Orfield. Chapel Hill: University of North Carolina Press, 2005.

Clotfelter, Charles, Helen F. Ladd, and Jacob L. Vigdor. "Federal Oversight, Local Control and the Specter of 'Resegregation' in Southern Schools." *American Law and Economics Review* (2006): 347–389.

Cobb, James C. *The Selling of the South: The Southern Crusade for Industrial Development, 1936–1980.* Baton Rouge: Louisiana State University Press, 1982.

———. *The Selling of the South: The Southern Crusade for Industrial Development, 1936–1980.* 2nd ed. Chicago: University of Illinois Press, 1993.

———. *The South and America Since World War II.* New York: Oxford University Press, 2011.

Cogan, John. "The Decline of Black Teenage Employment, 1950–1970." *American Economic Review* 72 (1982): 621–638.

Cohen, Lizabeth. *A Consumers' Republic: The Politics of Mass Consumption in Postwar America.* New York: Knopf, 2003.

Cohodas, Nadine. *Strom Thurmond and the Politics of Southern Change.* New York: Simon and Schuster, 1993.

Collins, William J. "The Labor Market Impact of State-Level Anti-Discrimination Laws, 1940–1960." *Industrial and Labor Relations Review* 56 (2003): 244–272.

———. "Race, Roosevelt, and Wartime Production." *American Economic Review* 91 (2001): 272–286.

Collins, William J., and Robert A. Margo. "The Economic Aftermath of the 1960s Riots in American Cities: Evidence from Property Values." *Journal of Economic History* 67 (2007): 849–883.

Conner, Catherine A. "Building Moderate Progress: Citizenship, Race, and Power in Downtown Birmingham, 1940–1992." Ph.D. diss., University of North Carolina, 2012.

Connerly, Charles E. *"The Most Segregated City in America": City Planning and Civil Rights in Birmingham, 1920–1980.* Charlottesville: University of Virginia Press, 2005.

Coombs, David W., M. H. Alsikafi, C. Hobson Bryan, and Irving L. Webber. "Black Political Control in Greene County, Alabama." *Rural Sociology* 42 (1977): 398–406.

Corrigan, Matthew T. *Race, Religion, and Economic Change: A Case Study of a Southern City.* Gainesville: University Press of Florida, 2007.

Cortner, *Civil Rights and Public Accommodations: The Heart of Atlanta and McClung Cases.* Lawrence: University Press of Kansas, 2001.

Couto, Richard A. *Ain't Gonna Let Nobody Turn Me Round.* Philadelphia: Temple University Press, 1991.

Cramer, M. Richard. "School Desegregation and New Industry: The Southern Community Leaders' Viewpoint." *Social Forces* 40 (1963): 384–389.

Crespino, Joseph. *In Search of Another Country: Mississippi and the Conservative Counterrevolution.* Princeton, NJ: Princeton University Press, 2007.

———. "Mississippi as Metaphor." In *The Myth of Southern Exceptionalism,* ed. Matthew D. Lassiter and Joseph Crespino. New York: Oxford University Press, 2010.

Daniel, Pete. *Lost Revolutions: The South in the 1950s.* Chapel Hill: University of North Carolina Press for the Smithsonian National Museum of American History, 2000.

Davidson, Chandler, and Bernard Grofman, eds. *Quiet Revolution in the South: The Impact of the Voting Rights Act, 1965–1990.* Princeton, NJ: Princeton University Press, 1994.

Davies, Gareth, and Martha Derthick. "Race and Social Welfare Policy: The Social Security Act of 1935." *Political Science Quarterly* 112 (1997): 217–235.

Davis, Ronald L. F. *Good and Faithful Labor: From Slavery to Sharecropping in the Natchez District, 1860–1890.* Westport, CT: Greenwood Press, 1982.

DeJarmon, LeMarquis. "Public Accommodations." In *With All Deliber-ate Speed,* ed. John H. McCord. Urbana: University of Illinois Press, 1969.

De Jong, Greta. *A Different Day: African American Struggles for Justice in Rural Louisiana, 1900–1970.* Chapel Hill: University of North Carolina Press, 2002.

Delgado, Richard, and Jean Stefancic, eds. *The Derrick Bell Reader.* New York: New York University Press, 2005.

Delton, Jennifer. "Before the EEOC: How Management Integrated the Workplace." *Business History Review* 81 (2007): 269–295.

———. *Racial Integration in Corporate America, 1940–1990.* New York: Cambridge University Press, 2009.

Dittmer, John. *The Good Doctors: The Medical Committee for Human Rights and the Struggle for Social Justice in Health Care.* New York: Bloomsbury Press, 2009.

Dobbin, Frank. *Inventing Equal Opportunity.* Princeton, NJ: Princeton University Press, 2009.

Donohue, John J., III. "Is Title VII Efficient?" *University of Pennsylvania Law Review* 134 (1986): 1411–1431.

Donohue, John J., III, and James Heckman. "Continuous versus Episodic Change: The Impact of Civil Rights Policy on the Economic Status of Blacks." *Journal of Economic Literature* 29 (1991): 1603–1643.

Donohue, John J., III, James J. Heckman, and Petra Todd. "The School-ing of Southern Blacks: The Roles of Legal Activism and Private Philanthropy, 1910–1960." *Quarterly Journal of Economics* 117 (2002): 225–268.

Douglas, Davison M. *Reading, Writing, and Race: The Desegregation of Charlotte Schools.* Chapel Hill: University of North Carolina Press, 1995.

Doyle, Don H. *New Men, New Cities, New South.* Chapel Hill: Univer-sity of North Carolina Press, 1990.

Draper, Alan. *Conflicts of Interests: Organized Labor and the Civil Rights Movement in the South, 1954–1968.* Ithaca, NY: ILR Press, 1994.

Drescher, Seymour. *Capitalism and Antislavery.* New York: Oxford Uni-versity Press, 1987.

Duncan, Cynthia M. *Worlds Apart: Why Poverty Persists in Rural America.* New Haven, CT: Yale University Press, 1999.

Dwyer, Owen J., and Derek H. Alderman. *Civil Rights Memorials and the Geography of Memory.* Chicago: Center for American Places at Columbia College, 2008.

Edsall, Thomas Byrne, with Mary D. Edsall. *Chain Reaction: The Impact of Race, Rights and Taxes on American Politics.* New York: Norton, 1992.

Ehle, John. *The Free Men.* New York: Harper & Row, 1965.

Eisinger, Peter K. "Black Employment in Municipal Jobs: The Impact of Black Political Power." *American Political Science Review* 76 (1982): 380–392.

Eldridge, H. T., and D. S. Thomas. *Population Redistribution and Economic Growth.* Philadelphia: American Philosophical Society, 1964.

Epstein, Richard. *Forbidden Grounds: The Case against Employment Discrimination Laws.* Cambridge, MA: Harvard University Press, 1992.

Eskew, Glenn T. *But for Birmingham: The Local and National Movements in the Civil Rights Struggle.* Chapel Hill: University of North Carolina Press, 1997.

———. "Memorializing the Movement: The Struggle to Build Civil Rights Museums in the South." In *Warm Ashes: Issues in Southern History at the Dawn of the Twenty-first Century,* ed. Winfred B. Moore Jr., Kyle S. Sinisi, and David White Jr. Columbia: University of South Carolina Press, 2003.

Fairbanks, Robert B. *For the City as a Whole: Planning, Politics, and the Public Interest in Dallas, Texas, 1900–1965.* Columbus: Ohio State University Press, 1998.

Fairclough, Adam. *Race and Democracy: The Civil Rights Struggle in Louisiana, 1915–1972.* Athens: University of Georgia Press, 1995.

———. *Teaching Equality: Black Schools in the Age of Jim Crow.* Athens: University of Georgia Press, 2001.

Fairlie, Robert W., and Alicia M. Robb. *Race and Entrepreneurial Success: Black, Asian and White-Owned Businesses in the United States.* Cambridge, MA: MIT Press, 2008.

Feldman, Glenn. *The Disfranchisement Myth: Poor Whites and Suffrage Restriction in Alabama.* Athens: University of Georgia Press, 2004.

Ferman, Louis A. *The Negro and Equal Employment Opportunities.* New York: Praeger, 1968.

Fischel, William A. *Making the Grade: The Economic Evolution of American School Districts.* Chicago: University of Chicago Press, 2009.

Fishback, Price V. "Can Competition among Employers Reduce Governmental Discrimination? Coal Miners and Segregated Schools in West Virginia in the Early 1900s." *Journal of Law and Economics* 32 (1989): 311–328.

Fishback, Price V., Michael R. Haines, and Skawn Kantor "The Impact of the New Deal on Black and White Infant Mortality in the South." *Explorations in Economic History* 38 (2001): 93–122.

Fite, Gilbert C. "Mechanization of Cotton Production Since World War II." *Agricultural History* 54 (1980): 190–207.

Fleming, Cynthia Griggs. *In the Shadow of Selma: The Continuing Struggle for Civil Rights in the Rural South.* Lanham, MD: Rowman & Littlefield, 2004.

Fleming, Douglas L. "The New Deal in Atlanta." In *Hope Restored,* ed. Bernard Sternsher. Chicago: Ivan R. Dee, 1999.

Fletcher, F. Marion. "The Negro in the Drugstore Industry." In *Negro Employment in Retail Trade.* Philadelphia: Wharton School of Finance and Commerce, University of Pennsylvania, 1972.

Florida, Richard. *The Rise of the Creative Class.* New York: Basic Books, 2002.

Foote, Christopher L., Warren C. Whatley, and Gavin Wright. "Arbitraging a Discriminatory Labor Market: Black Workers at the Ford Motor Company, 1918–1947." *Journal of Labor Economics* 21 (2003): 493–532.

Ford, Pearl K., ed. *African Americans in Georgia: A Reflection of Politics and Policy in the New South.* Macon, GA: Mercer University Press, 2010.

Fossett, Mark A., Omer R. Galle, and William R. Kelly. "Racial Occupational Inequality, 1940–1980: National and Regional Trends." *American Sociological Review* 51 (1986): 421–429.

Frankenberg, Erica, and Gary Orfield, eds. *Lessons in Integration: Realizing the Promise of Racial Diversity in American Schools.* Charlottesville: University of Virginia Press, 2007.

Franklin, John Hope. "History of Racial Segregation in the United States." *Annals of the American Academy of Political and Social Science* 304 (1956): 1–9.

Fredrickson, Mary. "Four Decades of Change: Black Workers in Southern Textiles, 1918–1981." In *Workers' Struggles, Past and Present,* ed. James Green. Philadelphia: Temple University Press, 1983.

Freeman, Richard B. "Black Economic Progress after 1964: Who Has Gained and Why?" In *Studies in Labor Markets,* ed. Sherwin Rosen. Chicago: University of Chicago Press, 1981.

———. *Black Elite: The Market for Highly Educated Black Americans.* New York: McGraw-Hill, 1976.

——— "The Changing Labor Market for Black Americans, 1948–1972." *Brookings Papers on Economic Activity* 1973 (1973): 67–131.

Frey, William H. "The New Great Migration: Black Americans' Return to the South, 1965–2000." In *Redefining Urban and Suburban America,* vol. 2, ed. Alan Berube, Bruce Katz, and Robert E. Lang. Washington, DC: Brookings Institution Press, 2005.

Friedman, Benjamin. *The Moral Consequences of Economic Growth.* New York: Vintage Books, 2005.

Frydl, Kathleen. *The GI Bill.* New York: Cambridge University Press, 2009.

Gaillard, Frye. *The Dream Long Deferred: The Landmark Struggle for Desegregation in Charlotte, North Carolina.* 3rd ed. Columbia: University of South Carolina Press, 2006.

Gainous, Jason, James Button, and Barbara Rienzo. "African Americans and Municipal Employment: A Test of Two Perspectives." *Social Science Journal* 44 (2007): 535–545.

Garrow, David J. *Protest at Selma: Martin Luther King, Jr., and the Voting Rights Act of 1965.* New Haven: Yale University Press, 1978.

Gerber, Jim. "Public School Expenditures in the Plantation States." *Explorations in Economic History* 28 (1991): 309–322.

Germany, Kent E. *New Orleans after the Promises: Poverty, Citizenship, and the Search for the Great Society.* Athens: University of Georgia Press, 2007.

Giles, "HEW versus the Federal Courts: A Comparison of School Desegregation Enforcement." *American Politics Quarterly* 3 (1975): 81–90.

Gilmore, Glenda Elizabeth. *Defying Dixie: The Radical Roots of Civil Rights, 1919–1950.* New York: W. W. Norton, 2008.

Gitterman, Daniel P., and Peter A. Coclanis, eds. *A Way Forward: Building a Globally Competitive South.* Chapel Hill: Global Research Institute, University of North Carolina at Chapel Hill, 2011.

Giuliano, Laura, David I. Levine, and Jonathan Leonard. "Manager Race and the Race of New Hires." *Journal of Labor Economics* 27 (2009): 589–631.

Goldfield, David. *Cotton Fields and Skyscrapers.* Baton Rouge: Louisiana State University Press, 1980.

Goldhagen, J., R. Remo, T. Bryant 3rd, P. Wludyka, A. Dailey, D. Wood, G. Watts, and W. Livingood. "The Health Status of Southern Children: A Neglected Regional Disparity." *Pediatrics* 116 (2005): 746–753.

Gourlay, Jack G. *The Negro Salaried Worker.* New York: American Management Association, 1965.

Graham, Hugh Davis. *The Civil Rights Era: Origins and Development of National Policy, 1960–1972.* New York: Oxford University Press, 1990.

Grant, Nancy L. *The TVA and Black Americans*. Philadelphia: Temple University Press, 1990.

Grawe, Nathan D., and Jenny B. Wahl. "Blacks, Whites and *Brown:* Effects on the Earnings of Men and Their Sons." *Journal of African American Studies* 13 (2009): 455–475.

Greeley, Andrew M., and Paul B. Sheatsley. "Attitudes toward Racial Integration." *Scientific American* 225 (December 1971): 13–19.

Greenberg, Jack. *Crusaders in the Courts*. 1994. New York: Twelve Tables Press, 2004.

Greenberg, Stanley. *Race and State in Capitalist Development*. New Haven, CT: Yale University Press, 1980.

Greene, Melissa Fay. *Praying for Sheetrock*. New York: Fawcett Columbine, 1991.

Gregory, James N. *The Southern Diaspora*. Chapel Hill: University of North Carolina Press, 2005.

Grose, Christian R. *Congress in Black and White: Race and Representation in Washington and at Home*. New York: Cambridge University Press, 2011.

Guryan, Jonathan. "Desegregation and Black Dropout Rates." *American Economic Review* 94 (2004): 919–943.

Habbe, Stephen. *Company Experience with Negro Employment*. New York: National Industrial Conference Board, 1966.

Hackler, Darrene. *Cities in the Technology Economy*. New York: M. E. Sharpe, 2006.

Halberstam, David. *The Children*. New York: Random House, 1998.

Hale, Grace Elizabeth. *Making Whiteness: The Culture of Segregation in the South, 1890–1940*. New York: Pantheon, 1998.

Halicoussis, Dennis, Kenneth Ng, and Nancy Virts. "Property Ownership and Educational Discrimination in the South." *Journal of Education Finance* 35 (2009): 128–139.

Hanchett, Thomas W. *Sorting Out the New South City: Race, Class and Urban Development in Charlotte, 1875–1975*. Chapel Hill: University of North Carolina Press, 1998.

Hanks, Lawrence J. *The Struggle for Black Political Empowerment in Three Georgia Counties*. Knoxville: University of Tennessee Press, 1987.

Harlan, Louis R. *Separate and Unequal: Public School Campaigns and Racism in the Southern Seaboard States, 1901–1915*. Chapel Hill: University of North Carolina Press, 1958.

Harris, Abram. *The Negro as Capitalist*. New York: Negro Universities Press, 1936.

Harris, Carl V. "Stability and Change in Discrimination against Black Public Schools: Birmingham, Alabama, 1871–1931." *Journal of Southern History* 51 (1985): 375–416.

Harris, J. William. "Plantations and Power: Emancipation on the David Barrow Plantations." In *Toward a New South,* ed. O. V. Burton and R. C. McMath. Westport, CT: Greenwood Press, 1982.

Harvey, Gordon E. *A Question of Justice: New South Governors and Education, 1968–1976.* Tuscaloosa: University of Alabama Press, 2002.

Hatch, Orrin. "Loading the Economy." In *Equal Employment Opportunity: Labor Market Discrimination and Public Policy,* ed. Paul Burstein. New York: Aldine de Gruyter, 1994.

Haveman, Robert, ed. *A Decade of Federal Antipoverty Programs: Achievements, Failures, and Lessons.* New York: Academic Press, 1977.

Hayes, Jack Irby. *South Carolina and the New Deal.* Columbia: University of South Carolina Press, 2001.

Haynie, Kerry L. *African-American Legislators in the American States.* New York: Columbia University Press, 2001.

Heckman, James J., and Brook Payner. "Determining the Impact of Federal Antidiscrimination Policy on the Economic Status of Blacks." *American Economic Review* 79 (1989): 138–177.

Heinemann, Ronald L. "Blue Eagle or Black Buzzard?" *Virginia Magazine of History and Biography* 89 (1981): 90–100.

Higgs, Robert. "Firm-Specific Evidence on Racial Wage Differentials and Workforce Segregation." *American Economic Review* 67 (1977): 236–245.

———. "Racial Wage Differentials in Agriculture: Evidence from North Carolina in 1887." *Agricultural History* 52 (1978): 308–311.

Hill, Joseph A. "Interstate Migration." In U.S. Bureau of the Census, *Special Reports: Supplementary Analysis and Derivative Tables.* Washington, DC: Government Printing Office, 1906.

Hill, Lance E. *The Deacons for Defense: Armed Resistance and the Civil Rights Movement.* Chapel Hill: University of North Carolina Press, 2004.

Holley-Walker, Danielle. "After Unitary Status: Examining Voluntary Integration Strategies for Southern School Districts." *North Carolina Law Review* 88 (2010): 877–910.

Holmes, Michael S. "The Blue Eagle as 'Jim Crow Bird': The NRA and Georgia's Black Workers." *Journal of Negro History* 57 (1972): 276–283.

Honey, Michael. *Southern Labor and Black Civil Rights: Organizing Memphis Workers*. Urbana: University of Illinois Press, 1993.

Hornsby, Alton. "A City That Was Too Busy to Hate." In *Southern Businessmen and Desegregation*, ed. Elizabeth Jacoway and David R. Colburn. Baton Rouge: Louisiana State University Press, 1982.

Howell, Susan E. *Race, Performance, and Approval of Mayors*. New York: Palgrave Macmillan, 2007.

Humphreys, Margaret. *Malaria: Poverty, Race and Public Health in the United States*. Baltimore: Johns Hopkins University Press, 2001.

Hunt, Larry L., Matthew O. Hunt, and William W. Falk. "Who Is Headed South? U.S. Migration Trends in Black and White, 1970–2000." *Social Forces* 87 (2008): 95–119.

Husted, Thomas A., and Lawrence W. Kenny. "The Effect of the Expansion of the Voting Franchise on the Size of Government." *Journal of Political Economy* (1997): 54–82.

Hyde, Timothy. "A Righteous Collusion: The Game Theoretical Implications of Title VII." Honors thesis, Stanford University, 2010.

Hyman, Herbert H., and Paul B. Sheatsley. "Attitudes toward Desegregation." *Scientific American* 211 (July 1964): 16–23.

Ingham, John N. "Building Businesses, Creating Communities: Residential Segregation and the Growth of African American Business in Southern Cities, 1880–1915." *Business History Review* 77 (2003): 639–665.

Irons, Jennifer. *Reconstituting Whiteness: The Mississippi Sovereignty Commission*. Nashville: Vanderbilt University Press, 2010.

Irons, Peter. *Jim Crow's Children: The Broken Promise of the Brown Decision*. New York: Viking Penguin, 2002.

Isenberg, Alison. *Downtown America*. Chicago: University of Chicago Press, 2004.

Jackson, Robert L., and William A. Person. "Educational Reform in Mississippi." In *School Reform in the Deep South,* ed. David J. Vold and Joseph L. DeVitis. Tuscaloosa: University of Alabama Press, 1991.

Jackson, Thomas F. *From Civil Rights to Human Rights: Martin Luther King, Jr., and the Struggle for Economic Justice*. Philadelphia: University of Pennsylvania Press, 2007.

Jacoway, Elizabeth. "Taken by Surprise: Little Rock Business Leaders and Desegregation." In *Southern Businessmen and Desegregation*, ed. Elizabeth Jacoway and David R. Colburn. Baton Rouge: Louisiana State University Press, 1982.

———. *Turn Away Thy Son*. New York: Free Press, 2007.

Jacoway, Elizabeth, and David R. Colburn, eds. *Southern Businessmen and Desegregation*. Baton Rouge: Louisiana State University Press, 1982.

Jacoway, Elizabeth, and C. Fred Williams. *Understanding the Little Rock Crisis*. Fayetteville: University of Arkansas Press, 1999.

Jaynes, Gerald David. *Branches without Roots: Genesis of the Black Working Class in the American South, 1862–1882*. New York: Oxford University Press, 1986.

Jeffrey, Julie Roy. *Education for the Children of the Poor: A Study of the Origins and Implementation of the Elementary and Secondary Education Act of 1965*. Columbus: Ohio State University Press, 1978.

Jenkins, Carol, and Elizabeth Gardner Hines. *Black Titan: A. J. Gaston and the Making of a Black American Millionaire*. New York: One World, 2004.

Jenkins, Robert L., and William A. Person. "Educational Reform in Mississippi: A Historical Perspective." In *School Reform in the Deep South*, ed. David J. Vold and Joseph L. DeVitis. Tuscaloosa: University Press of Alabama, 1991.

Johnson, Charles S. *Patterns of Negro Segregation*. New York: Harper, 1943.

Johnson, Rucker C. "Long-Run Impact of School Desegregation and School Quality on Adult Attainments." National Bureau of Economic Research, Working Paper 16664, 2011.

Joint Center for Political and Economic Studies. *Black Elected Officials*. Washington, DC: Joint Center for Political and Economic Studies, annual 1984–2002.

Jones, Lewis W., and Herman H. Long. *The Negotiation of Desegregation in Ten Southern Cities*. Nashville: Race Relations Department of the American Missionary Association, United Church Board for Homeland Missionaries at Fisk University, 1965.

Jones, Thomas Jesse. *Negro Education*. U.S. Bureau of Education Bulletin, vol. 1, no. 38. Washington, DC: Government Printing Office, 1917.

Jones, William P. *The Tribe of Black Ulysses: African American Lumber Workers in the Jim Crow South*. Urbana: University of Illinois Press, 2005.

Joseph, Peniel E., ed. *The Black Power Movement: Rethinking the Civil Rights–Black Power Era*. New York: Routledge, 2006.

Kahlenberg, Richard D. *Rescuing Brown vs. Board of Education*. New York: Twentieth Century Foundation, 2007.

Karsten, Peter. "'Bottomed on Justice': Breaches of Labor Contracts by Quitting or Firing in Britain and the United States, 1630–1880." *American Journal of Legal History* 34 (1990): 213–261.

Kasarda, J. D., M. D. Irwin, and H. L. Hughes. "The South Is Still Rising." *American Demographics* 8 (1986): 33–39.

Katznelson, Ira. *When Affirmative Action Was White*. New York: Norton, 2005.

Keech, William R. *The Impact of Negro Voting*. Chicago: Rand McNally, 1968.

Kennesaw State University Oral History Project. Cobb County Oral History Series No. 80. Interview with Hugh L. Gordon conducted by Joyce A. Patterson, 18 July 2000, transcript in KSU Archives.

Key, V. O. *Southern Politics in State and Nation*. New York: Knopf, 1949.

Kidder, Alice E. "Federal Compliance Efforts in the Carolina Industry." *Industrial Relations Research Association Proceedings* 1972, 353–361.

King, Ryan S., and Marc Mauer. *The Vanishing Black Electorate: Felony Disfranchisement in Atlanta, Georgia*. Washington, DC: The Sentencing Project, 2004.

Kirby, Jack Temple. "Black and White in the Rural South, 1919–1954." *Agricultural History* 58 (1984): 411–422.

———. *The Countercultural South*. Athens: University of Georgia Press, 1995.

———. *Rural Worlds Lost: The American South, 1920–1960*. Baton Rouge: Louisiana State University Press, 1987.

Kirk, John A. *Redefining the Color Line: Black Activism in Little Rock, Arkansas, 1940–1970*. Gainesville: University Press of Florida, 2002.

Kluger, Richard. *Simple Justice: The History of Brown v. Board of Education and Black America's Struggle for Equality*. 1975. New York: Knopf, 2004.

Konvitz, Milton R., and Theodore Leskes. *A Century of Civil Rights*. New York: Columbia University Press, 1961.

Korstad, Robert Rodgers. *Civil Rights Unionism: Tobacco Workers and the Struggle for Democracy in the Mid-Twentieth Century South*. Chapel Hill: University of North Carolina Press, 2003.

Korstad, Robert R., and James L. Leloudis. *To Right These Wrongs: The North Carolina Fund and the Battle to End Poverty and Inequality in 1960s America*. Chapel Hill: University of North Carolina Press, 2010.

Kotlowski, Dean J. *Nixon's Civil Rights: Politics, Principle, and Policy.* Cambridge, MA: Harvard University Press, 2001.

Kotz, Nick. *Judgment Days: Lyndon Baines Johnson, Martin Luther King, Jr., and the Laws That Shaped America.* Boston: Houghton Mifflin, 2005.

Kousser, J. Morgan. *Colorblind Injustice: Minority Voting Rights and the Undoing of the Second Reconstruction.* Chapel Hill: University of North Carolina Press, 1999.

———. "The Immutability of Categories and the Reshaping of Southern Politics." *American Review of Political Science* 13 (2010): 365–383.

———. "Progressivism for Middle-Class Whites Only: North Carolina Education, 1880–1910." *Journal of Southern History* 46 (May 1980): 169–194.

———. *The Shaping of Southern Politics: Suffrage Restrictions and the Establishment of the One Party South.* New Haven, CT: Yale University Press, 1974.

Krochmal, Max. "An Unmistakably Working-Class Vision: Birmingham's Foot Soldiers and Their Civil Rights Movement." *Journal of Southern History* 76 (2010): 923–960.

Kruse, Kevin. *White Flight: Atlanta and the Making of Modern Conservatism.* Princeton, NJ: Princeton University Press, 2005.

Kuklinski, James H., Michael D. Cobb, and Martin Gilens. "Racial Attitudes and the 'New South.'" *Journal of Politics* 59 (1997): 323–349.

Lamis, Alexander P., ed. *Southern Politics in the 1990s.* Baton Rouge: Louisiana State University Press, 1999.

———. *The Two-Party South.* 2nd ed. New York: Oxford University Press, 1990.

LaMonte, Edward Shannon. *Politics and Welfare in Birmingham, 1900–1975.* Tuscaloosa: University of Alabama Press, 1995.

Lassiter, Matthew D. *The Silent Majority: Suburban Politics in the Sunbelt South.* Princeton, NJ: Princeton University Press, 2006.

Lawrence, Charles R., III. "Forbidden Conversations: On Race, Privacy, and Community." *Yale Law Journal* 114 (2005): 1353–1403.

Lawson, Steven F. *Black Ballots: Voting Rights in the South, 1944–1969.* New York: Columbia University Press, 1976.

———. *In Pursuit of Power: Southern Blacks and Electoral Politics, 1965–1982.* New York: Columbia University Press, 1985.

Lefkowitz, Bonnie. *Community Health Centers: A Movement and the People Who Made It Happen.* New Brunswick, NJ: Rutgers University Press, 2007.

Leinberger, Christopher B. "New Kind of Growth Emerging for Charlotte." *Brookings Institution Opinions*, March 29, 2008.

Lemann, Nicholas. *The Promised Land: The Great Black Migration and How It Changed America*. New York: Vintage Books, 1991.

Leonard, Jonathan. "The Impact of Affirmative Action on Employment." *Journal of Labor Economics* 2 (1984): 439–463.

———. "The Impact of Affirmative Action Regulation and Equal Employment Law on Black Employment." *Journal of Economic Perspectives* 4 (Fall 1990): 47–63.

Lerman, Lisa Gabrielle, and Annette K. Sanderson. "Discrimination in Access to Public Places." *NYU Review of Law and Social Change* 215 (1978): 215–272.

Lewis, John. *Walking with the Wind*. New York: Simon and Schuster, 1988.

Lewis, Robert. "World War II Manufacturing and the Postwar Southern Economy." *Journal of Southern History* 73 (2007): 837–866.

Licht, Walter. *Getting Work: Philadelphia, 1940–1950*. Cambridge, MA: Harvard University Press, 1992.

Lieberman, Robert. *Shifting the Color Line*. Cambridge, MA: Harvard University Press, 1998.

Light, Steven Andrew. *"The Law Is Good": The Voting Rights Act, Redistricting, and Black Regime Politics*. Durham, NC: Carolina Academic Press, 2010.

Lin, Ann Chih, and David R. Harris, eds. *The Colors of Poverty: Why Racial and Ethnic Disparities Persist*. New York: Russell Sage Foundation, 2008.

Lipkin, Robert Justin. "Haunted by Brown." In *Choosing Equality*, ed. Robert L. Hayman and Leland Ware. University Park: Pennsylvania State University Press, 2009.

Litwack, Leon. *How Free Is Free? The Long Death of Jim Crow*. Cambridge, MA: Harvard University Press, 2009.

Liu, Baodong, and James M. Vanderleeuw. *Race Rules: Electoral Politics in New Orleans, 1965–2006*. Lanham, MD: Lexington Books, 2007.

Lowitt, Richard. "The TVA, 1933–1945." In *TVA: Fifty Years of Grass-Roots Bureaucracy*, ed. Erwin C. Hargrove and Paul K. Conklin. Urbana: University of Illinois Press, 1983.

Lublin, David. *The Republican South: Democratization and Partisan Change*. Princeton, NJ: Princeton University Press, 2004.

Luders, Joseph. "The Economics of Movement Success: Business Responses to Civil Rights Mobilization." *American Journal of Sociology* 111 (2006): 963–998.

Lutz, Byron F. "The End of Court-Ordered Desegregation." *American Economic Journal: Economic Policy* 3 (2011): 130–168.

MacLean, Nancy. *Freedom Is Not Enough: The Opening of the American Workplace.* Cambridge, MA: Harvard University Press, 2006.

Mangum, Charles. *The Legal Status of the Negro.* Chapel Hill: University of North Carolina Press, 1940.

Mangum, Vincent E. "Public Contracting, Political Barriers and the Role of Political Capital in the Growth of Black Entrepreneurship." *Journal of Public Management and Social Policy* (2010): 33–47.

Margo, Robert A. *Race and Schooling in the South, 1880–1950.* Chicago: University of Chicago Press, 1990.

———. *Disfranchisement, School Finance, and the Economics of Segregated Schools in the U.S. South, 1890–1910.* New York: Garland Press, 1985.

Markusen, Anne, and Greg Schrock. "The Distinctive City: Divergent Patterns in Growth, Hierarchy, and Specialization." *Urban Studies* 43 2006): 1301–1323.

Marshall, Burke. *Federalism and Civil Rights.* New York: Columbia University Press, 1964.

Marshall, Ray. *Negro Employment in the South.* Two unpublished volumes. Prepared for the Manpower Administration, February 1973. Jackson Business Library, Stanford University.

Marshall, Ray, and Virgin L. Christian Jr., eds. *Employment of Blacks in the South: A Perspective on the 1960s.* Austin: University of Texas Press, 1978.

Mason, T. David. "The Poverty Hurdle: Poverty as an Impediment to Development in the Mississippi Delta." In *A Social and Economic Portrait of the Mississippi Delta,* ed. Arthur G. Cosby, Mitchell W. Brackin, T. David Mason, and Eunice R. McCulloch. Mississippi State: Mississippi Agricultural and Forestry Experiment Station. Social Science Research Center, 1992.

McDonald, Laughlin. *A Voting Rights Odyssey: Black Enfranchisement in Georgia.* Cambridge: Cambridge University Press, 2003.

McElreath, J. Michael. "The Cost of Opportunity: School Desegregation's Complicated Calculus in North Carolina." In *With All Deliberate Speed: Implementing Brown vs. Board of Education,* ed. Brian J. Daugherity and Charles C. Bolton. Fayetteville: University of Arkansas Press, 2008.

McFayden, Elgie. "African-American Mayors: Impact on Georgia Municipalities." In *African Americans in Georgia: A Reflection of Politics and Policy in the New South,* ed. Pearl K. Ford. Macon, GA: Mercer University Press, 2010.

McHugh, Kevin E. "Black Migration Reversal in the United States." *Geographical Review* 77 (1987): 171–182.

Meier, August, and Elliott Rudwick. "The Boycott Movement against Jim Crow Streetcars, 1900–1906." *Journal of American History* 55 (1969): 756–775.

Meier, Kenneth J., and Robert E. England. "Black Representation and Educational Policy: Are They Related?" *American Political Science Review* 78 (1984): 392–403.

Meier, Kenneth J., Eric Gonzales Juenke, Robert D. Wrinkle, and J. L. Polinard. "Structural Choices and Representational Biases: Post-Election Color of Representation." *American Journal of Political Science* 49 (2005): 758–768.

Menifield, Charles E., and Stephen D. Shaffer, eds. *Politics in the New South: Representation of African Americans in Southern State Legislatures.* Albany: State University of New York Press, 2005.

Mickelson, Roslyn, Stephen Samuel Smith, and Stephanie Southworth. "Resegregation, Achievement, and the Chimera of Choice in Post-Unitary Charlotte-Mecklenburg Schools." In *Courtroom to Classroom,* ed. Claire E. Smrekar and Ellen B. Goldring. Cambridge, MA: Harvard Education Press, 2009.

Middleton, Earl M. *Knowing Who I Am: A Black Entrepreneur's Struggle and Success in the American South.* Columbia: University of South Carolina Press, 2008.

Miller, Melinda C. "Land and Racial Wealth Inequality." *American Economic Review* 101 (2011): 371–376.

Minchin, Timothy J. *The Color of Work: The Struggle for Civil Rights in the Southern Paper Industry, 1945–1980.* Chapel Hill: University of North Carolina Press, 2001.

———. "Federal Policy and the Racial Integration of Southern Industry." *Journal of Policy History* 11 (1999): 147–170.

———. *From Rights to Economics: The Ongoing Struggle for Black Equality in the U.S. South.* Gainesville: University Press of Florida, 2007.

———. *Hiring the Black Worker: The Racial Integration of the Southern Textiles Industry, 1960–1980.* Chapel Hill: University of North Carolina Press, 1999.

Minchin, Timothy J., and John A. Salmond. *After the Dream: Black and White Southerners since 1965.* Lexington: University Press of Kentucky, 2011.

Mingle, James R. *Black Enrollment in Higher Education: Trends in the Nation and in the South*. Atlanta, GA: Southern Regional Conference Board, 1978.

Minow, Martha. *In Brown's Wake: Legacies of America's Educational Landmark*. New York: Oxford University Press, 2010.

Mitchell, Glenford E., and William H. Peace III. *The Angry Black South*. New York: Corinth Books, 1962.

Moreno, Paul D. *Black Americans and Organized Labor: A New History*. Baton Rouge: Louisiana State University Press, 2006.

Morris, Aldon D. "Birmingham Confrontation Reconsidered: An Analysis of the Dynamics and Tactics of Mobilization." *American Sociological Review* 58 (1993): 621–636.

———. *The Origins of the Civil Rights Movement: Black Communities Organizing for Change*. New York: Free Press, 1984.

Murray, Pauli, ed. *States' Laws on Race and Color*. Cincinnati, OH: Methodist Church, 1950.

Muse, Benjamin. *The American Negro Revolution*. Bloomington: Indiana University Press, 1968.

———. *Ten Years of Prelude*. New York: Viking Press, 1964.

Myrdal, Gunnar. *An American Dilemma: The Negro Problem and Modern Democracy*. New York: Harper & Brothers, 1944.

National Advisory Commission on Civil Disorders. *Report*. Washington, DC: Government Printing Office, 1968.

National Planning Association. *Selected Studies of Negro Employment in the South*. Washington, DC: National Planning Association, 1955.

National Urban League. *State of Urban Business 2011: U.S. Cities That Lead the Way*. An Official Publication of the National Urban League, 2011.

The Negro Travelers' Green Book. New York: Victor H. Green and Company, 1956.

Nelson, Bruce. "CIO Meant One Thing for the Whites and Another Thing for Us: Steelworkers and Civil Rights, 1936–1974." In *Southern Labor in Transition, 1940–1995*, ed. Robert H. Zieger. Knoxville: University of Tennessee Press, 1997.

Nevin, David, and Robert E. Bills. *The Schools That Fear Built*. Washington, DC: Acropolis Books, 1976.

Newman, Harvey K. *Southern Hospitality: Tourism and the Growth of Atlanta*. Tuscaloosa: University of Alabama Press, 1999.

Newman, Katherine S., and Rourke L. O'Brien. *Taxing the Poor: Doing Damage to the Truly Disadvantaged*. Berkeley: University of California Press, 2011.

Nichol, Gene. "Southern Poverty, Southern Politics." In *A Way Forward: Building a Globally Competitive South,* ed. Daniel P. Gitterman and Peter Coclanis. Chapel Hill, NC: Global Research Institute, 2011.

Nicholls, William H. *Southern Tradition and Regional Progress.* Chapel Hill: University of North Carolina Press, 1960.

Norrell, Robert J. "Caste in Steel: Jim Crow Careers in Birmingham, Alabama." *Journal of American History* 73 (1986): 669–694.

Northrup, Herbert. *The Negro in the Paper Industry.* Philadelphia: Industrial Research Unit, Wharton School of Finance and Commerce, distributed by University of Pennsylvania Press, 1969.

Northrup, Herbert R., and Richard L. Rowan, eds. *The Negro and Employment Opportunities: Problems and Practices.* Ann Arbor: Bureau of Industrial Relations, Graduate School of Business, University of Michigan, 1965.

Nye, John V. C., Ilia Rainier, and Thomas Stratmann. "Do Black Mayors Improve Black Employment Outcomes?" Working Paper, George Mason University, April 2010.

Oakes, James. "The Present Becomes the Past: The Planter Class in the Postbellum South." In *New Perspectives on Race and Slavery in America: Essays in Honor of Kenneth M. Stampp,* ed. Robert H. Abzug and Stephen E. Maizlish. Lexington: University Press of Kentucky, 1986.

Odum, Howard. *Southern Regions of the United States.* Chapel Hill: University of North Carolina Press, 1935.

Onkst, David H. "First a Negro . . . Incidentally a Veteran: Black World War II Veterans and the G.I. Bill of Rights in the Deep South, 1944–1948." *Journal of Social History* 31 (1998): 517–543.

Oppenheimer, Martin. *The Sit-in Movement of 1960.* Brooklyn, NY: Carlson Publishing, 1989.

Orfield, Gary, and Susan E. Eaton. *Dismantling Desegregation: The Quiet Reversal of Brown v. Board of Education.* New York: New Press, 1996.

———. *Public School Desegregation in the United States, 1968–1980.* Washington, DC: Joint Center for Political Studies, 1983.

Orfield, Gary, and Chungmei Lee. *Historic Reversals, Accelerating Resegregation, and the Need for New Integration Strategies.* Report of the Civil Rights Project/Proyecto Derechos Civiles, UCLA, August 2007.

Palmore, Joseph R. "The Not-So-Strange Career of Interstate Jim Crow: Race, Transportation, and the Dormant Commerce Clause." *Virginia Law Review* 83 (1997): 1773–1817.

Parker, Frank R. *Black Votes Count: Political Empowerment in Mississippi after 1965.* Chapel Hill: University of North Carolina Press, 1990.

Paschall, Eliza K. *It Must Have Rained.* Atlanta: Center for Research in Social Change, Emory University, 1975.

Patterson, James T. *Brown v. Board of Education.* New York: Oxford University Press, 2001.

Payne, Charles M. *I've Got the Light of Freedom: The Organizing Tradition and the Mississippi Freedom Struggle.* Berkeley: University of California Press, 1995.

Perlman, J., and E. Frazier. "Entrance Rates of Common Laborers in 20 Industries." *Monthly Labor Review* 45 (1937): 1491–1510.

Perman, Michael. *Struggle for Mastery: Disfranchisement in the South, 1888–1908.* Chapel Hill: University of North Carolina Press, 2001.

Perry, Charles R. "The Negro in the Department Store Industry." In *Negro Employment in Retail Trade.* Philadelphia: Wharton School of Finance and Commerce, University of Pennsylvania, 1972.

Perry, Huey L. "The Socioeconomic Impact of Black Political Empowerment in a Rural Southern Locality." *Rural Sociology* 45 (1980): 207–222.

Perry, Hugh L. "The Evolution and Impact of Biracial Coalitions in Birmingham and New Orleans." In *Racial Politics in American Cities,* ed. Rufus P. Browning, Dale Rogers Marshall, and David H. Tabb. 3rd ed. New York: Longman, 2003.

Persky, Joseph J., and John F. Kain. "Migration, Employment, and Race in the Deep South." *Southern Economic Journal* 36 (1970): 268–276.

Phillips, Sarah T. *This Land, This Nation: Conservation, Rural America, and the New Deal.* New York: Cambridge University Press, 2007.

Plotnick, Robert D., and Felicity Skidmore. *Progress against Poverty: A Review of the 1964–1974 Decade.* New York: Academic Press, 1975.

Pollitt, Daniel H. "Dime Store Demonstrations: Events and Legal Problems of the First Sixty Days." *Duke Law Journal,* Summer 1960, 315–365.

Pomerantz, Gary M. *Where Peachtree Meets Sweet Auburn.* New York: Scribner, 1996.

Pope, Christie Farnham. "Southern Homesteads for Negroes." *Agricultural History* 44 (1970): 201–212.

Potter, Hillary, ed. *Racing the Storm: Racial Implications and Lessons Learned from Katrina.* Lanham, MD: Lexington Books, 2007.

Preuhs, Robert R. "The Conditional Effects of Minority Descriptive Representation: Black Legislators and Policy Influence in the American States." *Journal of Politics* 68 (2006): 585–599.

Price, Margaret. *The Negro and the Ballot in the South*. Atlanta, GA: Southern Regional Council, 1959.

———. *The Negro Voter in the South*. Atlanta, GA: Southern Regional Council, 1957.

Pride, Richard, and J. David Woodard. *The Burden of Busing: The Politics of Desegregation in Nashville, Tennessee*. Knoxville: University of Tennessee Press, 1985.

Quadagno, Jill. *The Color of Welfare*. New York: Oxford University Press, 1994.

———. "Promoting Civil Rights through the Welfare State: How Medicare Integrated Southern Hospitals." *Social Problems* 47 (2000): 68–89.

Rabinowitz, Howard N. *Race, Ethnicity, and Urbanization: Selected Essays*. Columbia: University of Missouri Press, 1994.

———. *Race Relations in the Urban South, 1865–1890*. Urbana: University of Illinois Press, 1980.

Raines, Howell. *My Soul Is Rested: Movement Days in the Deep South Remembered*. New York: Putnam, 1977.

Randolph, Lewis A., and Gayle T. Tate. *Rights for a Season: The Politics of Race, Class, and Gender in Richmond, Virginia*. Knoxville: University of Tennessee Press, 2003.

Ranis, Gustav. "Diversity of Communities and Economic Development: An Overview." Yale University Economic Growth Center, Discussion Paper 1001, 2011.

Ransom, Roger, and Richard Sutch. *One Kind of Freedom: The Economic Consequences of Emancipation*. New York: Cambridge University Press, 1977.

Reardon, Sean F., Elena Grewal, Demetra Kalogrides, and Erica Greenberg. "*Brown* Fades: The End of Court-Ordered School Desegregation and the Resegregation of American Public Schools." *Journal of Policy Analysis and Management* (forthcoming: online version published 3 July 2012).

Reber, Sarah J. "Court-Ordered Desegregation." *Journal of Human Resources* 40 (2005): 559–590.

———. "From Separate and Unequal to Integrated and Equal? School Desegregation and School Finance in Louisiana." NBER Working Paper 13192, 2007.

———. "School Desegregation and Educational Attainment for Blacks." *Journal of Human Resources* 45 (2010): 893–914.

Reed, Adolph L. "A Critique of Neo-progressivism in Theorizing about Local Development: A Case from Atlanta." In *The Politics of Urban Development*, ed. C. Stone and H. Sanders. Lawrence: University Press of Kansas, 1987.

"Rethinking 'Weber': The Business Response to Affirmative Action." *Harvard Law Review* 102 (January 1989): 658–671.

Roback, Jennifer. "The Political Economy of Segregation: The Case of Segregated Streetcars." *Journal of Economic History* 46 (1986): 893–917.

Robinson, Isaac. "Blacks Move Back to the South." *American Demographics* 8 (1986): 40–43.

Rodriguez, Daniel B., and Barry R. Weingast. "The Positive Political Theory of Legislative History: New Perspectives on the 1964 Civil Rights Act and Its Interpretation." *University of Pennsylvania Law Review* 151 (2003): 1417–1542.

Rogers, W. Sherman. *The African American Entrepreneur: Then and Now*. Santa Barbara, CA: Praeger, 2010.

Rossell, Christine, and Willis Hawley, eds. *The Consequences of School Desegregation*. Philadelphia: Temple University Press, 1983.

Rowan, Richard L. "The Negro in the Textile Industry." In *Negro Employment in Southern Industry*, ed. H. Northrup, R. Rowan, D. Barnum, and J. Howard. Philadelphia: University of Pennsylvania Press, 1970.

Rudder, Charles F. "Education Reform in Alabama, 1972–1989." In *School Reform in the Deep South*, ed. David J. Vold and Joseph L. DeVitis. Tuscaloosa: University Press of Alabama, 1991.

Rymer, Russ. *American Beach*. New York: HarperCollins, 1998.

———. "Integration's Casualties," *New York Times Magazine*, November 1, 1998, 48–50.

St. John, Nancy. *School Desegregation: Outcomes for Children*. New York: Wiley, 1975.

Salmond, John A. *Southern Struggles*. Gainesville: University Press of Florida, 2004.

Sandoval-Strausz, A. K. *Hotel: An American History*. New Haven: Yale University Press, 2007.

Schmidt, Christopher W. "The Sit-ins and the State Action Doctrine." *William and Mary Bill of Rights Journal* 18 (2010): 767–829.

Schofield, Janet Ward. "Review of Research on School Desegregation's Impact on Elementary and Secondary School Students." In *Handbook of Research on Multicultural Education*. New York: Macmillan, 1995.

Schulman, Bruce. *From Cotton Belt to Sunbelt: Federal Policy, Economic Development, and the Transformation of the South, 1938–1980*. New York: Oxford University Press, 1991.

Schwab, Stewart. "Is Statistical Discrimination Efficient?" *American Economic Review* 76 (1986): 228–234.

Scribner, Christopher MacGregor. *Renewing Birmingham: Federal Funding and the Promise of Change, 1929–1979*. Athens: University of Georgia Press, 2002.

Scroggs, William O. "Interstate Migration of the Negro Population." *Journal of Political Economy* 25 (1917): 1034–1043.

Shafer, Byron E., and Richard Johnston. *The End of Southern Exceptionalism*. Cambridge, MA: Harvard University Press, 2006.

Shlomowitz, Ralph. "The Squad System on Postbellum Cotton Plantations." In *Toward a New South*, ed. O. V. Burton and R. C. McMath. Westport, CT: Greenwood Press, 1982.

Sitkoff, Harvard. *A New Deal for Blacks: The Emergence of Civil Rights as a National Issue. The Depression Decade*. 30th Anniversary ed. New York: Oxford University Press, 2009.

Smith, David Barton. *Health Care Divided: Race and Healing a Nation*. Ann Arbor: University of Michigan Press, 1999.

———. "The Politics of Racial Disparities: Desegregating the Hospitals in Jackson, Mississippi." *Milbank Quarterly* 83 (2005): 247–269.

Smith, Douglas L. *The New Deal in the Urban South*. Baton Rouge: Louisiana State University Press, 1988.

Smith, James P. "Race and Human Capital." *American Economic Review* 74 (1984): 685–698.

Smith, James, and Finis Welch. "Black Economic Progress Since Myrdal." *Journal of Economic Literature* 27 (1989): 519–564.

Smith, Robert Samuel. *Race, Labor and Civil Rights: Griggs versus Duke Power and the Struggle for Equal Employment Opportunity*. Baton Rouge: Louisiana State University Press, 2008.

Smith, Stephen Samuel. *Boom for Whom? Education, Desegregation, and Development in Charlotte*. Albany: State University of New York Press, 2004.

———. "Development and the Politics of School Desegregation and Resegregation." In *Charlotte, NC: The Global Evolution of a New South City*, ed. William Graves and Heather A. Smith. Athens: University of Georgia Press, 2010.

———. "Still Swimming against the Tide? A Suburban Southern School District in the Aftermath of *Parents Involved*." *North Carolina Law Review* 88 (2010): 1145–1208.

Smith, Suzanne. *To Serve the Living: Funeral Directors and the African American Way of Death.* Cambridge, MA: Belknap Press of Harvard University Press, 2010.

Sokol, Jason. *There Goes My Everything: White Southerners in the Age of Civil Rights.* New York: Knopf, 2006.

Soss, Joe, Richard C. Fording, and Sanford F. Schram. "The Color of Devolution: Race, Federalism, and the Politics of Social Control." *American Journal of Political Science* 52 (2008): 536–553.

Soss, Joe, Sanford F. Schram, Thomas Vartanian, and Erin O'Brien. "Setting the Terms of Relief: Explaining State Policy Choices in the Devolution Revolution." *American Journal of Political Science* 45 (2001): 378–395.

Southern Regional Council. *The Negro and Employment Opportunities in the South.* Atlanta, GA: Southern Regional Council, 1961–1962.

Spitzberg, Irving J. *Racial Politics in Little Rock, 1954–1964.* New York: Garland, 1987.

Stainback, Kevin, Corre L. Robinson, and Donald Tomaskovic-Devey. "Race and Workplace Integration." *American Behavioral Scientist* 48 (2005): 1200–1228.

Stanley, Harold W. "The Latino Vote in 2008." In *Presidential Elections in the South,* ed. Branwell DuBose Kapeluck, Robert P. Steed, and Laurence W. Moreland. Boulder, CO: Lynne Rienner, 2010.

———. *Voter Mobilization and the Politics of Race.* New York: Praeger, 1987.

Stein, Lana, and Stephen E. Condrey. "Integrating Municipal Workforces: A Comparative Study of Six Southern Cities." *Publius* 17 (1987): 93–103.

Stephan, Walter G. "School Desegregation: Short-Term and Long-Term Effects." In *Opening Doors: Perspectives on Race Relations in Contemporary America,* ed. Harry J. Knopke, Robert J. Norrell, and Ronald W. Rogers. Tuscaloosa: University of Alabama Press, 1999.

Stern, Mark. *Calculating Visions: Kennedy, Johnson and Civil Rights.* New Brunswick, NJ: Rutgers University Press, 1992.

Stoll, Michael A. "Race, Place, and Poverty Revisited." In *The Colors of Poverty: Why Racial and Ethnic Disparities Persist,* ed. Ann Chih Lin and David R. Harris. New York: Russell Sage Foundation, 2008.

Stoll, Michael A., Steven Raphael, and Harry J. Holzer. "Black Job Applicants and the Hiring Officer's Race." *Industrial and Labor Relations Review* 57 (2004): 267–287.

Strausz, A. K. *Hotel: An American History.* New Haven, CT: Yale University Press, 2007.

Sugrue, Thomas J. *Sweet Land of Liberty: The Forgotten Struggle for Civil Rights in the North.* New York: Random House, 2008.

Sullivan, Patricia. *Days of Hope: Race and Democracy in the New Deal Era.* Chapel Hill: University of North Carolina Press, 1996.

Sundstrom, William A. "Half a Career: Discrimination and Railroad Internal Labor Markets." *Industrial Relations* 29 (1990): 423–440.

———. "Last Hired, First Fired? Unemployment and Urban Black Workers in the Great Depression." *Journal of Economic History* 52 (1992): 415–429.

Swain, Carol. *Black Faces, Black Interests.* Enlarged ed. Cambridge, MA: Harvard University Press, 1995.

Tarr, Joel A. "Sewerage and the Development of the Networked City in the United States." In *Technology and the Rise of the Networked City in Europe and America,* ed. Joal A. Tarr and Gabriel Dupuy. Philadelphia: Temple University Press, 1988.

Thernstrom, Abigail M. *Voting Rights—and Wrongs: The Elusive Quest for Racially Fair Elections.* Washington, DC: AEI Press, 2009.

———. *Whose Votes Count? Affirmative Action and Minority Voting Rights.* Cambridge, MA: Harvard University Press, 1987.

Thernstrom, Stephan, and Abigail Thernstrom. *America in Black and White.* New York: Simon and Schuster, 1997.

Thompson, Joel A. "The Voting Rights Act in North Carolina: An Evaluation." *Publius* 16 (1986): 139–153.

Thornton, J. Mills. *Dividing Lines.* Tuscaloosa: University of Alabama Press, 2002.

Timpone, Richard J. "Mass Mobilization or Government Intervention? The Growth of Black Registration in the South." *Journal of Politics* 57 (1995): 425–442.

Tindall, George B. *The Emergence of the New South, 1913–1945.* Baton Rouge: Louisiana State University Press, 1967.

Tolnay, Stewart E. "Educational Selection in the Migration of Southern Blacks, 1880–1990." *Social Forces* 77 (1998): 487–514.

Troesken, Werner. *Water, Race, and Disease.* Cambridge, MA: MIT Press, 2004.

Turner, Sarah, and John Bound, "Closing the Gap or Widening the Divide: The Effects of the G.I. Bill and World War II on the Educational Outcomes of Black Americans." *Journal of Economic History* 63 (2003): 145–177.

U.S. Bureau of the Census. *Survey of Minority-Owned Business Enterprises*. Washington, DC: Government Printing Office, 1972–.

———. *Current Population Reports*. Series P-60, No. 119, "Characteristics of the Population Below the Poverty Level: 1979." Washington, DC: U.S. Government Printing Office, 1981.

———. *Historical Statistics of the United States to 1970*. Washington, DC: Government Printing Office, 1975.

U.S. Commission on Civil Rights. *Becoming Less Separate? School Desegregation, Justice Department Enforcement, and the Pursuit of Unitary Status*. Washington, DC: Commission on Civil Rights, 2007.

———. *Civil Rights '63*. Washington, DC: Government Printing Office, 1963.

———. *Political Participation*. Washington, DC: Government Printing Office, 1968.

———. *Twenty Years after Brown: Equality of Economic Opportunity*. Washington, DC: Government Printing Office, 1975.

———. *The Voting Rights Act: Ten Years After*. Washington, DC: Government Printing Office, 1975.

U.S. Department of Agriculture. Economic Research Service. *Statistics on Cotton and Related Data, 1920–1973*. Washington, DC: U.S. Government Printing Office, 1974.

U.S. Department of Education, Institute of Educational Sciences, National Center for Education Statistics. *Achievement Gaps: How Black and White Students in Public Schools Perform in Mathematics and Reading on the National Assessment of Educational Progress*. NCES 2009-455, 2009.

U.S. Department of Justice. *Annual Report of the Attorney General*. 1965–1977. Washington, DC: U.S. Department of Justice, Office of the Attorney General.

U.S. Federal Works Agency. *Final Report on the WPA Program, 1935–1943*. Washington, DC: Government Printing Office, 1947.

U.S. Industrial Commission. *Final Report*. Washington, DC: Government Printing Office, 1902.

Valelly, Richard M. "Net Gains: The Voting Rights Act and Southern Local Government." In *Dilemmas of Scale in America's Federal Democracy*, ed. Martha Derthick. Washington, DC: Woodrow Wilson Center Press, 1999.

———. *The Two Reconstructions: The Struggle for Black Enfranchisement*. Chicago: University of Chicago Press, 2004.

Valentino, Nicholas A., and David O. Sears. "Old Times There Are Not Forgotten: Partisan Realignment in the Contemporary South." *American Journal of Political Science* 49 (2005): 672–688.

Vedder, Richard K., and Lowell Gallaway. "Racial Differences in Unemployment in the United States, 1890–1990." *Journal of Economic History* 52 (1992): 696–702.

Vigdor, Jacob L. "The New Promised Land: Black-White Convergence in the American South, 1960–2000." NBER Working Paper 12143, March 2006.

———. "The Pursuit of Opportunity: Explaining Selective Black Migration." *Journal of Urban Economics* 51 (2002): 391–417.

Vigdor, Jacob L., and Jens Ludwig. "Segregation and the Test Score Gap." In *Steady Gains and Stalled Progress: Inequality and the Black-White Test Score Gap,* ed. Katherine Magnuson and Jane Waldfogel. New York: Russell Sage Foundation, 2008.

Vigdor, Jacob, and Thomas Nechyba. "Peer Effects in North Carolina Public Schools." In *Schools and the Equal Opportunity Problem,* ed. P. E. Peterson and L. Woessman. Cambridge, MA: MIT Press, 2007.

Walker, Anders. *The Ghost of Jim Crow.* New York: Oxford University Press, 2009.

Walters, Pamela Barnhouse, David R. James, and Holly J. McCammon. "Citizenship and Public Schools: Accounting for Racial Inequality in Education in the Pre- and Post-Disfranchisement South." *American Sociological Review* 62 (1997): 34–52.

Watkins, Steve. *The Black O: Racism and Redemption in an American Corporate Empire.* Athens: University of Georgia Press, 1997.

Watters, Pat, and Reese Cleghorn. *Climbing Jacob's Ladder: The Arrival of Negroes in Southern Politics.* New York: Harcourt, Brace and World, 1967.

Wayne, Michael. *The Reshaping of Plantation Society: The Natchez District, 1860–1880.* Baton Rouge: Louisiana State University Press, 1983.

Weems, Robert E., Jr. "A Crumbling Legacy: The Decline of African American Insurance Companies in Contemporary America." *Review of Black Political Economy* 23 (1994): 25–37.

———. *Desegregating the Dollar: African American Consumerism in the Twentieth Century.* New York: New York University Press, 1998.

Weiser, Wendy R., and Lawrence Norden. *Voting Law Change in 2012.* Report, Brennan Center for Justice at New York University School of Law, 2012.

Welke, Barbara Young. *Recasting American Liberty: Gender, Race, Law and the Railroad Revolution, 1865–1920.* Cambridge: Cambridge University Press, 2001.

Wendt, Simon. "The Roots of Black Power?" In *The Black Power Movement: Rethinking the Civil Rights–Black Power Era,* ed. Peniel Joseph, 145–165. New York: Routledge, 2006.

Whalen, Charles W. *The Longest Debate: A Legislative History of the Civil Rights Act.* Cabin John, MD: Seven Locks Press, 1985.

Whatley, Warren. "Getting a Foot in the Door: 'Learning,' State Dependence, and the Racial Integration of Firms." *Journal of Economic History* 50 (1990): 913–926.

———. "Labor for the Picking: The New Deal in the South." *Journal of Economic History* 43 (1983): 905–929.

———. "Southern Agrarian Labor Contracts as Impediments to Cotton Mechanization." *Journal of Economic History* 47 (1987): 45–70.

Whatley, Warren, and Gavin Wright. "Race, Human Capital, and Labour Markets in American History." In *Labour Market Evolution,* ed. George Grantham and Mary MacKinnon. London: Routledge, 1994.

Whayne, Jeannie M. *A New Plantation South: Land, Labor, and Federal Favor in Twentieth-Century Arkansas.* Charlottesville: University Press of Virginia, 1996.

Wheat, Leonard F., and William H. Crown. *State Per-Capita Income Change Since 1950: Sharecropping's Demise and Other Causes of Convergence.* Westport, CT: Greenwood Press, 1995.

Wiese, Andrew. "African-American Suburbanization and Regionalism in the Modern South." In *The Myth of Southern Exceptionalism,* ed. Matthew D. Lassiter and Joseph Crespino. New York: Oxford University Press, 2010.

Williamson, Joel. *The Crucible of Race.* New York: Oxford University Press, 1984.

Willis, John C. *Forgotten Time: The Yazoo-Mississippi Delta after the Civil War.* Charlottesville: University Press of Virginia, 2000.

Wilson, Franklin D. "The Ecology of a Black Business District." *Review of Black Political Economy* 5 (1975): 353–375.

Wilson, William Julius. *The Declining Significance of Race: Blacks and Changing American Institutions.* Chicago: University of Chicago Press, 1978.

Wirt, Frederick M. *Politics of Southern Inequality: Law and Social Change in a Mississippi County.* Chicago: Aldine, 1970.

———. *"We Ain't What We Was": Civil Rights in the New South.* Durham, NC: Duke University Press, 1997.

Wolff, Miles. *Lunch at the Five and Ten: The Greensboro Sit-ins.* New York: Stein and Day, 1970.

Wolters, Raymond. *The Burden of Brown: Thirty Years of School Desegregation.* Knoxville: University of Tennessee Press, 1984.

———. *Negroes and the Great Depression.* Westport, CT: Greenwood Press, 1975.

———. *Race and Education, 1954–2007.* Columbia: University of Missouri Press, 2008.

Woodard, Michael. *Black Entrepreneurs in America.* New Brunswick, NJ: Rutgers University Press, 1997.

Woodman, Harold D. *New South, New Law: The Legal Foundations of Credit and Labor Relations in the Postbellum Agricultural South.* Baton Rouge: Louisiana State University Press, 1995.

———. "The Political Economy of the New South." In *Origins of the New South Fifty Years Later,* ed. John B. Boles and Bethany Johnson. Baton Rouge: Louisiana State University Press, 2003.

Woodward, C. Vann. *Origins of the New South, 1877–1913.* Baton Rouge: Louisiana State University Press, 1951.

———. *The Strange Career of Jim Crow.* New York: Oxford University Press, 1955.

———. *Tom Watson, Agrarian Rebel.* 1938. New York: Oxford University Press, 1963.

Worthman, Paul. "Black Workers and Labor Unions in Birmingham, Alabama, 1897–1904." *Labor History* 10 (1969): 375–406.

Wright, Gavin. "Cheap Labor and Southern Textiles, 1880–1930." *Quarterly Journal of Economics* 96 (1981): 605–629.

———. "The Civil Rights Revolution as Economic History." *Journal of Economic History* 59 (1999): 267–289.

———. "The Economics of the Civil Rights Revolution." In *Toward the Meeting of the Waters: Currents in the Civil Rights Movement of South Carolina During the Twentieth Century,* ed. Winfred B. Moore Jr. and Orville Vernon Burton. Columbia: University of South Carolina Press, 2008.

———. "The New Deal and the Modernization of the South." *Federal History,* January 2010, 58–73.

———. *Old South, New South: Revolutions in the Southern Economy Since the Civil War.* New York: Basic Books, 1986.

———. "Persisting Dixie: The South as an Economic Region." In *The American South in the Twentieth Century,* ed. Craig S. Pascoe,

Karen Trahan Leathem, and Andy Ambrose. Athens: University of Georgia Press, 2005.

Wright, Marion A. "Public Accommodations." In *Legal Aspects of the Civil Rights Movement,* ed. Donald B. King and Charles W. Quick. Detroit: Wayne State University Press, 1965.

ACKNOWLEDGMENTS

Because this book has evolved over such an extended time, it would not be possible to list all of those whose advice and inspiration helped to shape the end result. But special thanks are due to the individuals who offered comments on chapter drafts or presentations: Tony Badger, Leah Boustan, David Chappell, James Cobb, Peter Coclanis, Frank Dobbin, Peter Eckstein, Ted Eisenberg, John Luke Gallup, George Grantham, Jim Grossman, Tim Guinnane, Carol Heim, Alison Isenberg, Gerald Jaynes, Mark Kanazawa, Mary King, Naomi Lamoreaux, Alan Olmstead, Randy Patton, Dan Pope, Craig and Janet Swan, Rick Valelly, Jenny Wahl, Ebonya Washington, Warren Whatley, and Eleanor Wilking. As much as I have gained from these interactions, no one named should be held responsible for any opinions or interpretations presented in this book.

Several generations of Stanford students contributed essential research assistance, including: Nick Baldo, Derek Knowles, Betsy Walls, and Randy Zabaneh. Ben Schneer's assistance with the IPUMS runs was vital. Sam Zarnegar's work with the department store sales data was especially valuable, and Danny Lynn Schaden's overhaul of the graphs was indispensable. Tim Hyde's honors thesis on consumer-based employment discrimination added new insights to my understanding of that phenomenon.

The draft manuscript was completed during a sabbatical at the Woodrow Wilson International Center for Scholars during 2010–11. I am grateful to the Center for providing an ideal work environment, and particularly to the library staff for its indefatigable support work. The congenial setting was further enriched by stimulating conversations with Don Doyle, Jo Freeman, David Greenberg, Joseph Inikori, Bob Kaiser, Sonia Michel, and Marjorie Spruill, among others. My interns at the Center, John Boone and Simone Oyekan, were helpful beyond measure.

I owe special gratitude to Michael Aronson, who encouraged me to pursue the project with Harvard University Press and stuck with it despite delays. Mike's editorial advice has been consistently good, and Kathi Drummy's help navigating the editorial process is also much appreciated. Isabelle Lewis did an outstanding job with the maps.

My deepest debts are personal. My wife, Cathe, has encouraged and supported this project from beginning to end. Although economics is not exactly her thing, Cathe has nonetheless sat through countless Civil Rights presentations, and I have come to count on her always-reliable counsel. This book is dedicated to our grandchildren, Daisy and Agnita, who should learn that hopeful things can sometimes happen in this world.

INDEX

Aaron, Henry, 29
Abbott, Carl, 103, 209
Affirmative action, 139–140, 221, 247–248, 251–252
AFL-CIO, 125
Alabama, 98–99, 189, 207, 218, 221. *See also* Birmingham (AL); Montgomery (AL)
Alabama Christian Movement for Human Rights (ACMHR), 14
Albany (GA) boycotts, 77, 81–82
Allen, Ivan, 92
Allen v. State Board of Education, 190
Almond, Douglas, 238
Andrews, Kenneth, 272n55
Applebome, Peter, 3, 74, 173, 223–224
Arkansas. *See* Little Rock (AR) desegregation
Arrington, Richard, 210, 212, 231–232
Arrow, Kenneth, 38, 106
Ashenfelter, Orley, 164
Askew, Reubin, 214, 219
Atlanta (GA): sewer project in, 63–64; desegregation in, 85,

87–89, 91–92, 100, 158; occupational status in, 130; in-migration to, 144; economic growth of, 208–209, 212–213; black businesses and, 231, 232
Atlantic Steel Company, 284n36
Ayers, Edward, 52

Badger, Anthony, 64
Baker, Ella, 13
Baker, Scott, 248
Baker v. Carr, 216
Baldwin, James, 226
Baldwin, William H., 48
Baltimore (MD) desegregation, 84
Barnes, Joy, 234
Baseball and desegregation, 29, 273n61
Becker, Gary, 19, 148
Bell, Derrick, 16, 102
Birmingham (AL): New Deal funding and, 63; desegregation in, 89, 100–101, 212; occupational status in, 132; economic growth in, 210–212; black businesses and, 226, 227, 231–234; poverty and, 235

registration and, 183, 185–186, 187–188, 262; black representation and, 183–184, 199, 203, 205–213, 217, 221–222, 230–234; legislation and, 183–184, 185–188; early efforts and, 184–186; black elected officials and, 188–197, 202–213, 247; vote dilution and, 189–190; regional character of, 190–193; race-conscious voting and, 193–197; economic gains and, 198–213; two-party South and, 213–214, 215, 220; racist rhetoric and, 214–215; public policy and, 216–220, 221–222; end of Second Reconstruction and, 220–222
Voting Rights Act (1965), 19–23, 183–184, 186–188, 190

Wages: in Jim Crow South, 38–41, 47–48, 49–51, 105; New Deal and, 66–67
Wake County (Raleigh) schools, 182
Walker, Anders, 248
Wallace, George, 216
Waller, William, 219
Waring, J. Waties, 153
War on Poverty, 240–242, 250
Warren, Earl, 155
Washington, Ebonya, 202
Watt, Melvin, 190–191

Weems, Robert E., Jr., 224
Wendt, Simon, 270n24, 300n69
West, John, 214, 215, 218
Whatley, Warren, 5
"White flight," 159–160, 167–168; reverse, 177
White southerners: economic views of, 18, 25, 26, 65, 71; disfranchisement, education and, 43–46, 127; labor market desegregation and, 146–149; school desegregation and, 150–151, 159–160, 166–170; voting rights and, 205–213; hospital desegregation and, 240
Wiese, Andrew, 180
Wilder, Douglas, 193
Williams, Hosea, 226
Williams, Juan, 247
Wilson, William Julius, 247
Wilson, Woodrow, 56
Wirt, Frederick, 207
Wolkon, Shari, 164
Wolters, Raymond, 3, 68, 166, 248
Woodward, C. Vann, 42, 51, 73
Woolworth's, 79–80, 81, 82, 95, 279n29
Works Progress Administration (WPA), 58–59, 64, 66, 67

Yarmolinsky, Adam, 241
Yoon, Albert, 164
Young, Andrew, 103–104
Young, Whitney, 14–15, 136